Game Audio Programming 3

Game Audio
Programming 3
Principles and Practices

Edited by
Guy Somberg

CRC Press
Taylor & Francis Group
Boca Raton London New York

CRC Press is an imprint of the
Taylor & Francis Group, an **informa** business

First edition published 2021
by CRC Press
6000 Broken Sound Parkway NW, Suite 300, Boca Raton, FL 33487-2742

and by CRC Press
2 Park Square, Milton Park, Abingdon, Oxon, OX14 4RN

ISBN: 978-0-367-35413-8 (hbk)
ISBN: 978-0-367-34804-5 (pbk)
ISBN: 978-0-429-33125-1 (ebk)

Typeset in Minion
by codeMantra

Visit the companion website: https://www.routledge.com/9780367348045

*To Emily, who is (hopefully) not yet sick of
these books getting dedicated to her.*

Contents

Preface

INTRODUCTION

Welcome to the third volume of *Game Audio Programming: Principles and Practices*! It is always exciting to me when these books come together. So many audio programmers pour their expertise onto the page, and I get the privilege of collecting that knowledge into one place that can be shared with the world. As an added bonus, I get to be the first one to read the chapters and to learn from them. As with all of the books in this series, all of the contributors worked very hard, and this volume would not exist without their hard work and dedication.

Game audio programming is a job that requires many layers of expertise. We have to be tools programmers, pipeline managers, build engineers, experts in using our chosen middleware (both tools and APIs), and more. We need to have an understanding of audio design and the tools, techniques, and terminology that they use. There are many fundamental techniques that apply globally, but each game genre has its own set of specific challenges that require their own distinctive solutions. Small wonder, then, that there is always more to write about and always more to learn.

THIS BOOK

The chapters in this book touch on only some of these techniques that are critical to our jobs. Some of them dive deep into a topic and provide specific solutions to individual problems, while others are broad overviews of a subject and provide a concept of the scope of the problem and the kinds of questions you may need to ask.

Here are brief summaries of all of the chapters in this book:

- **Sound Effect: Categories** by Florian Füsslin—Any game project, no matter the genre or scale, will follow a pattern in the types of audio assets that it requires. This chapter takes a tour of the various categories that sound effects live in and the sorts of features that will be necessary in order to feed the content. It is intended as a starting point and a common frame of reference in creating a dialog between the audio designers and the audio programmers.

- **Complex Numbers: A Primer for DSP Programming** by Robert Bantin—Complex numbers show up a lot in DSP programming, but they can feel a little bit mystical without the proper background. This chapter uses an alternating current as a practical demonstration of how complex numbers are useful in solving real-world problems. With this primer, the math of DSPs will be more approachable.

- **Building Dynamic Analog-Style Filters: Bi-Quadratic Cascades vs Digital Integrator Cascades** by Robert Bantin—The ubiquitous biquad filter and the "cookbook" formulas by Robert Bristow-Johnson have been implemented in innumerable audio engines, and they work well for the most part. However, they exhibit some undesirable properties when their parameters are adjusted rapidly. Digital Integrator Cascades, a technique by Hal Chamberlin, are an alternative to the biquad filter that have some better properties for this particular purpose.

- **Modeling Atmospheric Absorption with a Low-Pass Filter** by Nic Taylor—Attenuation settings are often implemented in games as a set of parameters, including a low-pass filter to model atmospheric absorption. This chapter explores using the atmospheric features of air temperature and humidity to provide a systematic way of setting a low-pass filter cutoff for sound propagation.

- **Software Engineering Principles of Voice Pipelines** by Michael Filion—Managing and delivering voice lines can be among the most complex processes in a game project. This chapter takes a tour and overview of the sorts of challenges that you are likely to run into and some of the questions that you will need to ask.

- **A Stimulus-Driven Server Authoritative Voice System** by Tomas Neumann—Spoken words are often at the core of why players connect and relate to the characters within a video game. This chapter presents some techniques for creating a voice system based on an authoritative server that directs which lines are chosen, picks who says something, and which client should play these lines.

- **Building the Patch Cable** by Ethan Geller—In analog audio, any point in the signal chain can be split off and plugged into any device by using a patch cable. When we think about abstractions for game audio, we tend to think of base classes and hierarchies, but this chapter takes a different tactic with a more generic abstraction: the patch cable. This chapter builds up a fully thread-safe multi-producer multi-consumer patch abstraction.

- **Split Screen and Audio Engines** by Aaron McLeran—When implementing a split-screen game where multiple players are all on the same physical device, it can be difficult to figure out how to render the audio. This chapter provides a simple solution, along with the background math, and explanations of why it is the best solution to the problem.

- **Voice Management and Virtualization** by Robert Gay—Game audio engines, at their core, are about managing which sounds are currently playing. This chapter discusses techniques for managing real and virtual voice queues, and how to virtualize and realize the currently playing sounds.

- **Screen-Space Distance Attenuation** by Guy Somberg—When making a game like an ARPG where the camera is up in the sky looking down at the action, it can be difficult for sound designers to find appropriate min/max distances for 3D sounds. We can create a meaningful value for sound designers by redefining the concept of distance from "world distance to attenuation position" to "distance in screen space."

- **Under the Influence: Using Influence Maps for Audio** by Jon Mitchell—Influence maps are a technology that comes from the AI world, and are used a lot in RTS games. Applying the techniques from influence maps to audio can create some extremely useful features. This chapter discusses how to create and update influence maps, and how to apply them to game audio.

- **An Importance-Based Mixing System** by Guy Somberg—Most of the mixing tools that are in our toolbox are offline—that is, the decisions are made at content authoring time, even if they are applied at runtime. However, any mixing decision that is made at authoring time can be negated by a particular situation in-game. This chapter goes through the algorithm of creating a mixing system based on the concept of "importance," which is calculated at runtime based on what's happening in the game.

- **Voxel-Based Emitters: Approximating the Position of Ambient Sounds** by Nic Taylor—When implementing volumetric sounds based on voxel emitters, there are many edge cases and corners to understand and deal with. This chapter dives deep into these dark corners, and provides mathematical and code solutions to them.

- **Improvisational Music** by Charlie Huguenard—Implementing a dynamic note-based music system can be an effective way to author music that changes with gameplay. Taking it one step further, we can apply the lessons of jazz to author music on the fly. This chapter goes through how to build such a system, and provides code examples and homework assignments to improve the system.

PARTING THOUGHTS

My first job out of college was writing a software mixer for a slot machine operating system, and that is where I got my first taste of (and love for) audio programming. As I transitioned to working on video games, I learned some good ways of solving game audio problems and some bad ways, but I never had a resource like this book or the previous two volumes. I wish I had it at the time, but I am excited that it exists now. I hope that it is inspiring, educational, and valuable.

Guy Somberg

Acknowledgments

Thanks to my contributors. Books like this don't exist without your hard work and expertise, and your determination to write it all down.

Thanks to Brian Fitzgerald, David Brevik, and Tyler Thompson, who all gave me chances to prove myself and from whom I have learned a lot.

Thanks again to Thomas Buckeyne, who started me on my audio programming journey.

Thanks to David Steinwedel, who was with me on my first big game title, and whose partnership and friendship were both instrumental in cementing my love of game audio programming.

Thanks once again to David Steinwedel, Jordan Stock, Andy Martin, Pam Aranoff, Michael Kamper, Michael Csurics, and Erika Escamez—the sound designers who have accompanied me on my audio programming journey.

Thanks to Rick Adams, Jessica Vega, and the rest of the team at CRC Press. I appreciate all of your hard work on my behalf in making this book a reality.

And thanks to my wife Emily who is always helpful and supportive of my work on this book.

Editor

Guy Somberg has been programming audio engines for his entire career. From humble beginnings writing a low-level audio mixer for slot machines, he quickly transitioned to writing game audio engines for all manner of games. He has written audio engines that shipped AAA games like *Hellgate: London*, *Bioshock 2*, *The Sims 4*, and *Torchlight 3*, as well as smaller titles like *Minion Master*, *Tales from the Borderlands*, and *Game of Thrones*. Guy has also given several talks at the Game Developer Conference, the Audio Developer Conference, and CppCon.

When he's not programming or writing game audio programming books, he can be found at home reading, playing video games, and playing the flute.

Contributors

Aaron McLeran is a game audio veteran with AAA development experience as an interactive music composer, sound designer, and audio programmer for a number of award-winning games. He is currently the lead audio programmer at Epic Games working on the audio engine for UE4.

Charlie Huguenard is a musician who learned how to code. For about a decade, he's made interactive experiences and tools for making interactive sound at companies like Facebook, Meow Wolf, Telltale Games, Magic Leap, and Funomena. In his free time, he can be found poking around the wilderness with a backpack and a hammock, taking in the beauty of the Southwest from the highway, and narrowly avoiding injury at one of the Bay Area's many skate parks.

Ethan Geller is an audio programmer working on the Unreal Engine, which is used by several games. Prior to working at Epic Games, Ethan worked at Dolby and PlayStation, received his master's degree from CCRMA at Stanford, and went to undergrad for music composition at Indiana University. Ethan's primary research interests are HRTF personalization, optimal filter design, and wave field capture/synthesis. He also plays drums.

Florian Füsslin had a 10-year music background when entering the game industry with Crytek in 2006. During the past 14 years, he has contributed to the audio pipeline of CRYENGINE and shipped all major Crytek titles on multiple platforms, including the *Crysis Franchise, Ryse: Son of Rome*, the VR titles *The Climb* and *Robinson*, and *HUNT: Showdown*. Being a dedicated gamer and living the passion for game audio, he is leading the audio team in the role of an Audio Director. He is lecturing at the Hochschule Darmstadt (h_da) and School of Audio Engineering in Frankfurt (SAE), and has given talks at multiple international conferences.

Jon Mitchell has worked as an audio programmer for United Front Games, Radical Entertainment, and Codemasters, and is currently working with the wonderfully talented and friendly people at Blackbird Interactive on *Homeworld 3*. He lives in Vancouver with his partner, two destructive cats, and the World's Cutest Baby.

Michael Filion has been developing video games for his entire career of more than 10 years with Ubisoft Québec, with the majority in the world of audio. When explaining his work and passion to friends and family, he often oversimplifies by stating that he is "responsible for ensuring the bleeps and bloops are functional in video games." He has had the opportunity to work with many talented people on games such as *Assassin's Creed*, *Child of Light*, and *Tom Clancy's The Division*. In between delivering great titles, he enjoys traveling with his daughter and searching out different craft brews from around the world.

Nic Taylor has 10 years of experience working on audio engines in the video game industry. He started programming writing casual games for Windows in the late 1990s as well as audio plug-ins for his own music projects. Nic's first audio engine integration from scratch was for Red 5 Studio's custom MMO engine which was an early adopter of Wwise. Nic has since done other audio engine integrations and feature work using well-known engines. His last game project was with the *Diablo* team at Blizzard Entertainment. Nic now has a different role in audio working on language understanding of music queries at Google. On the side, he continues to produce music applying his interest in DSP and room acoustics.

Robert Bantin has been writing audio code for rather a long time. While at school, he was an active member of the Amiga demo scene. At Salford University, he studied acoustics and brought his coding experience to his studies in the form of DSP and audio-focused applications. Upon graduating, he was recruited by Philips ASA Labs in Eindhoven in order to join the MPEG technology program. After returning to the UK, he worked at Thorn-EMI and brushed with their spin-off game audio middleware: Sensaura GameCODA. He also worked at Yamaha and FXpansion on several well-known DAW plug-ins, as well as writing some of Auro Technologies' first shippable code. Robert has since worked on a number of AAA games such as *Guitar Hero Live*, *Dirt 4*, and *Tom Clancy's The Division 2*. When he's not programming, he can be found at home building flying models with his son, attempting to shred on guitar, and playing video games when no one is looking.

Robert Gay has been working in games ever since he graduated from the University of Washington with a Bachelor of Science in Electrical Engineering and a Bachelor of Fine Arts in Digital Arts & Experimental Media. Starting as a Sound Designer in 2010 and then moving to being a Technical Sound Designer, he finally moved to audio programming full time while working at ArenaNet. Since then, he has worked at Amazon as a Lead Game Audio Programmer and is currently a Senior Audio Programmer working at Epic Games on the Unreal Engine.

Tomas Neumann has focused on improving audio technology in the game industry for 15 years. By improving the audio capabilities and workflows of CryEngine, he contributed to the development of the critically acclaimed CRYSIS series. At Blizzard Entertainment, he developed the audio technology and voice system used for the award-winning *Overwatch* and contributed to *World of Warcraft* and *Warcraft 3 Reforged*. Currently Tomas is defining the audio pipeline and features of Blizzard's shared game engine development.

CHAPTER 1

Sound Effect Categories

Florian Füsslin

Crytek GmbH

CONTENTS

1.1 PREAMBLE

In the last two years, I have lectured on the subject of Game Audio at various universities and audio schools. While giving those talks, I realized that I ended up explaining terminology in greater detail than I had anticipated. The general split of game audio production into dialog, music, and sound effects makes sense to everyone. When I tried to break it into smaller pieces, however, there were many follow-up questions on sound effects in particular. Some people had either never heard of some sound effect categories or didn't associate anything with them. I consulted with colleagues in the game industry about this observation, and it turns out that even within this group of audio specialists, definitions and terminologies of sound effect categories vary. This chapter felt like a great opportunity to tackle the topic, and provide an overview of a potential project structure, common complexity, and possible challenges. It can function as a basis for a nomenclature for the project naming convention, and can build the foundation for communication and collaboration between audio designers and audio programmers. The goal is to enable you to handle all sound effect requirements and requests coming your way in a structured fashion.

1.1.1 Interactive Media

Most of the terminology around sound effects has been adopted from film and audio post production, thinking in scenes and stems. Atmospheres set the mood and background of a scene; foley effects support on-screen sounds to add details and enhance drama; designed special effect sounds create emotional reactions and support the actions. We have full control of audio in this kind of linear media environment, so all of our sound effects will play back exactly once and can be perfectly designed, timed, balanced, and mixed to fit that particular scene.

But because games are interactive with player input, we have a lot less control. Therefore, we have to think in sources (where is the sound emitter), situations (when is it playing), and conditions (what states it is in). We need a lot more assets to cover all potential scenarios and multiple variations to avoid repetition. In theory, every sound could play at any time and be the most important sound playing at that moment, which requires a constant shift in priorities and adjustment of the mix in real time. With this complexity, game audio needs to develop new sub-categories within the sound effects group.

1.1.2 The Big Three

The sound effects for most modern games usually fall into three major categories:

1. **World**—The game environment including ambiences, weather conditions, particle effects, and physics.

2. **Character**—All protagonists and antagonists, their movement, and their interactions.

3. **Feedback**—Audio cues for menu, heads-up display, and enrichment of the user experience.

It's easy to see how these categories can map to the sounds for games like an FPS or an MMORPG, but they are also applicable to other genres. For example, in a soccer game, the world is the stadium, the character is the ball, and feedback is the situational crowd reaction. In an RTS game, the world is the battlefield, the units are the characters, and feedback is the information about mission status, resources, and production.

These "big three" main categories can function as a starting point for how we structure and manage our audio data in the project or audio middleware. In a soccer game, for example, we would need specific groups and folders for each stadium, but we could treat and structure the crowd globally. This line of thinking works for other categories as well. If our game will always be in sunny daylight for all levels, then we don't need any weather effects, and we can treat our ambiences globally with no real-time conditions.

In another scenario, we have an open world with different environments ranging from a dense jungle to vast deserts, extreme weather conditions, and a complete 24-hour day/night cycle featuring all four seasons. In this case, we will probably design and structure per environment, including dawn, day, dusk, and night layers. We will repeat this procedure per season, and support extreme weather conditions like seasonal types of rain in the jungle and various sandstorms in the desert. All of this must be driven by parameters so that our environments and conditions can adapt in real time.

There are always exceptions to the rules, and each project has different requirements, which is why it is important to ask the following questions:

Do I need this (sub) category in my project? Do I see this category used globally, or is it specific to one section of the game? Do I have to react to real-time conditions, and if yes, what are they?

With these questions in mind, let's dive deeper into the sub-categories of the big three.

1.2 THE WORLD

The world represents the game environment and consists of the following sub-categories:

- **Environment**—Ambiences and spot effects.

- **Weather**—All elements like rain or thunderstorms.

- **Particle effects**—Fires, sparks, steam, etc.

- **Physics**—Everything related to rolling, sliding, bending, collision, and destruction.

1.2.1 Environment

Unless you are in space, there is always some noise. It can be a subtle room tone, a rustling forest, or a cold mountain wind. This is called ambience, sound bed, or atmosphere. Even if it is very subtle, it grounds the player in the world and functions as the noise floor and threshold from which we can build our audio mix and dynamic range. This base layer is usually designed as a static loop or a granular loop which is rather sparse and steady to hide its repetition. To reduce the potential monotony, we can add details which don't need visual support such as blooms or falling dust.

Once we have the base loop, we can build on it. Wind gusts can help to make the ambience feel more dynamic, ideally driven by a parameter like wind_intensity. If our project supports a full day and night cycle, we will want to consider sweeteners for dawn, day, dusk, and night and drive them via a time_of_day parameter. If our game ranges across all seasons, we might use a season parameter to provide variants for spring, summer, autumn, and winter.

In addition to the ambiences, we can use spot effects for positional details to the environment. This can be a constant emitter like a waterfall, a generator, or a windmill, or it can be randomly occurring like an insect flyby, wind gust, or distant rumble. Ideally there is a corresponding visual representation or a landmark we want the player to pay attention to, but even without that, playing these sounds can still enliven and add depth to the player's environment.

1.2.2 Weather

Weather can be a big part of the perceived environment and ambience. Due to its complex nature and the strong visual component, it makes sense to treat it as a separate sub-category. Rain, for example, can range from a sprinkle to a thunderstorm to a full-blown hurricane and will need to blend between these via a parameter like rain_intensity. Wind can go from a gentle breeze to a full storm all the way to a tornado, again driven by a wind_intensity value.

If our weather simulation is dynamic, we also have to consider the time before and the time after the effect. For example, a thunderstorm usually starts with gusts of wind which increase in intensity. Then they suddenly stop before the rain starts to fall with a couple of big drips before the shower begins. Eventually the wind increases again during the rainfall before it quiets down again. Finally, there is the aftermath. The ground is wet with puddles, rivulets, and small streams. It is dripping from the roofs and trees, and gurgling in the downspouts.

Even less noisy weather can have a strong impact on the audio. With fog, for example, we may want to make everything sound more muted as the fog gets thicker. Snow has a very similar effect. Falling snowflakes are not very noisy, but they swallow all reflections, which reduces audibility over distance. The acoustic difference is prominent.

1.2.3 Particle Effects

Similar to weather, particle effects also have a strong and very dynamic visual component which can range in scale and size drastically. Because they are often reused across the whole game, it makes sense to treat them in their own environment sub-category. For example, a fire effect can range from a small match all the way to a firestorm. The visual part often does a copy and paste, treating it as more of the same scaled up or down. For audio, playing the sound of a burning match one thousand times still won't make it a firestorm, and attempting to do so will not help our performance.

Given this disparity, it makes sense to create assets for a fixed range of scale and size such as small, medium, and large. In addition, we can

drastically reduce the load on the audio engine and help to build a convincing, manageable, and flexible toolkit by including parameters such as
size to drive a pitch effect or amount to trigger additional sweeteners like
an additional rumble or sizzle, or to switch the asset to a plural version of
the individual sound.

1.2.4 Physics

Physics describes everything that can collide, roll, slide, bend, or break in
our game world. While this is often tied to the actions the characters can
perform, it makes sense to keep it a global system and therefore tied to the
world and environment.

With physics, small design requests can quickly result in a very complex system with a large number of assets needed. For example, maybe the
player can throw a stone to distract enemies. For audio, this feature means
that we need multiple stone impacts for all possible surface types in the
game like wood, metal, stone, and water. If the player can hold the throw
input to throw harder, we add an intensity from soft to hard. If the sizes
of the throwable rocks also vary, we also need to cater from pebble to brick
for all surface types. It is easy to end up with a couple hundred assets just
for the collision of one thing.

The closer we get to a real-world simulation, the more complex and
difficult it becomes to create believable outcomes. Just as with particles,
audio doesn't scale with size: many small stone impacts don't sound like
a big rock collision. To make it manageable to create these assets, we take
shortcuts by generating groups such as size (small, medium, large), throw-
ing intensity (soft, regular, hard), and use real-time parameters such as
mass, velocity, speed, and amount to drive real-time effects such as pitch
or volume. Also, we can design multi-impact sweeteners that trigger once
a certain threshold of "impacts per time" is reached.

While grouping can get us a fair distance, there will always be exceptions where we have to use original assets. A barrel is a good example.
While its surface is made of sheet metal, its internal resonance gives it
a distinct sound which will require a bespoke asset. A similar rule also
applies to breakable objects. A tree might consist of multiple sizes of wood
which splinter when the tree is destroyed, but simply playing the wood
splintering sound is unlikely to be convincing when the whole tree breaks
and comes down, for both the trunk and branches with leaves and foli-
age. Once again, we will need to design a bespoke asset in order to sound
realistic.

Sometimes it can make sense to move some elements to another category based on what triggers them, even though the assets share a strong relationship. For example, when the wind moves vegetation about (driven by a `wind_intensity` parameter), it makes sense to keep it in the world physics category. However, vegetation shuffle sounds caused by player actions (such as walking through the vegetation or hitting it) would go into the character category.

1.3 CHARACTERS

The category of characters includes everything that is related to player and non-player assets with the following sub-categories:

- **Movement**—Clothes and footsteps.

- **Interactions**—Player control and everything the player can manipulate.

1.3.1 Movement

In movies, the term "foley" describes the sounds that are added and replaced during post production, either because they were not possible to record properly on set or require special sound design. This includes footsteps on surfaces and sounds of cloth movement, as well as specific prop sounds like a squeaking door for example. These sounds are often exaggerated to increase the drama and intensity of the scene. As video games are silent from the start, we end up with a large amount of assets required to cover our bases like basic movement of the main character. If our game supports character customization or user-generated content with a wide range of possible clothing styles, this can scale out of control, so we share and reuse assets where possible.

For clothing sounds like cloth rustles and movement, we can group our assets by speed (slow, medium, fast) or intensity (soft, regular, hard). For different clothing styles, we can split our design into multiple layers, such as fabric (the soft cloth-on-cloth movement), leather (typical correspondent jacket crunch), and jingle (zippers, buttons, and chains). If we tie parameters to each layer and give clothing a specific layer value, we can create a solid wardrobe of very-different-sounding clothes. There might be some exceptions which need additional sweeteners because they have a specific and unique-sounding element, like backpacks or gun belts. Together with real-time effects and asset blending, a matrix like this should hold up for the majority of our character movements.

For footsteps, it is pretty common that we also need different movement speeds (sneak, walk, and run/sprint), turning on the spot (shuffle), or quickly accelerating/stopping (scuff). If our game supports jumping, we also need a landing sound. If our character can fall, we have to think about more heavy body-falls. This task becomes massive if we also have to support different shoe types (e.g. boots, flip-flops, sneakers), different character sizes, all genders, and even weather with dry and wet variants for all surface types.

In order to manage the number of assets, we share the surface types across all characters by splitting tip and toe and make the boot type an iconic sweetener. A similar approach can work for landing and body-fall where we share the surface and create generic assets for each type. We can use size and gender as real-time parameters to drive a pitch or a delay effect to manipulate the timing of how the individual assets are granularly stitched together.

There will usually be exceptions to this matrix. Water is one as moving in puddle-, ankle-, knee-, and hip-deep water all sound very different. A parameter like depth can help to find a good balance between the amount of assets, and real-time blending and modification.

Also specific boot types can require exceptions. While cowboy boots with spurs is probably solved with the typical jingle added to the standard boot, the distinct sound of high heels makes it tricky to share assets. One possible shortcut could be to group the surface type as hard and soft or to build our matrix around parameters like resonant and solid to cater for the game we are making.

1.3.2 Interactions

Most of the sounds required for a game are based on the actions of the player and the control inputs. This can range from a simple activity such as opening a door or operating a rifle all the way to complex mechanics like driving a car.

Most of the time, we can split an interaction into five consecutive steps:

1. **Attempt**—The initial control input: the player wants to perform an action.

2. **Execution**—The attempt put into action.

3. **Condition**—Check plausibility and possible outcomes of the action.

4. **Result**—The action based on the condition.

5. **Reaction**—The game world responding to the result.

Let's see how this works with a few examples:

Action: *Opening an old rusty wooden door*

Attempt	Reaching for the latch
Execution	Pushing down the door handle
Condition	Check whether the door is locked
Result	Either rattling the locked door or the door actually opening
Reaction	The resonance of the creaking wood when slowly granting access complemented by the reverb of the surroundings

Action: *Shooting a gun*

Attempt	Aiming down the sights
Execution	Pulling the trigger
Condition	Check whether a bullet is in the chamber
Result	Either the dry fire click or the muzzle-flash and the bullet leaving the barrel
Reaction	Gun tail and reflections of the surroundings

Action: *Braking while driving a vehicle*

Attempt	Putting the foot on the pedal resulting in engine reducing its stress and potentially dropping in rpm
Execution	Pushing down on the pedal
Condition	Check whether the braking is strong enough to make the wheels stop turning with a surface-type-based squeak or the anti-lock braking system kicking in with a rumble
Result	Decrease in speed, less wind noise, and audibility of the tires
Reaction	Dust settling

If we have a piece of complex machinery that the player can operate, it can make sense to keep "attempt" and "execution" in the character category and move "condition," "result," and "reaction" to the world category. For example, operating the button to call an elevator is very character driven, but the elevator moving, arriving, and opening its door is part of the world.

1.4 FEEDBACK

The player is constantly providing input to the game, so we will need a stream of acoustic feedback and additional audio cues to make the player aware about the status of the game, the overall progress, important moments, and critical events.

There are three sub-categories to feedback:

1. **Menu**—Sounds required for the landing page.

2. **Interface**—Elements for the in-game heads-up display.

3. **Experience**—Emotional sound cues to trigger player excitement.

1.4.1 Menu

The menu is the first contact between the player and our product. The game begins with the main menu, where players start their onboarding by creating an avatar; setting difficulty, graphic, and sound options; or adjusting the controls to their needs. Going in or out of a submenu, slider movement, and button presses usually have sound attached to support the physical interaction of the input device. Ideally these sounds should be themed to our product. For example, in an ancient Roman action game, we might want using sword whooshes for moving between the menu pages, a shield smash to cancel, and a sword hit to confirm. The main menu also offers an option to give a first glimpse of the game world by playing an ambience or moody soundscape. In our example, this could be the sound of a distant battle or marching soldiers.

1.4.2 Interface

The interface plays a major role in giving the player helpful information about the status, progress, and events of the game. These events might be acoustic support for banners and tutorial hints, flashing icons that highlight the controls, notifications of mission success, or warnings that focus the player's attention to a certain area of the screen or to an important event which is about to happen. Like the menu, these sounds should be themed to our product. We want to give these events a strong audible identity while maximizing player readability. Using our Roman action game example, we can support the banners with a sword pulling from the sheath on appearance and holstering it when it disappears, highlighting controls with a drum roll to underline the haptic nature, or playing battle horn sounds to make the player aware that an attack is underway.

1.4.3 Experience

The user experience is deeply connected to the emotional aspects of playing a game. Audio can play a big role in achieving a memorable gaming

experience. HUD sounds are part of that, giving the player vital information regarding the game status, critical events, or important information.
This can be an alert sound when your base is under attack in a real-time
strategy game, the heartbeat sound when running out of health in an
action game, or the ticking of the timer when falling behind in a racing
game.

Often, these sounds are unrealistic and designed to enhance the drama
or provide satisfaction. A good example is the successful hit feedback,
which is designed and exaggerated to celebrate the victorious moment, or
low-tone sub-bass rumbles which increase tension and build up a sense of
fear and danger long before the actual game event.

1.5 WRAP-UP

While this structure has been proven to work for a solid range of titles,
there will always be elements which might not fit into an existing category
and require a different structure based on the game you are making. The
list in Section 1.5.1 is meant to be a first check to give you a starting point
regarding your asset requirements, technical implementation, and project
structure.

1.5.1 Sound Effects Category Check List

- **World**
  - Environment (e.g. ambiences, spot FX)
  - Weather (e.g. rain, snow)
  - Particle (e.g. fire, spark)
  - Physics (e.g. collision, destruction)
- **Character**
  - Movement (e.g. clothes, footsteps)
  - Interaction (e.g. abilities, features)
- **Feedback**
  - Menu (e.g. options, buttons)
  - Interface (e.g. mini-map, events)
  - Experience (e.g. hit feedback, health indicator)

- **Questions to answer:**
  - Do I need this (sub) category in my project?
  - Do I see this category used globally or specifically?
  - Do I have to react to real-time conditions, and if yes, what are they?

1.6 CONCLUSION

It is important for us to talk about the sound effect requirements and potential challenges early in production. The common use of audio middleware and the high standard of audio implementation with visual scripting in game engines allow the audio designers to build complex audio behavior with minimum help from audio programmers. However, with great power comes great responsibility: we want to enable audio designers to build complex game audio with maximum flexibility, while keeping maintenance, performance, and costs in consideration. I hope the sound effect categories help you to avoid some pitfalls, master the challenges, and strengthen the communication and collaboration between audio programmers and audio designers.

I

DSP

CHAPTER 2

Complex Numbers

A Primer for DSP Programming

Robert Bantin

Massive Entertainment — an Ubisoft Studio

CONTENTS

2.1 INTRODUCTION

Although it may not be intuitively obvious, the concept of a "complex number" (i.e. a compound value containing a *real* and an *imaginary* component) can be very powerful when you are modeling something that has both magnitude and phase. Consider the model of a spiral in Figure 2.1. When you compare each point along the graph with the next, two properties can be observed:

1. The relative angle from the origin increasing linearly.

2. The relative distance from the origin growing geometrically.

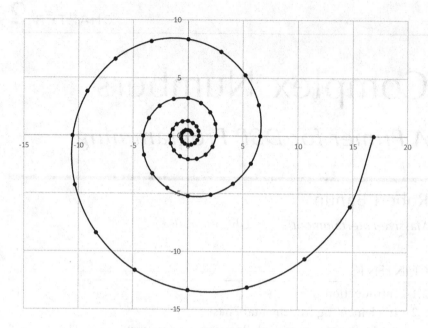

FIGURE 2.1   A spiral graph.

We can say that the angle here is our *phase*, while the distance is our *magnitude*. Modeling this graph with mathematics is precisely the sort of thing that complex numbers are for.

2.2 IMPLEMENTING INCREMENTAL PHASE

With the aim of producing this spiral graph using complex numbers, let's backtrack a little bit and examine how the phase of our model is incrementing. Consider the simpler model of a circle in Figure 2.2. If we look at each point's position on the horizontal axis, we could just as easily plot these values on a horizontal time plot as vertical values and get a sinusoidal wave, as shown in Figure 2.3.

Let us imagine that this circle model simulates an A.C. voltage generator and that these amplitude values in time are the *real* voltage output from this model. On the circular graph, this output traces along each point's horizontal coordinate, so let's say the horizontal axis is the *real*, or *Re*, axis. The vertical axis is necessary to help track the steady phase rotation of the model, but each point's coordinate on this axis is not part of the *real* output, so we'll call this axis the *imaginary*, or *Im*, axis. If we set the significance of these labels aside, we can just treat them as alternative *x* and *y* labels.

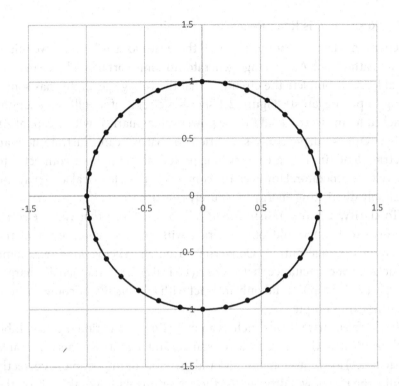

FIGURE 2.2   A circle graph.

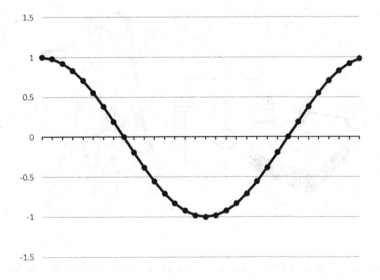

FIGURE 2.3   Time plot of the real axis.

2.2.1 Resistance Is Real; Reaction is Imaginary

The reason why we're bothering with these two axes is because we might want to attach our A.C. voltage generator to some sort of load (i.e. an electrical load to complete the circuit so that the voltage generator has something to push against). Figure 2.4 shows a circuit of a voltage generator attached to an electric load for the power cable (marked with a capital Z). This circuit is purposefully simplified so that we can illustrate how an electrical load (in this case a very long power cable) might be connected to our voltage generator. However, the contents of this electrical load may not be simply dissipating energy in a purely resistive way.

To clarify, a *purely resistive load* (e.g. a resistance that turns electric energy into heat) would only interact with the *real* component of the generator's voltage output. Conversely, a *purely reactive load* (e.g. some inductance or capacitance that stores electrical energy and then discharges it in particular way) would only interact with the *imaginary* component of the generator's output.

Real-life electrical loads such as a power line on a national grid exhibit both *resistive* (in this case, cable resistance) and *reactive* (in this case, cable capacitance) load components. It would therefore be impossible to correctly predict the *real* power drop across the power line without taking both the *resistive* and *reactive* load components into account. As an example, it's possible for *reactance* to act like an open circuit (i.e. infinite resistance)

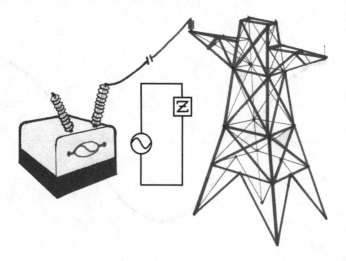

FIGURE 2.4 Circuit of a voltage generator attached to an electric load for the power cable (marked with a capital Z).

below a certain frequency and act like a closed circuit (i.e. very low resistance) above a certain frequency. In this case, how much power dissipation actually occurs with this type of *reactance* in parallel to the *resistance* could depend greatly on the oscillation frequency of our generator, as well as the length of the cable (because as the cable gets longer, the *resistance* and *reactance* increase at different rates). This is why power engineers are so careful about cable selection when designing power lines.

2.2.2 The Voltage Before the Load

Let's look at the voltage generation before the load. If we take the *Re* and *Im* values of each point in the circle model as Cartesian-style coordinates, we can describe each point of our circle model at time interval t as a 2D vector:

$$S_t = [a_t, b_t]$$

where a and b are the *real* and *imaginary* voltage states of the generator at time interval t. Just think of t as a discrete time index: $t = [0, 1, 2, 3,$ etc.].

If we were to attempt to progress the phase within S using vector math, we could define a constant rotation vector as

$$Q = \begin{bmatrix} \cos\theta \\ \sin\theta \end{bmatrix}$$

where θ is the phase increment between each time interval t.

Q would be applied to S of the current time interval to get the value of S at the next time interval as follows:

$$S_{t+1} = S_t \times Q = [a_t \cos\theta - b_t \sin\theta, a_t \sin\theta + b_t \cos\theta]$$

You could then apply this incremental rotation in our simulation by reapplying the same vector operation to each time interval of S to get the next time interval of S. You can thereby model the alternator turning over at an angular rate of θ per time interval t.

For implementing this in code, the above equations would all work just fine. However, in an era when a computer was a person, the mathematicians of the day came up with a different approach that fit the tool they had at the time: Algebra.

They might have approached this problem by declaring S and Q as follows:

$$S_t = a_t + ib_t$$

$$Q = \cos\theta + i\sin\theta$$

The value i is a special coefficient that cannot be resolved into a *real* number until it is squared, at which point it becomes -1. The i is therefore used to signify that the value on its own is "imaginary"—opposite to the normal "real" numbers that always produce a positive result when multiplied by themselves. The value i is often described as "the square root of -1." While this is technically true, it is not a terribly helpful definition, so this chapter will stick to the definition $i^2 = -1$.

Within the context of our circle model, what we are saying here is that when an *Im* axis component is multiplied with another *Im* axis component, the result is transformed into an inverted *Re* axis component. Conversely, when a *Re* axis component is multiplied with an *Im* axis component, the result is transformed into an *Im* axis component.

So, let's apply this to S and Q using an algebraic product:

$$S_t = a_t + ib_t$$

$$Q = \cos\theta + i\sin\theta$$

$$S_{t+1} = S_t Q = (a_t + ib_t)(\cos\theta + i\sin\theta)$$

Open out the brackets:

$$S_{t+1} = S_t Q = a_t\cos\theta + ia_t\sin\theta + ib_t\cos\theta + i^2 b_t\sin\theta$$

Remember that $i^2 = -1$, so applying that here gives us:

$$S_{t+1} = S_t Q = a_t\cos\theta + ia_t\sin\theta + ib_t\cos\theta - b_t\sin\theta$$

And then re-factorize the four terms into *real* and *imaginary* chunks:

$$S_{t+1} = S_t Q = (a_t\cos\theta - b_t\sin\theta) + i(a_t\sin\theta + b_t\cos\theta)$$

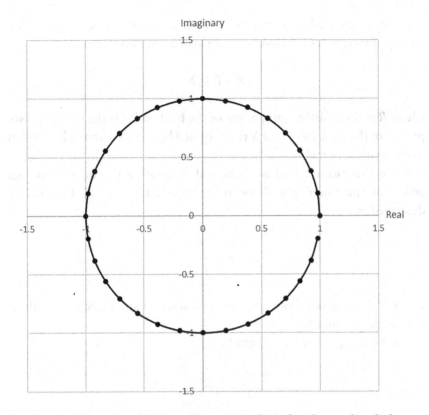

FIGURE 2.5   The circle graph from Figure 2.2 achieved with complex algebra.

You may begin to see that this little algebraic trick with $i^2 = -1$ is what's doing the work of that vector operation for us, albeit with a somewhat different style of notation. *That's really all it is.*

In any case, any complex number can be plotted on this *Re/Im* graph (known as an Argand diagram after its creator, J.D. Argand) by treating its *real* and *imaginary* components as Cartesian-style coordinates.

Now that we've got our phase progression correctly worked out using complex numbers, we can reproduce the circle graph that we built in Figure 2.2 by using complex numbers (Figure 2.5). Note that Figures 2.2 and 2.5 are identical, even though they were constructed using different mechanisms.

2.2.3 The Voltage After the Load

Now that we have a way to simulate the complex voltage at the generator source, let's see how we could apply a load that's both *resistive* and *reactive.* When we lump these two properties together, we usually call it an *impedance*, so let's declare a simple load as an impedance Z:

$$Z = R + iX$$

where R is the resistive component of the load and X is the reactive component of the load. Note that X is multiplied by i to show that it lives solely in the *imaginary* realm.

Since this electric load is connected in series with our A.C. voltage generator, the power drop P due to the impedance factor Z of the load is described by

$$P = \frac{\overline{S^2}}{Z}$$

where $\overline{S^2}$ is all of our plotted values for S squared and averaged, resulting in a single *real* number.

Substituting Z for $(R + iX)$ gives us

$$P = \frac{\overline{S^2}}{(R + iX)}$$

Now, to perform the division of this complex denominator, there's another trick. If we multiply the top and bottom of this fraction with the same number, the overall effect will cancel out, so what we do is choose another complex number for this purpose that nullifies the *imaginary* component in the denominator. That's actually pretty easy—we just take the existing complex denominator and flip the sign of the *imaginary* component. This number with the negated *imaginary* component is called the complex conjugate. In this case, it is simply

$$R - iX$$

Multiplying the numerator and denominator by this complex conjugate gives us

$$P = \frac{\overline{S^2}(R - iX)}{(R + iX)(R - iX)}$$

Opening out the brackets of the denominator eliminates the *imaginary* component in the denominator:

$$P = \frac{\overline{S^2}(R - iX)}{R^2 + X^2}$$

Now the denominator is purely *real*. We just need to open the brackets of the numerator:

$$P = \frac{\overline{S^2}R - i\overline{S^2}X}{R^2 + X^2}$$

To be clear then, the *real* and *imaginary* components of the power drop are

$$P_{real} = \frac{\overline{S^2}R}{R^2 + X^2}, \; P_{imag} = \frac{-i\overline{S^2}X}{R^2 + X^2}$$

Hopefully you can now see that if we ignored the cable capacitance of the power line, our simulation of the power drop across the load would only be $\frac{\overline{S^2}}{R}$. That estimate would make our prediction way off with even the slightest amount of *reactance*—even though we said the *reactance* of the load was purely *imaginary*.

To summarize thus far, what we are saying is that since our A.C. voltage generator simulation needs to predict the effect of a load that can be both *resistive* and *reactive*, we can pretend that there is a second, *imaginary* voltage working orthogonally to the *real* one, and this helps us correctly understand how the power would drop over that kind of combined load.

2.3 IMPLEMENTING GEOMETRIC GROWTH

Going back to the spiral model from Figure 2.1, we would need to grow the magnitude geometrically to get the desired effect. Ideally, we'd need to choose a growth factor and translate it into a *real* and *imaginary* factor for S. Since the *real* and *imaginary* components are always orthogonal, we can view these growth factors like a right-angled triangle and apply the Pythagoras theorem:

$$C^2 = A^2 + B^2$$

where C is our growth factor, and A and B are the respective *real* and *imaginary* components of that factor.

Since A and B will apply their scale equally, they need to be the same, so we say

$$C^2 = 2A^2$$

And therefore

$$B = A = \sqrt{\frac{C^2}{2}}$$

If we restate that S per interval of time t as

$$S_t = a_t + ib_t$$

our constant growth factor Q would be

$$Q = A + iB$$

Substituting for A and B, we get

$$Q = \sqrt{\frac{C^2}{2}} + i\sqrt{\frac{C^2}{2}}$$

which we can factorize as

$$Q = \sqrt{\frac{C^2}{2}}(1+i)$$

And we can then apply the growth factor for each point of S as before:

$$S_{t+1} = S_t Q$$

2.4 COMBINING INCREMENTAL PHASE WITH GEOMETRIC GROWTH

In order to combine the rotational increment and the growth factor into a single spiraling modifier for S, we can define Q as an aggregate of the last two definitions:

$$Q = A\cos\theta + iB\sin\theta$$

where A and B are our respective *real* and *imaginary* growth components, and θ is the phase increment between each time interval t.

Based on the formula we've been using for generating S along time interval t,

$$S_{t+1} = S_t Q$$

We can generate our spiral model with the following formula:

$$S_{t+1} = S_t Q = S_t \left(A\cos\theta + iB\sin\theta \right)$$

Open out the brackets:

$$S_{t+1} = S_t Q = A\left(a_t \cos\theta - b_t \sin\theta \right) + iB\left(a_t \sin\theta + b_t \cos\theta \right)$$

$$S_{t+1} = S_t Q = Aa_t \cos\theta - Ab_t \sin\theta + iBa_t \sin\theta + iBb_t \cos\theta$$

Re-factorize for the *real* and *imaginary* chunks:

$$S_{t+1} = S_t Q = \left(Aa_t \cos\theta - Ab_t \sin\theta \right) + i\left(Ba_t \sin\theta + Bb_t \cos\theta \right)$$

Because of the equivalence $\{A \equiv B\}$,

$$S_{t+1} = S_t Q = A\left(\left(a_t \cos\theta - b_t \sin\theta \right) + i\left(a_t \sin\theta + b_t \cos\theta \right) \right)$$

And since we've already stated that

$$B = A = \sqrt{\frac{C^2}{2}}$$

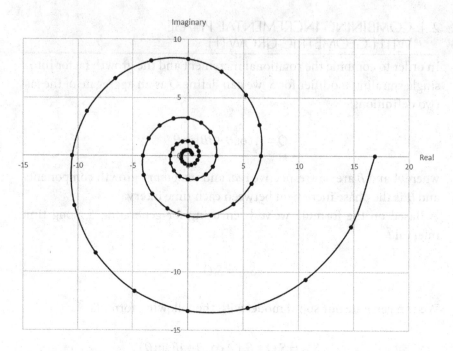

FIGURE 2.6   The spiral graph from Figure 2.1 achieved with complex algebra.

we can substitute that here:

$$S_{t+1} = S_t Q = \sqrt{\frac{C^2}{2}} \left((a_t \cos\theta - b_t \sin\theta) + i(a_t \sin\theta + b_t \cos\theta) \right)$$

Let's pick some values now and graph them out. For growth factor C, we're going to pick the first golden ratio $= \frac{3}{2}$, and for the rotational increment, we're going to pick $\theta = \frac{\pi}{8}$. The resulting graph is in Figure 2.6. Now that we have our magnitude and phase properties worked out using complex numbers, we can see that the spiral graph in Figure 2.6 is identical to Figure 2.1.

2.5 NOTATION USED BY DSP PROGRAMMERS

Electrical engineers use complex algebra a lot, but they tend to use the letter i for alternating current. (Capital I is used for direct current.) To avoid potential mix-ups, they opt for the letter j when referring to the *imaginary* coefficient. For example, our load impedance would instead be described as

$$Z = R + jX$$

where R is the resistive load and X is the reactive load.

Since signal processing and DSP historically grew out of branches of electrical engineering, you will mostly see j notation used in books and papers, so be aware that j is not just some mystery scale factor. It's the *imaginary* coefficient getting its hands dirty.

For example, you might see the Discrete Fourier Transform defined as

$$X_k = \sum_{n=0}^{N-1} x_n e^{\frac{-j\omega kn}{N}}$$

You will see this pairing of j and ω (frequency in radians) a lot in signal processing. In the world of digital audio, they're almost inseparable—particularly with the natural exponent e and the sample period (the time duration of a single audio cycle) T:

$$e^{-j\omega T}$$

where ωT is frequency in radians-per-sample.

Since Euler's formula states that

$$e^{ix} = \cos x + i \sin x$$

$$e^{-ix} = \cos x - i \sin x$$

these appearances with the natural exponent and the sample period are nothing more than shorthand notation for

$$e^{-j\omega T} = \cos \omega T - j \sin \omega T$$

And while the left-hand side is shorter to write down, the right-hand side is easier to implement in code using either interleaved arrays or an array of some kind of container that encapsulates both the *real* and *imaginary* components of each element. In C++, using a container class such as `std::complex` also allows the coder to make use of the overloaded math operators of add, subtract, multiply, and divide in order to apply the special complex number rules opaquely, which makes objects of such a container class visibly cleaner to use in code (and with no additional impact to performance).

2.6 CONCLUSION

A complex number consists of a *real* and an *imaginary* component. Using complex numbers, we can represent both amplitude and phase together. Complex numbers work just like normal algebra, except that when an *imaginary* component is multiplied with an *imaginary* component, the result is an inverted *real* component. When a *real* component is multiplied with an *imaginary* component, the result is an *imaginary* component, so multiplying complex numbers needs to use the trick $i^2 = -1$ to get to the right answer. Conversely, dividing by a complex number requires multiplying the numerator and denominator of the fraction by the *complex conjugate* (the same complex number with an inverted *imaginary* component), thereby eliminating the *imaginary* component in the denominator. (Note that electrical engineers often use j instead of i to avoid confusing the *imaginary* component with the standard symbol for alternating current.)

Finally, Euler's formula allows us to use e^{ix} shorthand in cases where the *real* and *imaginary* components are *cosine* and *sine* functions, respectively. This means that in code, we don't usually implement the exponential function with an *imaginary* power and instead prefer to implement a two-element container type that gets multiplied by *cosine* and *sine* accordingly.

CHAPTER 3

Building Dynamic Analog-Style Filters

Bi-Quadratic Cascades vs Digital Integrator Cascades

Robert Bantin

Massive Entertainment — an Ubisoft Studio

CONTENTS

3.1 INTRODUCTION

It's a fairly regular occurrence that DSP coders get asked by sound design-ers about dynamic filters (i.e. filters that can move their corner frequency as they process) and why a particular dynamic filter sounds "harsh" or "weird." If it's a simple low-pass or high-pass filter, the most likely reason is that it was implemented using the ubiquitous "bi-quadratic filter" (or "bi-quad") structure. While this approach is generally excellent, it seems to fall apart when modulating its cut-off or center frequency rapidly.

Prior to the bi-quad being widely adopted across the audio industry, Hal Chamberlin [1] had been developing his own ideas in isolation and came up with a vastly different approach to the one that later came to popular research papers and textbooks. Neither approach is necessarily superior to the other—there are pros and cons to both, and some will be outlined in this chapter. However, Chamberlin's approach really shines in two important respects: Firstly, in its natural ability to emulate classic Butterworth-type filter alignments (meaning those with a flat-as-possible pass-band) and secondly, in the structure's stability—particularly when modulating the cut-off or center frequency rapidly. It is for these two aspects that Chamberlin's approach is measurably superior at building dynamic analog-style filters. However, before diving headlong into some of Hal Chamberlin's work, let's have a quick look at a more traditional digital filter structure.

3.2 THE INFINITE IMPULSE RESPONSE (IIR) FILTER

The IIR filter gets its name because if you throw a single amplitude value at an IIR filter followed by digital silence, the output tails off forever, or at least until all the filter states fall into the noise floor. This is due to the filter structure performing weighted averages of previous outputs as negative feedback to the input processing, which could also be a weighted average of current and/or previous inputs. The impulse response length is governed by the amount of feedback.

Arguably the most famous of these filter structures (shown in a generalized form in Figure 3.1) is the bi-quadratic filter, a name it gets from the fact that the Z-plane design method leads you to a ratio of polynomials and the quadratic or second-order polynomial ratio is quite versatile, particularly when cascaded with others.

$$y_k = \sum_{n=0}^{N-1} b_n x_{k-n} - \sum_{m=1}^{M-1} a_m y_{k-m} \tag{3.1}$$

where k is the sample time index, y is the output, x is the input, b is a collection of N input coefficients, n is the input coefficient index in the range $\{0 \le n < N\}$, a is a collection of M output coefficients, and m is the output coefficient index in the range $\{1 \le m < M\}$.

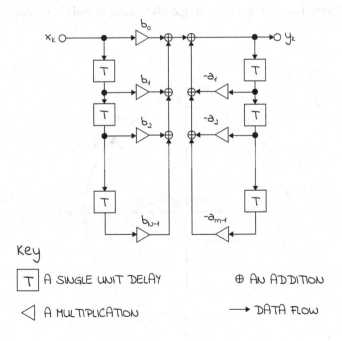

FIGURE 3.1   IIR schematic using "Direct Form-I."

3.2.1 Pole-Zero Maps, the Z-Plane, the Unit Circle, and the Inverse-Z Transform

To apply the Z-plane design method, we first create a "pole-zero map": a 2D graph that plots complex numbers as coordinates along a *real* axis and an *imaginary* axis as shown in Figure 3.2. It's an adaption of the Argand diagram that treats complex numbers as 2D vectors. For more information about complex numbers and algebra, refer to Chapter 2 "Complex Numbers: A Primer for DSP Programming."

The Z-plane is a plane along these two axes, so for simplicity, think of the page that Figure 3.2 is on as the Z-plane. We place a "unit circle" on the origin of the graph with a radius of 1.0. We can then plot a vector called Z as a point that follows this unit circle based on its angle to the *real* axis, ωT in radians-per-sample. This means that for any place along the unit circle, Z is describing a frequency in radians that is normalized with the sample rate in the range $\{0 \leq \omega T \leq 2\pi\}$, or equally $\{-\pi \leq \omega T \leq \pi\}$, as Z will wrap around the circle indefinitely making these two ranges equivalent.

The Z-plane design method allows the designer to place two other types of data, one called a "pole" and the other called a "zero." This is not the numerical value zero, rather the shape of zero as you might describe the O's in tic-tac-toe. Using the strategic placement of poles and zeros inside

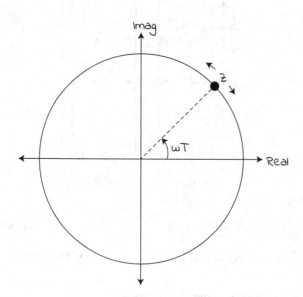

FIGURE 3.2   A pole-zero map.

the unit circle, a transfer function of a digital filter can be designed with respect to the angle (i.e. frequency) of Z:

$$H(Z)=\frac{\prod_{q=0}^{Q-1}Z-z_q}{\prod_{r=0}^{R-1}Z-p_r} \tag{3.2}$$

where H is the transfer function of the filter with respect to the frequency described by Z, Q is the number of zero points z_q (of which q is the index), and R is the number of pole points p_r (of which r is the index).

In other words, the transfer function $H(Z)$ is equal to the product of all distances between Z and each zero, divided by the product of all distances between Z and each pole. This gives importance to the unit circle as it presents the designer with a strict limit—one that ensures that these data points' gain effect is between 0 and unity. There is sometimes reason to place a zero point outside the unit circle as the product of all the zero points controls the DC gain of the filter. However, putting a pole point outside of the unit circle will make the filter unstable.

The next step is to apply the Inverse-Z transform, which turns this map of poles and zeros into a discrete time function of current and previous inputs, and previous outputs, that you can implement as a discrete-time algorithm in code.

Crucially, though, you should think of the angle ωT at π or $-\pi$ radians per sample as the frequency at the Nyquist limit (i.e. the sample rate divided by two). This implies that we are encouraged to design filters with poles and zeros beyond the Nyquist limit or with negative frequency. While this might seem counterintuitive, it is in fact necessary. If you were to place a single pole or zero in the upper half of the unit circle, the time-domain filter that came out of the Inverse-Z transform would have a complex number output. Since we usually want a filter that takes a purely *real* input and generates a purely *real* output, we can mirror the poles and zeros of the upper half of the unit circle in the lower half of the unit circle (doubling the filter order). Each mirror point is a complex conjugate of the original, so when they multiply together in the transfer function $H(Z)$, the *imaginary* components will cancel each other out. There's only one case where this isn't necessary: when the poles and/or zeros are lying on the real axis, implying that the data point is only working around 0 Hz (also known as D.C.) and/or the Nyquist limit (the maximum frequency expressible at a given sample rate). Most of the time you will want to design filters what work in between those two limits, so as a natural consequence, the minimum number of poles or zeros is usually two each and increases in steps of two. When resolving a pole-zero map with just two poles and two zeros, the transfer function $H(Z)$ is then a ratio of two quadratic polynomials - in other words, a bi-quadratic.

$$H(Z) = \frac{b_0 Z^2 + b_1 Z + b_2}{Z^2 + a_1 Z + a_2} \qquad (3.3)$$

where H is the transfer function of the filter with respect to the frequency described by Z, using input coefficients $[b_0\ b_1\ b_2]$ and output coefficients $[a_1\ a_2]$.

Equation 3.3 is the transfer function $H(Z)$ as a bi-quadratic in one its standardized forms. Note that the a_0 coefficient is missing because this term will eventually become the output parameter y_k in Equation 3.1.

The challenge, then, is to fit the transfer function $H(Z)$ as described in Equation 3.2 into the function $H(Z)$ described in Equation 3.3. Once this has been done, the Inverse-Z transform converts all the terms as either current and/or past inputs or past outputs. This is decided by $H(Z)$ as any terms with which it is multiplied become output terms, while the rest become input terms. Every multiple of Z shifts a term's sample time index one unit into the future, such that a term like $b_0 Z^2$ becomes $b_0 x_{k+2}$. Likewise, dividing by Z shifts a term's sample time index one unit into the past, such that $b_0 Z^{-1}$ becomes $b_0 x_{k-1}$.

3.2.2 Example: Math to Create a Notch Filter from Two Poles and Two Zeros

Here is a simple scenario where we want to attenuate a very specific frequency band while leaving the rest of the frequency spectrum relatively untouched. If we stipulate that the notch should attenuate as much as it can, the top half of the ratio in $H(Z)$ should be zero (or almost zero) at our desired frequency ωT.

According to function $H(Z)$ in Equation 3.2, this means that a pole should have no distance from Z at frequency ωT. We can achieve this by placing a zero on the unit circle at an angle from the origin of ωT. We then mirror this zero on the other side of the *real* axis to ensure a purely *real* output from these zeros when their terms are multiplied together.

For the latter side of that ratio, we could leave it at 1 and have no poles at all. However, you'd end up with a very wide notch with lots of ripple on either side of it, so let's instead place a pole along the same angle ωT but slightly closer to the origin. Let's call that distance D, ensuring that it's in the range $\{0 \le D < 1\}$ to keep the filter stable. Let's also mirror the pole on the other side of the *real* axis to ensure a purely *real* output from these poles when their terms are multiplied together.

If we then trace Z around the unit circle, we can see that the ratio of distances from Z to any pole and zero is almost 1.0 all the way around until we get close to the angle ωT or $-\omega T$, whereupon the ratio (and therefore the gain of the filter) falls to nothing because the distance to one of the zero points is nothing (Figure 3.3).

Since this pole-zero map is in fact an Argand diagram, the position of either pole or zero point above the *real* axis can be described as Equation 3.4, and the position of either pole or zero point below the real axis can be described as Equation 3.5. This is all thanks to Euler's theorem.

$$e^{j\omega T} \equiv \cos\omega T + j\sin\omega T \tag{3.4}$$

$$e^{-j\omega T} \equiv \cos\omega T - j\sin\omega T \tag{3.5}$$

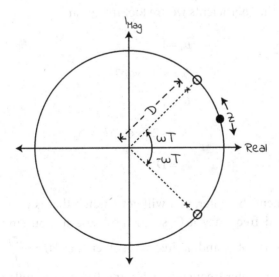

FIGURE 3.3 A pole-zero map with two poles and zeros configured to make a notch filter.

where ωT is the angle from the real axis and j is the engineers' equivalent of the imaginary number i (such that $j^2 = -1$).

The transfer function $H(Z)$ for this specific pole-zero map then looks like this:

$$H(Z) = \frac{\left(Z - e^{j\omega T}\right)\left(Z - e^{-j\omega T}\right)}{\left(Z - De^{j\omega T}\right)\left(Z - De^{-j\omega T}\right)} \tag{3.6}$$

Multiplying out the brackets and working through the terms gives us

$$H(Z) = \frac{Z^2 - Ze^{j\omega T} - Ze^{-j\omega T} + e^0}{Z^2 - ZDe^{j\omega T} - ZDe^{-j\omega T} + D^2 e^0} \tag{3.7}$$

$$H(Z) = \frac{Z^2 - Z\cos\omega T - Zj\sin\omega T - Z\cos\omega T + Zj\sin\omega T + 1}{Z^2 - ZD\cos\omega T - ZDj\sin\omega T - ZD\cos\omega T + ZDj\sin\omega T + D^2} \tag{3.8}$$

$$H(Z) = \frac{Z^2 - 2Z\cos\omega T + 1}{Z^2 - 2ZD\cos\omega T + D^2} \tag{3.9}$$

If you then compare the bi-quadric equation with its standardized form in Equation 3.3, the coefficients we are looking for are

$$b_0 = 1$$

$$b_1 = -2\cos\omega T$$

$$b_2 = 1$$

$$a_1 = -2D\cos\omega T$$

$$a_2 = D^2$$

If you implement this filter, you will get a notch that is centered around the normalized frequency ωT, so to modulate it, you simply need to update the values of b_1 and a_1. Just remember that $\omega T = \dfrac{2\pi f}{f_s}$, where f in this case is your center frequency in Hz and f_s is your sample rate. Setting D close to 1 (say 0.95) will get you a tight notch with minimal ripple, but the attenuation of the notch will be small. Setting D to a lower value like 0.75 will not only increase the attenuation of the notch band, but will also widen the notch band and increase the ripple on either side of it. Figure 3.4 shows the difference between a tight notch and a wide notch.

The only thing left to do is apply the Inverse-Z transform so we can see how this transfer function becomes something implementable in the time domain. This can be done providing you take the formula in Equation 3.3 and multiply both sides by the denominator in that ratio. This should give you Equation 3.10.

$$H(Z)\left(Z^2 + a_1 Z + a_2\right) = b_0 Z^2 + b_1 Z + b_2 \tag{3.10}$$

Applying the Inverse-Z transform, we arrive at the following time domain:

$$y_{k+2} + a_1 y_{k+1} + a_2 y_k = b_0 x_{k+2} + b_1 x_{k+1} + b_2 x_k \tag{3.11}$$

Since we can't practically work in the future, the only way to really implement this time domain equation is by shuffling all the sample time indexes k two units into the past:

$$y_k + a_1 y_{k-1} + a_2 y_{k-2} = b_0 x_k + b_1 x_{k-1} + b_2 x_{k-2} \tag{3.12}$$

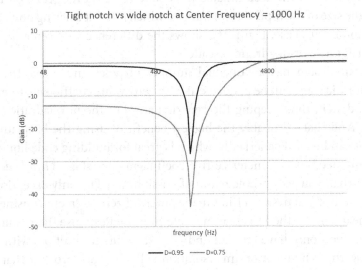

FIGURE 3.4   Tight notch ($D = 0.95$) vs wide notch ($D = 0.75$) at 1,000 Hz.

If we then subtract both sides by $(a_1 y_{k-1} + a_2 y_{k-2})$ to solve for the current output y_k, we end up with

$$y_k = b_0 x_k + b_1 x_{k-1} + b_2 x_{k-2} - a_1 y_{k-1} - a_2 y_{k-2} \qquad (3.13)$$

This is the same as Equation 3.1, just described in the more specific bi-quadratic form of three input terms and two previous output terms.

3.2.3 Going Beyond a Bi-Quadratic Filter

A designer may want to create a higher-order filter using the same method. They will just add more poles and zeros to suit—and lo and behold, the transfer function $H(Z)$ will be a ratio of higher-order polynomials. To be clear, though, you don't need to have equal numbers of poles and zeros. The reason why filters implemented as higher-order polynomials are less common in practice is that the accumulated filter state values within the filter structure get larger as the order increases, and this can lead to precision issues and instabilities. There have been various alternative structures derived to combat the issue of stability (lattice, ladder, a hybrid of the two), but largely speaking, they don't match the clinical simplicity of breaking up a high-order structure into a series of second-order (bi-quadratic) structures that can be cascaded together to get the same intended effect. Each bi-quadratic stage adds an extra multiplication and addition to the computation, but the accumulated filter state values never get larger than twice the size of the input/output ranges, which a 32-bit floating point unit can handle with ease. Figure 3.5 shows the difference between a higher-order IIR and a bi-quadratic cascade.

If your design has an unequal number of poles and zeros, the last bi-quadratic stage can be padded out with zero-value coefficients to make up the deficit, thus keeping the generic nature of the bi-quadratic filter intact. And that's probably the biggest benefit of using the bi-quadratic filter: it can be used generically, which is great for building code libraries. You only need to parameterize five coefficients per stage: $[b_0 \, b_1 \, b_2 \, a_1 \, a_2]$; and for that, you get a whole realm of possibilities. The only exception to this trend is if you design a filter made purely of zeros—in effect using the Z-plane design method to create a Finite Impulse Response filter. Since in this case you only have current and/or past inputs to multiply with and sum together, the most optimal solution is likely a dot-product that has been made more efficient using blocks of SIMD operations.

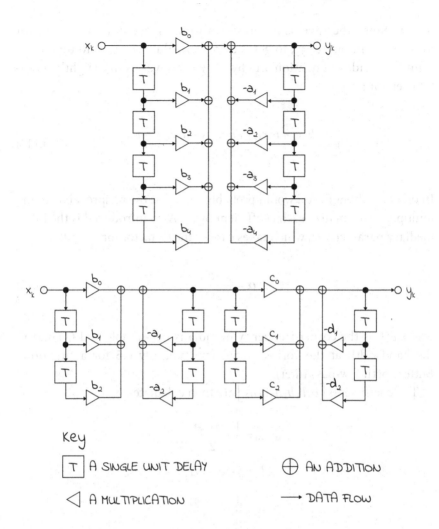

Key

$\boxed{\mathsf{T}}$ A SINGLE UNIT DELAY $\oplus$ AN ADDITION

$\triangleleft$ A MULTIPLICATION $\longrightarrow$ DATA FLOW

FIGURE 3.5   Higher-order IIR vs bi-quadratic cascade.

3.2.4 Robert Bristow-Johnson's Cookbook

Robert Bristow-Johnson worked out a cookbook of formulas for approximating the classic Butterworth-shapes using bi-quadratic filter structures [2], and no doubt these formulas have since been implemented by expedient DSP coders many, many times over.

3.2.4.1 Digital Butterworth Low-Pass Bi-Quadratic Coefficients Derived from Analog Butterworth Control Parameters

The original source material not only quotes the bi-quadratic coefficients we are familiar with, but also includes the one we normally leave out: a_0. Since the Inverse-Z transform would place a_0 as a scale factor to the current output y_k, to get the correct value, we need to divide the right-hand side of Equation 3.13 by a_0, which gives us this slightly modified version:

$$y_k = \frac{b_0 x_k + b_1 x_{k-1} + b_2 x_{k-2} - a_1 y_{k-1} - a_2 y_{k-2}}{a_0} \tag{3.14}$$

In practice, though, you would probably work out the reciprocal of a_0 and multiply or normalize each coefficient by a_0. Also introduced is the intermediary parameter α, which takes care of the Q-factor for our filter:

$$\alpha = \frac{\sin \omega T}{2Q} \tag{3.15}$$

where ωT is the corner frequency in radians-per-sample and Q controls the bandwidth at the corner frequency (typically 0.5 for a first-order Butterworth low-pass filter).

The coefficients $\left[b_0\, b_1\, b_2\, a_0\, a_1\, a_2 \right]$ are then calculated by

$$b_0 = \frac{1 - \cos \omega T}{2}$$

$$b_1 = 1 - \cos \omega T$$

$$b_2 = \frac{1 - \cos \omega T}{2}$$

$$a_0 = 1 + \alpha$$

$$a_1 = -2 \cos \omega T$$

$$a_2 = 1 - \alpha$$

However, these "Digital Butterworth filters" don't match their analog equivalents exactly. Figure 3.6 shows a plot comparing the bi-quadratic cookbook low-pass filter and the analog cascade.

Even if the filter response differences are not that critical to you, consider that the design method used to derive these coefficients assumes that the filter structure is in a steady state, which it only gets to after processing

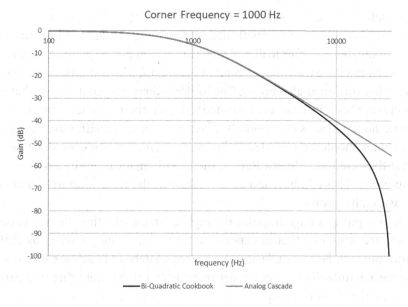

FIGURE 3.6 Bi-quadratic cookbook low-pass magnitude plot, with analog cascade comparison.

potentially hundreds of sample points due to the nested feedback paths with different delay lengths. For a filter that is designed to move and then stay put (like a parametric equalizer band), that's fine, but if you're aiming to build a truly dynamic filter, then you can't realistically expect this implementation to behave as intended when the control parameters are moving all the time. The intermediary results will be very unpredictable.

Lastly, all these bi-quadratic coefficients from the cookbook recipes need to be recalculated every time just one of the control parameters changes, which is potentially once per sample while any control parameter is moving.

Therefore, a bi-quadratic implementation of a Butterworth filter with rapidly moving control parameters is at best cumbersome and at worst not fit for purpose.

3.3 DIGITAL IMPLEMENTATION OF A RESISTOR-CAPACITOR (RC) NETWORK

It seems that the digital techniques we have examined thus far are sub-optimal facsimiles for the real thing. The issue with these techniques is either that they focused on the inputs and outputs of an analog device or somehow warped themselves until their magnitude spectrum got close to the original. Hal Chamberlin's approach was significantly different because he was already very familiar with analog filter design and instead attempted to upgrade those circuits to digital ones using a component-based approach.

Let us examine the simple circuit in Figure 3.7, which shows an RC low-pass filter into an analog buffer. The buffer is there only to illustrate that if several of these circuits were cascaded together, their individual behaviors would not change as they don't "see" each other. The resistor and capacitor values should be regarded as lumped parameters, since we don't care what they are individually. Rather, their mathematical product is what is important. This combination *RC* is known as the time constant τ and is measured in seconds.

If you put a voltage impulse through a circuit like this, the response afterward would be that of exponential decay at a rate governed by that time constant. For example, it takes approximately 4τ to achieve 98% discharge. Chamberlin's approach began by attempting to replicate *that* part of an analog filter digitally.

3.3.1 The Digital Integrator (DI) Filter

The digital integrator (DI) is the filter structure that Chamberlin created to replace that buffered RC circuit. Figure 3.8 shows a schematic of the DI.

$$K = 1 - e^{-\omega T} \tag{3.16}$$

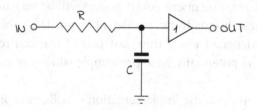

FIGURE 3.7   RC low-pass into an analog buffer.

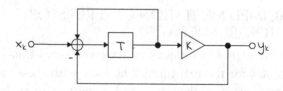

FIGURE 3.8   DI schematic.

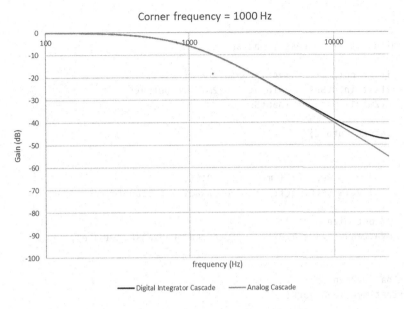

FIGURE 3.9   DI cascade magnitude plot, with analog cascade comparison.

where K is the attenuation factor and ωT is the corner frequency in radians-per-sample.

The DI makes use of feedback, so it is actually another form of IIR filter, albeit one made of a single pole and some additional feedback. It also has just one filter state, so the time it takes to stabilize is miniscule compared to a bi-quadratic IIR filter. This is already good news if we're intending to modulate it rapidly. There's only one coefficient K to worry about too and nothing nearly as difficult to derive as one of Robert Bristow-Johnson's cookbook formulas. Figure 3.9 shows a DI cascade magnitude plot compared with an analog cascade.

3.3.2 Example Code

```
#ifndef _DIGITAL_INTEGRATOR_INCLUDED_
#define _DIGITAL_INTEGRATOR_INCLUDED_

#include <math.h>

class DigitalIntegrator
{
public:
  DigitalIntegrator()
    : myZmin1(0.0f)
    , myAttenuatorK(1.0f)
```

```
{}

inline float Process(float anInput)
{
   float output   = myAttenuatorK * myZmin1;
   float inputSum = anInput + myZmin1 - output;
   myZmin1        = inputSum;

   return output;
}

inline void Reset() { myZmin1 = 0.0f; }
inline void SetFreq(float aFreqInRadiansPerSample)
{
   // optimize expf()
   myAttenuatorK = 1.0f - expf(-aFreqInRadiansPerSample);
}
private:
  float myZmin1;
  float myAttenuatorK;
};

#endif // defined(_DIGITAL_INTEGRATOR_INCLUDED_)
```

3.3.3 A Fast e^x Implementation

Since we are talking about modulating corner frequencies at sample rate, we should also address the matter of the $e^{-\omega T}$ term in Equation 3.16. In the example code, we used expf() from <math.h> for clarity, but realistically you'll want to implement something more efficient in your code.

Option 1—Taylor Series

There is a Taylor series polynomial that approximates e^x with increasing accuracy as the number of terms used increases:

$$e^x \approx \sum_{n=0}^{\infty} \frac{x^n}{n!} = \frac{x^0}{0!} + \frac{x^1}{1!} + \frac{x^2}{2!} + \frac{x^3}{3!} + \cdots \qquad (3.17)$$

Option 2—A Bespoke Polynomial Fit

Given that our range for x is limited to $\{0 \leq x < \pi\}$, it might be better to perform a regression on values for e^{-x} in that range and see if you can get a good curve with less terms than the Taylor series expansion. Microsoft Excel with the "Data Analysis Toolpak" enabled can help you do this.

Option 3—A Self-Interpolating Lookup Table

Lookup tables are commonplace in optimizations, but in this case, the values need a high degree of accuracy. Fortunately, the key property of e^x is that it is its own gradient, so you can use the table to interpolate between the points in the table. Heavy recursion should be avoided, but you may be surprised at how accurate you can get with just a handful of recursions. As an example, using 8.24 fixed-point arithmetic possible on a 32-bit ARM CPU, three iterations will already exceed the precision of the number system itself.

3.4 BUILDING STANDARD BUTTERWORTH FILTER SHAPES WITH DI NETWORKS

Now that we have our basic DI building block, let's see how it works in networks.

3.4.1 Butterworth Low-Pass Filter

For a first-order Butterworth low-pass filter, the DI building block is unchanged. To increase the order, cascade separate instances of the DI together as shown in Figure 3.10.

3.4.2 Butterworth High-Pass Filter

For a first-order Butterworth high-pass filter, take a single DI building block and subtract it from the input. To increase the order, cascade separate instances of this network together as shown in Figure 3.11.

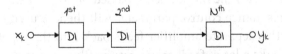

FIGURE 3.10   DI low-pass cascade.

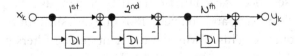

FIGURE 3.11   DI high-pass cascade.

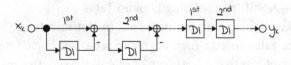

FIGURE 3.12   DI band-pass or notch cascade.

3.4.3 Butterworth Band-Pass and Notch Filters

Using the rules set in the previous two examples, cascade a low-pass DI network with a high-pass DI network. Set the low-pass network's corner frequency above the high-pass network's corner frequency to get a band-pass filter, and do the reverse for a notch filter. To increase the order, cascade separate instances of this network together as shown in Figure 3.12.

3.5 DEALING WITH RESONANCE

It's hard to ignore the question of resonance when talking about dynamic filters, as many dynamic filters in the analog domain either have resonance or its reciprocal parameter "Q" as a control parameter. Resonance in small amounts will add emphasis around the corner or center frequency of a filter, and in larger amounts, it can get the filter to self-oscillate. Both extremes are musically interesting, particularly when the corner or center frequency is modulating rapidly.

3.5.1 The Concept

Analog filter circuits will achieve resonance using some kind of controlled feedback, typically by tapping off the immediate output of the filter into a separate amplifier such that the feedback path is buffered and doesn't interact with the output being passed on to the next stage of the circuit. The resonance control parameter will then be used to vary how much signal this separate amplifier feeds back into the input of the filter. It doesn't take a lot of feedback to get the filter to self-oscillate (a few percent), so the resonance amplifier will always attenuate to a varying degree. If such a filter circuit is a cascade of multiple first-order filters, then the feedback path is typically sent around the entire cascade. This is crucial for resonance, as each first-order filter stage adds a 90° phase shift at its corner frequency, and you need 180° of phase shift for the feedback to cause resonance. This is why the resonant analog filters common to musical applications are either second order or fourth order with a negative feedback path.

3.5.2 The Moog Ladder Filter Example

3.5.2.1 Why the First Thing People Try Doesn't Work Quite Right

Ignoring the clever overdriving features of this filter, the circuit can be viewed as four first-order low-pass filters cascaded together with a negative feedback path going from the final output to the first input. Figure 3.13 shows a Moog ladder filter schematic.

Since we now know how to build these filter stages using DIs, it would be fair to assume that implementing such a filter digitally is pretty straightforward. However, once tested out, you might notice that the resonant peak around the corner frequency isn't exhibiting the properties of "constant Q" (i.e. constant width on a logarithmic axis) and in fact gets narrower and taller as the corner frequency increases. Worse, pushing that frequency far enough will create a peak so large that the code will actually overflow. Obviously, this is not what we want, so what's caused this?

It is an unfortunate fact that many analog circuits are designed without taking propagation delay into account because it's so small that it's not really a factor. This is one of the ways in which digital simulations of analog circuits fail: the digital version will be working at a discrete sample rate, and in our case, the output is four samples later than the input. At very low corner frequencies, this delay translates to a very minor phase shift, so the digital filter will appear to be working correctly. Go up in frequency, and suddenly it's a very different story.

For many years, the received wisdom was to oversample the filter so that this phase gap between the output and input could be narrowed, and without worrying about CPU performance, this does help a great deal. Additionally, the corner frequency can be limited in range to prevent the user from putting the code into a state where it will overflow. Nonetheless, what this means is that building a decent-sounding digital recreation of a resonant analog filter this way can be very CPU intensive, which is undesirable for game audio.

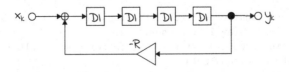

FIGURE 3.13   Moog ladder filter schematic.

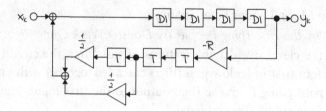

FIGURE 3.14 Moog ladder filter schematic with added feedback delay of 2.5 samples.

3.5.2.2 The Feedback Delay Fix

Tim Stilson and Julius Smith [3] and Antti Houvilainen [4] have published research on this topic and have reasoned that it's easier to further delay the feedback path so that the signal fed back to the input is back-in-phase "enough" to get the resonance behaving correctly at the range of corner frequencies that we're interested in. Figure 3.14 shows a Moog ladder filter schematic with an added feedback delay of 2.5 samples.

2.5 samples' delay is the preferred amount for a sample rate of 48 kHz and can be achieved using some linear interpolation. The fractional delay code shown below should be flexible enough to deal with this and higher sample rates as required.

3.5.2.3 Example Code

```
#ifndef _FRACTIONAL_DELAY_INCLUDED_
#define _FRACTIONAL_DELAY_INCLUDED_

#include <cassert>
#include <cstring>

#define FRACTIONAL_DELAY_LENGTH (8)
#define FRACTIONAL_DELAY_MASK   (FRACTIONAL_DELAY_LENGTH - 1)

static_assert((FRACTIONAL_DELAY_LENGTH & FRACTIONAL_DELAY_MASK) == 0,
              "FRACTIONAL_DELAY_LENGTH must be 2^N power");

class FractionalDelay
{
public:
  explicit FractionalDelay(float inFractionalDelay)
    : myFractionalDelay(inFractionalDelay)
    , myWholeNumberedDelay(static_cast<int>(inFractionalDelay))
    , myLERP(myFractionalDelay -
             static_cast<float>(myWholeNumberedDelay))
    , myWriteCursor(0)
```

```
    , myReadCursorA((myWriteCursor - myWholeNumberedDelay) &
        FRACTIONAL_DELAY_MASK)
    , myReadCursorB((myReadCursorA - 1) & FRACTIONAL_DELAY_MASK)
  {
    assert (myWholeNumberedDelay < FRACTIONAL_DELAY_LENGTH);
    Reset();
  }

  inline float Process(float anInput)
  {
    mySampleBuffer[myWriteCursor & FRACTIONAL_DELAY_MASK] = anInput;

    float output = myLERP * mySampleBuffer[myReadCursorB]
      + (1.0f - myLERP) * mySampleBuffer[myReadCursorA];

    ++myWriteCursor;
    myWriteCursor &= FRACTIONAL_DELAY_MASK;

    ++myReadCursorA;
    myReadCursorA &= FRACTIONAL_DELAY_MASK;

    ++myReadCursorB;
    myReadCursorB &= FRACTIONAL_DELAY_MASK;

    return output;
  }

  inline void Reset()
  {
    memset(
      mySampleBuffer, 0,FRACTIONAL_DELAY_LENGTH * sizeof(float));
  }

private:
  FractionalDelay() = delete;

  float myFractionalDelay;
  int   myWholeNumberedDelay;
  float myLERP;
  int   myWriteCursor;
  int   myReadCursorA;
  int   myReadCursorB;
  float mySampleBuffer[FRACTIONAL_DELAY_LENGTH];
};

#endif // defined(_FRACTIONAL_DELAY_INCLUDED_)
```

Despite this lo-fi approach, the digital artefacts it produces are minimal, so most DSP coders are happy to live with it.

3.6 CONCLUSIONS

While the bi-quadratic filter is flexible, it doesn't perform well when emulating analog Butterworth-type filters, both in a steady state and while being modulated. The unpredictable results account for that "harshness" or "weirdness" that a sound designer might notice. The digital integrator is less flexible in that it *only* works with Butterworth-type filters, but when that's what the sound designer actually wants, it's the ideal choice. Special consideration has to be given when introducing resonance, but a fractional delay in the feedback path can overcome this without the need to oversample.

REFERENCES

1. H. Chamberlin. *Musical Applications of Microprocessors*, p. 488, Second Edition, Hayden Books, Indianapolis, 1985.
2. R. Bristow-Johnson. Cookbook formulae for audio EQ biquad filter coefficients. http://www.musicdsp.org/files/Audio-EQ-Cookbook.txt.
3. T. Stilson and J. Smith. Analyzing the Moog VCF with considerations for digital implementation. In "Proceedings of the International Computer Music Conference," pp. 398–401, Hong Kong, China, August 1996.
4. A. Houvilainen. Non-linear digital implementation of the Moog ladder filter. In "Proceedings of the International Conference on Digital Audio Effects," pp. 61–64, Naples, Italy, October 2004.

CHAPTER 4

Modeling Atmospheric Absorption with a Low-Pass Filter

Nic Taylor

CONTENTS

4.1 INTRODUCTION

Air temperature, humidity, and atmospheric pressure (not to be confused with acoustic pressure) change how sound is absorbed over distance. This atmospheric absorption has the strongest effect on high frequencies and so is often modeled as a low-pass filter as one component of the overall attenuation settings for a sound instance. The attenuation settings, including the low-pass filter, are exposed to the sound designer as a function of distance and for the most part are then static.

This chapter explores using the atmospheric features of air temperature and humidity to provide a systematic way of setting a low-pass filter cutoff for sound propagation. The cutoff frequency can audibly change based on temperature and humidity. By plotting the frequency response of atmospheric absorption, we can see that the low-pass filter is a good approximation of the real-world values.

4.2 MOTIVATIONS

I was motivated to explore using atmospheric features to adjust attenuation settings for two primary reasons:

1. While working on open world games where the player could travel from extreme environments such as Arctic-like zones to dense jungle or desert, there was a desire to find subtle ways to influence sound so that the environment would feel different without relying on ambient sounds. Similar to how air temperature changes drastically between day and night, the goal also included having a subtle change in perception in the same zone at different times of day.

2. One common issue I had observed working on games was inconsistencies in attenuation settings resulting in bugs typically caught toward the end of production. More than once, these inconsistencies required a large refactoring of attenuation settings across the entire game, so it seemed worthwhile to find a systematic way to address attenuation. When it comes to the low-pass filter, using well-understood atmospheric features like temperature and humidity can set a decent starting point even if the attenuation settings were still static in game.

4.3 REVIEW

Attenuation of a point source as a function of distance, r, can be modeled by the following equation [1]:

$$L_p = L_W - 10\log 4\pi r^2 - \alpha r \qquad (4.1)$$

where L_W is the sound pressure level of the source in decibels (dB), $10\log 4\pi r^2$ is the geometric attenuation, and αr is the atmospheric absorption.

In game audio, the geometric attenuation (GA) is often modeled as a curve that terminates at a given distance. And even though GA can be computed infinitely, audio engines have an absolute threshold or cutoff below which sounds are culled. The end of the attenuation curve can be considered the distance at which the sound will reach the cutoff.

The atmospheric absorption, α, is often modeled as a low-pass filter.[1] α is dependent on temperature, pressure, and humidity with a value in decibels/meter. It is also dependent on frequency for which the frequency response resembles a low-pass filter. This model will assume an idealized atmosphere without wind and having a uniform temperature.[2]

4.4 EXTREME RANGES

Observing environments on Earth, temperature and humidity change the atmospheric absorption coefficient the most. Atmospheric pressure even at high elevations is almost negligible, so we can treat atmospheric pressure as a constant.

The extreme ranges of temperature and humidity give some intuition as to how variable the cutoff will be. Using Figure 4.1 as a guide, sounds that are all near field or within 25 meters will have an effect that is perhaps not audible. Past 250 meters, the change in cutoff from a hot, dry environment to a cold, dry environment can be in entirely different frequency bands. This difference is potentially significant enough to impact the mixdown of the game.

---

[1] Some audio engines also include a high-pass filter which sound designers use to remove distant low-frequency content so that closer sounds have better low-end clarity.

[2] A non-uniform temperature, where the ground temperature is different from that of the air above, has interesting effects on sound propagation but is outside the scope of this chapter. See [1] for more details.

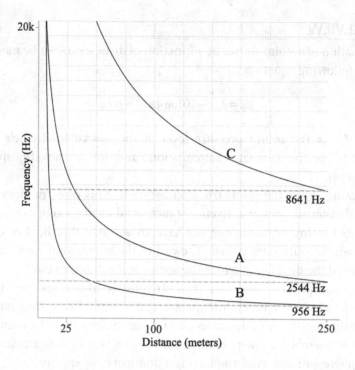

FIGURE 4.1 Cutoff frequencies by distance: (A) 70% humidity, 65°F; (B) 5% humidity, 100°F; and (C) 5% humidity, −5°F.

As a loose rule, cold temperatures have highest absorption with moderate to high humidity, and hot temperatures have highest absorption with dry humidity, as shown in Figure 4.2. For example, in Antarctica where temperatures are often below −20°F, the humidity can almost approach zero percent, and so it would be expected that there is relatively less atmospheric absorption [2]. The Acoustics Wikibook [3] includes a comprehensive table of absorption coefficients at different temperatures and humidity values.

4.5 A LOOK AT THE LOW-PASS FILTER

The frequency response of atmospheric absorption is mostly flat out to a point where the frequencies begin to fall off. The falloff becomes nearly linear on a logarithmic scale, so it shares key traits with the Butterworth filter which is flat in the passband and also falls off linearly on a logarithmic plot as in Figure 4.3.[3]

---

[3] All plots should line up together at −3 dB. However, there is a slight rounding issue as the filters were approximated.

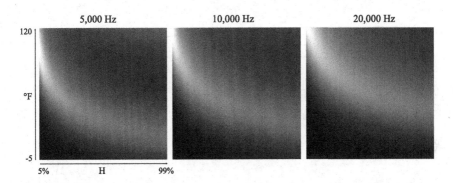

FIGURE 4.2 Absorption coefficients plotted by temperature and humidity. Plots have been normalized by the range at each frequency to highlight relative adsorption. From left to right: 5,000 Hz with a coefficient span of 0.46–17.9 dB/hm, 10,000 Hz with a span of 1.58–41.7 dB/hm, and 20,000 Hz with a span of 6.0–90.8 dB/hm.

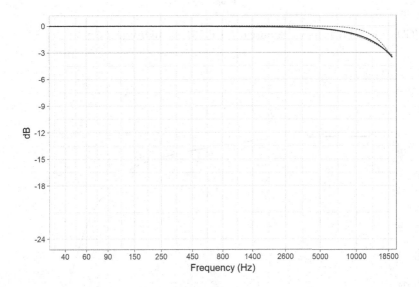

FIGURE 4.3   Frequency response of 75°F, 75% humidity at 10 m.

In Figures 4.3–4.8, the bold line is the computed atmospheric absorption, and the dashed and dash-dotted lines are the frequency responses of a first- and second-order Butterworth filter.

The damping amount at the cutoff frequency of the Butterworth filter is −3 dB. The filters are solved such that the cutoff frequency equals the point where the atmospheric coefficient at the given distance, αr, is also −3 dB.

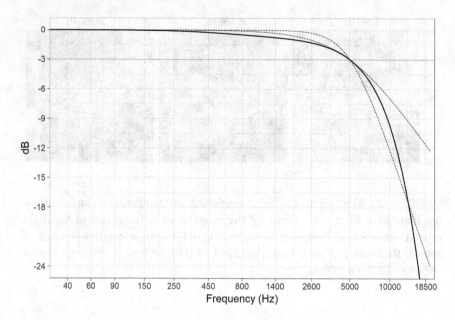

FIGURE 4.4   Frequency response of 75°F, 75% humidity at 100 m.

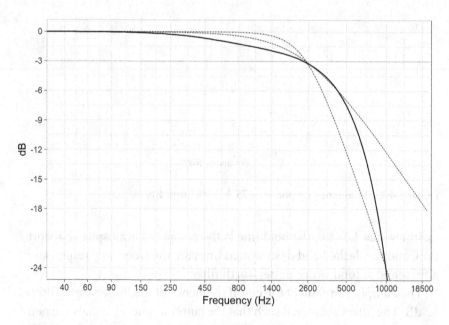

FIGURE 4.5   Frequency response of 75°F, 75% humidity at 250 m.

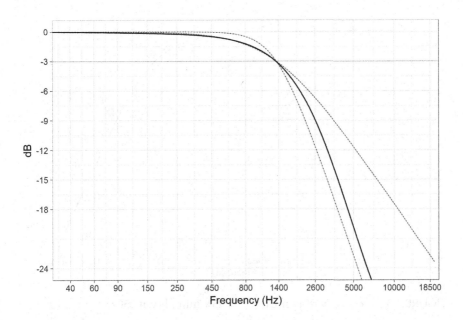

FIGURE 4.6   Frequency response of 110°F, 3% humidity at 250 m.

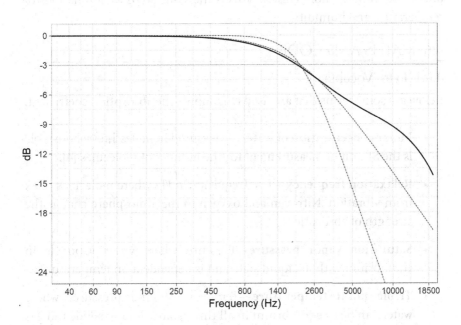

FIGURE 4.7   Frequency response of 20°F, 50% humidity at 250 m.

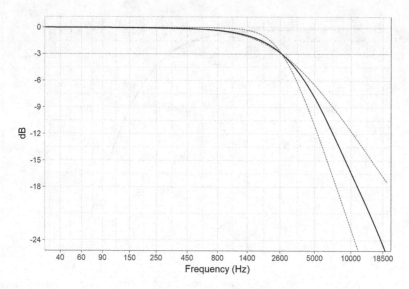

FIGURE 4.8   Frequency response of 20°F, 95% humidity at 250 m.

Notice that before the cutoff frequency, the first-order filter is almost identical with the atmospheric absorption. After the cutoff, the second-order filter follows more closely. This is the same across combinations of temperature and humidity.

4.6 MATHS AND CODE

4.6.1 Extra Vocabulary

Below are some terms that are used to compute the absorption coefficient.

- **Molar concentration of water**—Measured in moles/liter where mole is the SI unit of measurement for the number of molecules [4].

- **Relaxation frequency**—The frequency in Hz where molecules relax from vibration. Nitrogen and oxygen in the atmosphere change the strength of absorption.

- **Saturation vapor pressure**—Pressure where water vapor is in equilibrium with its liquid state and is dependent on temperature.

- **Triple point temperature**—Temperature (and pressure) where water can be in equilibrium in all three states: liquid, solid, and gas (273.16 K).

4.6.2 Math

The equation for the attenuation coefficient is [1, 3, 5]:

$$\alpha = 8.686 f^2 \tau_r^{1/2} \left(1.84 \times 10^{-11} P_r^{-1} + \tau_r^{-3} (b_1 + b_2) \right) \tag{4.2}$$

$$b_1 = \frac{0.1068^{-3352/T} f_{rN}}{f_{rN}^2 + f^2} \tag{4.3}$$

$$b_2 = \frac{0.01275^{-2239.1/T} f_{rO}}{f_{rO}^2 + f^2} \tag{4.4}$$

where b_1 and b_2 are terms dependent on f_{rN} and f_{rO}, the relaxation frequencies in Hz of nitrogen and oxygen. τ_r is the ratio of the given temperature in Kelvin and the reference air temperature. Similarly, P_r is the ratio of the ambient atmospheric pressure in kilopascals and the reference ambient atmospheric pressure [5].

To find the filter cutoff frequency requires solving for frequency f given the coefficient α. To begin to solve for f, Equation 4.2 must be expanded. Because of the large number of constants, some placeholders are introduced: a_1, a_2, a_3 for combined coefficients, N for nitrogen (or f_{rN}), O for oxygen (or f_{rO}), and finally $F = f^2$ to avoid confusion with exponents. a_4 which is negative α is used for consistency. Substituting these in Equation 4.2 yields

$$0 = a_1 F + \frac{a_2 NF}{N^2 + F} + \frac{a_3 OF}{O^2 + F} + a_4 \tag{4.5}$$

Creating common denominators and expanding out the equation will put equation 4.6.1 in a form that can be solved as cubic equation of F:

$$0 = \frac{a_1 F \left(N^2 + F \right) \left(O^2 + F \right) + a_2 NF \left(O^2 + F \right) + a_3 OF \left(N^2 + F \right) + a^4 \left(N^2 + F \right) \left(O^2 + F \right)}{\left(N^2 + F \right) \left(O^2 + F \right)} \tag{4.6}$$

As the denominator is guaranteed to be greater than zero, it can be ignored. The coefficients are consolidated to form the cubic polynomial. New placeholders will be used for the coefficients of the cubic equation:

$$0 = aF^3 + bF^2 + cF + d$$

$$a = a_1$$

$$b = a_1\left(N^2 + O^2\right) + a_2 N + a_3 O + a_4 \tag{4.7}$$

$$c = a_1 N^2 O^2 + a_2 O^2 N + a_3 N^2 O + a_4\left(N^2 + O^2\right)$$

$$d = a_4 N^2 O^2$$

The absorption coefficient is a function of frequency, and there is some frequency at which there is minimal or no absorption and a different, greater frequency where the absorption is greater than the dampening at the cutoff frequency (−3 dB for a Butterworth filter). Therefore, there will exist a real root solution to the cubic equation. Appendix B contains more discussion on finding roots of cubic equations.

4.6.3 API

For the implementation, a class `FilterCutoffSolver` will encapsulate an environment's atmosphere and expose a function, `Solve()`, which returns the cutoff frequency given a distance.

Because several factors in Equation 4.2 are independent of distance, these factors are computed once and stored in variables based on Equation 4.6.

```
const double kPressureSeaLevelPascals = 101325.0;

class FilterCutoffSolver {
public:
  FilterCutoffSolver(const double humidity_percent,
    const double temperature_farenheit,
    const double pressure_pascals = kPressureSeaLevelPascals);

  double Solve(const double distance,
    const double cutoff_gain = 3.0) const;
private:
  double nitrogen_relax_freq;
  double oxygen_relax_freq;

  // Pre-computed coefficients independent of the absorption
  // coefficient.
  double a1, a2, a3;
};
```

4.6.4 Helper Functions

These functions do not need to be exposed by the API but help in unit testing by being extracted from the FilterCutoffSolver class.

```cpp
const double kReferenceAirTemperature = 293.15;

double FarenheitToKelvin(const double farenheit)
{
  return (farenheit + 459.60) * 5 / 9.0;
}

// Convert humidity to molar concentration of water vapor as a
// percentage
static double HumidityConcentration(
  const double humidity_percent, // 0 to 100.0
  const double temperature_kelvin,
  const double pressure_normalized)
{
  const double triple_point_temperature_water = 273.16;
  // Exponent to compute molar concentration
  const double csat = -6.8346 * pow(
    triple_point_temperature_water / temperature_kelvin, 1.261
  ) + 4.6151;
  // Saturation vapor pressure
  const double psat = pow(10, csat);
  // Humidity to molar concentration of water vapor
  return humidity_percent * psat / pressure_normalized;
}

static double NitrogenRelaxationFrequency(
  const double humidity_concentration,
  const double temp_normalized,
  double pressure_normalized)
{
  const double nitrogen_relax_factor = 9 +
    280 * humidity_concentration *
    exp(-4.170 * (pow(temp_normalized, -1.0 / 3) - 1.0));
  // An approximate expected value is 200 Hz.
  return pressure_normalized *
    (1.0 / sqrt(temp_normalized)) * nitrogen_relax_factor;
}

static double OxygenRelaxationFrequency(
  double humidity_concentration,
  double pressure_normalized)
{
  const double oxygen_relax_factor = 24 +
    40400 * humidity_concentration *
```

```
    (0.02 + humidity_concentration) /
    (0.391 + humidity_concentration);
  // An approximate expected value is 25,000 Hz.
  return pressure_normalized * oxygen_relax_factor;
}
```

4.6.5 Implementation

The constructor performs the substitutions from Equation 4.6 to be stored and cached for repeated calls to Solve().

```
FilterCutoffSolver::FilterCutoffSolver(
  const double humidity_percent,
  const double temperature_farenheit,
  const double pressure_pascals)
{
  const double temperature_kelvin =
    FarenheitToKelvin(temperature_farenheit);
  const double temp_normalized =
    temperature_kelvin / kReferenceAirTemperature;
  const double pressure_normalized =
    pressure_pascals / kPressureSeaLevelPascals;

  const double humidity_concentration =
    HumidityConcentration(humidity_percent,
    temperature_kelvin, pressure_normalized);

  // Low frequencies are affected more by nitrogen relaxation
  nitrogen_relax_freq = NitrogenRelaxationFrequency(
    humidity_concentration, temp_normalized, pressure_normalized);
  // Very high frequencies are affected more by oxygen relaxation
  oxygen_relax_freq = OxygenRelaxationFrequency(
    humidity_concentration, pressure_normalized);

  const double temp_norm_inv_cube =
    1.0 / (temp_normalized * temp_normalized * temp_normalized);
  const double nitrogen_relax_coefficient =
    temp_norm_inv_cube * 0.1068 *
    exp(-3352.0 / temperature_kelvin);
  const double oxygen_relax_coefficient =
    temp_norm_inv_cube * 0.01275 *
    exp(-2239.10 / temperature_kelvin);

  const double pressure_coefficient = 1.84e-11 / pressure_normalized;
  // Factor multiplied to the absorption quantities
  const double outer_coefficient = 8.686 * sqrt(temp_normalized);

  // Re-arrange the equation as a cubic polynomial with the
```

```
// absorption_coefficient as the constant factor -a4
// 0 = a1*f^2 + a2*n*f^2/(n^2+f^2) + a3*o*f^2/(o^2+f^2) + a4 where
// f is the variable frequency, n and o are nitrogen/oxygen
// relaxation frequencies
a1 = outer_coefficient * pressure_coefficient;
a2 = outer_coefficient * nitrogen_relax_coefficient;
a3 = outer_coefficient * oxygen_relax_coefficient;
}
```

Solve() collects the factors into the coefficients which form a cubic polynomial and returns the largest root as the filter cutoff frequency in Hz.

```
double FilterCutoffSolver::Solve(const double distance,
  const double cutoff_gain) const
{
  const double absorption_coefficient = cutoff_gain / distance;
  const double a4 = -absorption_coefficient;

  const double nitrogen_sq =
    nitrogen_relax_freq * nitrogen_relax_freq;
  const double oxygen_sq =
    oxygen_relax_freq * oxygen_relax_freq;

  // Expand the denominators (which can then be ignored)
  // and collecting terms
  const double a = a1;
  const double b = a1 * (nitrogen_sq + oxygen_sq) +
    a2 * nitrogen_relax_freq +
    a3 * oxygen_relax_freq + a4;
  const double c = a1 * nitrogen_sq * oxygen_sq +
    a2 * oxygen_sq * nitrogen_relax_freq +
    a3 * nitrogen_sq * oxygen_relax_freq +
    a4 * (nitrogen_sq + oxygen_sq);
  const double d = a4 * oxygen_sq * nitrogen_sq;

  const double root = FindFirstRoot(a, b, c, d);
  const double frequency_hz = sqrt(root);
  return frequency_hz;
}
```

4.7 INTEGRATION

From a performance viewpoint, it should be fine to compute the filter cutoff per game object per frame. Alternatively, a table of cutoffs at different distances could be computed once—for example, when loading into a zone. Using a pre-computed table, game objects could linearly interpolate the cutoff value between the two nearest keys. Having a table in memory also has the benefit of being able to visually inspect what the cutoff frequency is across distances.

For fast moving objects, the filter cutoff may need to be interpolated with a slight delay over time or smoothing function to avoid sudden jumps in the filter cutoff.[4]

Sound designers sometimes rely on an attenuation test world where they can test a sound at different intervals and perform mix balancing. The addition of humidity and temperature parameters would complicate this work. As a result, instead of allowing a near infinite set of potential humidity and temperature combinations, the team can decide on a few "atmosphere profiles" that the game will use. This should include an easy mechanism to switch between these profiles so that testing can be done without changing the game world or zones. Keep in mind that sound designers may also want a way to override the atmospheric absorption cutoff value.

4.8 FUTURE WORK

I acknowledge that the math and number of constants involved in the computation of the frequency cutoff is heavy handed. Future work would be attempting to determine whether the entire model could be simplified to a linear equation. This approximation may not be too large a simplification as the equations used here are only accurate to ±10% in the ideal range in the first place [5].

This model assumes an ideal atmosphere without wind. Wind is a very large component of sound propagation and one that I personally find very interesting. However, wind's impact on sound may not "sound" correct without other cues to convey it. As an example, I have tried to add a "speed of sound" feature to a couple of game engines but always ended up removing it. At a typical speed of 340 m/s, it seemed like the delay would easily come across for sounds just a hundred meters away. However, the implementation would feel as if the sound engine was being unresponsive or lagging. Perhaps the reason is that there are other subtle cues missing that the brain requires for processing images and audio—cues that might become available with continued improvements in areas like VR and 3D sound.

---

[4] Wwise supports this behavior with Interpolation Mode Slew Rate from the Game Parameter properties [6].

APPENDIX A: ABSORPTION COEFFICIENT

It is useful to compute the absorption coefficient given a frequency to test the FilterCutoffSolver. Below is the implementation used to develop FilterCutoffSolver.

```
double AbsorptionCoefficient(const double frequency_hz,
  const double humidity_percent,
  const double temperature_farenheit,
  const double pressure_pascals)
{
  const double temperature_kelvin =
    FarenheitToKelvin(temperature_farenheit);
  const double temp_normalized =
    temperature_kelvin / kReferenceAirTemperature;
  const double pressure_normalized =
    pressure_pascals / kPressureSeaLevelPascals;

  const double humidity_concentration = HumidityConcentration(
    humidity_percent, temperature_kelvin, pressure_normalized);

  const double nitrogen_relax_freq = NitrogenRelaxationFrequency(
    humidity_concentration, temp_normalized, pressure_normalized);
  double nitrogen_quantity =
    0.1068 * exp(-3352.0 / temperature_kelvin);
  nitrogen_quantity /= (nitrogen_relax_freq + frequency_hz *
    (frequency_hz / nitrogen_relax_freq));

  const double oxygen_relax_freq = OxygenRelaxationFrequency(
    humidity_concentration, pressure_normalized);
  double oxygen_quantity =
    0.01275 * exp(-2239.10 / temperature_kelvin);
  oxygen_quantity /= (oxygen_relax_freq +
    (frequency_hz * frequency_hz) / oxygen_relax_freq);

  const double pressure_quantity =
    1.84e-11 / pressure_normalized;
  const double relaxation_quantity =
    (nitrogen_quantity + oxygen_quantity)
    / (temp_normalized * temp_normalized * temp_normalized);

  double absorption_coefficient = 8.686 * sqrt(temp_normalized) *
    (pressure_quantity + relaxation_quantity);
  absorption_coefficient *= frequency_hz * frequency_hz;
  return absorption_coefficient;
}
```

APPENDIX B: ROOT FINDING

The form of the cubic equation used for atmospheric absorption has three real roots, and the solution for frequency happens to be the largest real root.[5] Figure 4.9 shows an example taken from a typical temperature and humidity pair.

4.B.1 Newton's Method

There are multiple ways to find the root of a cubic equation. Newton's method is nice because it is easy to visualize and converges quickly in quadratic fashion to the root nearest the starting value [7].

We know that our root will be somewhere in the range of 5,000–20,000 Hz squared. Therefore, the starting value of Newton's method needs to be greater than the root to avoid converging on one of the lower, possibly negative roots. Since the frequency squared becomes quite large, I have found that it takes more than ten iterations to converge by starting at a value greater than half the sampling rate squared. One optimization would be to use an intermediate function to estimate where the root is.

If you are interested in using Newton's method, here is a naive implementation that can be used as a starting point.

```
double FindRootNewton(const double a, const double b,
   const double c, const double d,
   const double epsilon, const double start) {
   // First derivative
   const double a_prime = a * 3;
   const double b_prime = b * 2;
   const double c_prime = c;
```

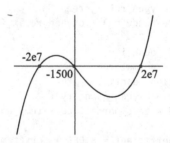

FIGURE 4.9   Typical cubic to be solved. Recall that the root is the frequency cutoff squared.

---

[5] The span of cubic equations was found by evaluating many combinations of temperature, humidity, and distance.

```
  double x = start;
  double delta = epsilon;
  while (fabs(delta) >= epsilon) {
    const double cubic = ((a * x + b) * x + c) * x + d;
    const double quadratic = (a_prime * x + b_prime) * x +
      c_prime;
    delta = cubic / quadratic;
    x = x - delta;
  }
  return x;
}
```

4.B.2 Trigonometric Solver

The option I opted for was to solve the root directly by converting the cubic equation into a depressed form as described on Wikipedia [8]. Because the leading coefficient is always greater than zero, the implementation skips extra checks to validate the result.

```
double FindFirstRoot(const double a, const double b,
  const double c, const double d) {
  // Trigonometric Cubic Solver
  // Assumes a, b, c, and d are all real and that a is > 0,
  // so at least one real root must exist.
  // Also assumes the first root is the largest and correct solution.

  // Convert to depressed cubic using change of variable.
  const double p = (3.0 * a*c - b*b) / (3.0 * a*a);
  const double q = ((2.0 * b*b*b) - (9.0 * b*a*c) +
    (27.0 * a*d*a)) / (27.0 * a*a*a);

  const const double theta = (3.0 * q * sqrt(-3.0 / p)) / (2.0 * p);
  const double depressed_root =
    2.0 * sqrt(-p / 3.0) * cos(acos(theta) / 3.0);

  // For debugging here are the other real roots:
  //const double t2 = -2.0 * sqrt(-p / 3.0) *
  //  cos(acos(-theta) / 3.0);
  //const double t1 = -depressed_root - t2;

  const double root = depressed_root - b / (3.0 * a);
  return root;
}
```

One optimization here would be to replace acos with an approximation[6] and/or rewrite using SIMD.

---

[6] Cubic approximations have been solved for arccos, and your game engine may already be using one.

REFERENCES

1. Erik M. Salomons. *Computational Atmospheric Acoustics*. Springer Science, Heidelberg, 2001, pp. 108–111.
2. Antarctic's Climate: The Key Factors, https://discoveringantarctica.org.uk/oceans-atmosphere-landscape/atmosphere-weather-and-climate/key-factors-behind-antarcticas-climate/.
3. Engineering Acoustics/Outdoor Sound Propagation, https://en.wikibooks.org/wiki/Engineering_Acoustics/Outdoor_Sound_Propagation#Sound_attenuation.5B3.5D.
4. Molar Concentration, https://en.wikipedia.org/wiki/Molar_concentration. Last modified date: 21 June 2020.
5. International Standard. *Acoustics - Attenuation of Sound during Propagation Outdoors* (ISO 9613-1:1993(E)), 1993, pp. 1–3.
6. Property Editor: Game Parameter, *Wwise Help*, https://www.audiokinetic.com/library/edge/?source=Help&id=game_parameter_property_editor.
7. Forman S. Acton. *Numerical Methods that Work*, Harper & Row, New York, 1970, pp. 180.
8. Cubic Equation – Trigonometric Solution, https://en.wikipedia.org/wiki/Cubic_equation#Trigonometric_solution_for_three_real_roots. Last modified date: 22 June 2020.

II

Voice

CHAPTER 5

Software Engineering Principles of Voice Pipelines

Michael Filion

Ubisoft

CONTENTS

5.1 INTRODUCTION

As games continue to grow larger, the number of spoken lines continues to increase. As a result, the challenges for managing and delivering the lines have increased as well. Designing and implementing a flexible and robust voice pipeline becomes important in order to deliver the highest quality voice in-game. There are many challenges, both human and technological, related to any voice pipeline. Providing the necessary tools and removing repetitive tasks allows the people responsible for voice to focus on quality. Additionally, providing the proper debugging tools and information allows programmers to empower less technical members of the team to address problems as they arise in an efficient manner without programmer intervention.

While this chapter will specifically discuss the design and implementation of voice pipelines for large-scale game productions (i.e. anything related to a spoken line in the game on the audio side), the important points can be adapted to a variety of different pipelines and contain reminders of many solid software design principles.

5.2 DEFINITIONS

This chapter uses a number of terms that we will define here for clarity:

- **Line**—Any written or spoken piece of text that is used in-game.

- **Voice**—Any spoken text that is the product of a recording[1] for the game. Both line and voice can, at times, be used interchangeably.

- **Pipeline**—A collection of processes and/or related steps undertaken in an ordered fashion. Explained differently, it is the method that we use to take an input (i.e. written text) and produce an output (i.e. spoken line triggered in the game). Figure 5.1 shows an example of a basic pipeline.

- **Continuous Integration**—The process of automatically integrating multiple developers' work into a shared base.

- **Digital Audio Workstation (DAW)**—A tool that is used in the recording, editing, and production of audio files.

FIGURE 5.1   An example of a basic pipeline for taking written text and producing and implementing an audible voice line in-game.

---

[1] Or produced through some other mechanism.

5.3 DEFINING REQUIREMENTS

Before implementing or beginning any cursory design of the required voice pipeline, it is important to list all the requirements for your project. Even between two different projects of comparable size and complexity, small details can make all the difference.

What is the expected line count? Will it be 100 or 100,000 lines? This means the difference between developing tools and automated processes to deal with the massive quantity of files, and simply dragging and dropping the files from one location to the next. This number will allow a proper evaluation of the time invested versus the potential time savings. There is no sense in spending 10 hours developing some tools where it would take only 1 hour to manually treat all of the lines with an existing toolset.

In what manner will the text be delivered to the department for recording? Will text be sent as it is written, or will it only be sent once approved by the parties responsible? How will you track which lines have been approved and/or already recorded? A spreadsheet will help, but what is the potential for human error in this flow? Will adding any sort of tools for validation and approval into this allow for greater quality control, or will one person become a bottleneck?

Once the lines are recorded, how will they be sent from the recording studio to the development team? There are well-known transfer methods that can easily be automated such that the files are moved with existing third-party tools (such as FTP or transfer to a NAS). Other solutions might require more or less manual intervention depending on how those tools/protocols were built.

Where will all of the files be stored before being integrated into the game engine? Will they be stored in a revision control system such as Perforce or Plastic SCM, or will they simply be stored on a NAS somewhere accessible to all members responsible for working with these files?

What type of processing will need to be performed on the files before being integrated into the engine? Will you need to enforce loudness standards, projection levels, file formats, sample rates, etc.?

Are you using middleware for your audio engine or is it a custom-developed solution? This is the difference between doing a search online to see if there are any third-party tools that can already perform many (if not all) of the tasks that you need when treating your sound data and knowing that you need to develop everything yourself.

How will these files be stored once integrated? If these files will reside alongside other game assets, there isn't any extra work necessary. However, the audio middleware might store them as raw WAV files which need to be converted before being used in-game.

While the answers to these questions will reveal many details about your requirements, there are still many more that have not been listed here. It is important to review all of the requirements in conjunction with the rest of the team and to bear in mind that something that worked for the first release of SuperAwesome Game might not work for SuperAwesome Game 2.

5.4 DESIGN

With the list of requirements in hand, now the time has come to define the pipeline. The first version will almost never look like the final version used at the end of production. It is important to iterate on the pipeline design continually throughout the implementation process as new requirements and technical challenges arise.

Starting with the individual steps in the pipeline, determining what resources are required at each step will help flush out the overall design. Sometimes the resources may seem obvious, but it is important to document them for a new member of your team that joins several months after the pipeline design has been completed and implementation has started. This has the additional advantage of someone looking at the design and pointing out errors or questions of concern.

5.4.1 Expecting the Unexpected

In an ideal world, all edge cases would be handled, and every possible combination has an actionable item. Programming never exists in an ideal world, and software users always find new ways to break tools that should be impossible. Undoubtedly someone will think of a way to try and simplify their workflow or execute some action incorrectly, leaving you with an unexpected result. In a worst-case scenario, it ends up corrupting data (or at least results in data that is less than optimal), which could result in a bug in-game that never gets fixed because of time constraints.

Let's be clear that there is no magic solution to prevent every user misstep or mistake. The important question will be: "How quickly can we handle User X's new action?" If it takes a week to implement a solution, how many other users will invent new and creative ways to use the pipeline in that time?

5.4.2 Platform Agnostic

This ties into the previous section's principle in that you should not rely on any particular piece of software when possible. Today your company's servers are running Windows, but will they be running Linux next year? Your production is currently using Jenkins, but perhaps they will switch to something like TeamCity because of the reduced manpower cost or the budget suddenly opening up to purchase a commercial license. Tightly integrating with any specific software, internal or third-party, may prove detrimental in the future when someone makes decisions without fully realizing their impact.

Some design choices will have little to no impact in any future software migrations; others could render your pipeline absolutely useless or at the very least require hours of additional work for migration. Having an understanding from the outset of these potential hurdles will help make informed decisions with other members of the production when considering changes.

5.4.3 Automation

Most game productions have already mastered continuous integration for code and most types of data, including sound. However, automation can be a real time saver when dealing with the large amounts of voice files with different statuses that are being moved through the pipeline. Amazingly, people often don't think to ask for automation or are too afraid to request it, even if they are executing the same repetitive tasks time and time again by the same group of people.

There are many different options for how to implement your automation. Continuous Integration systems (such as Jenkins, JetBrains TeamCity, or Atlassian Bamboo) are easy options, especially if they're already present in the wider game development pipeline. Many of these Continuous Integration systems allow for easy integration using web UIs and don't always require the help of a build system or automation engineer. As an additional bonus, they provide easy and graphical scheduling capabilities.

Another route is to use the Windows Task Scheduler, cron, or an equivalent tool that is available on each system to schedule the process locally. While this is definitely the least advantageous for a number of reasons (what happens if there is a power outage, the workstation is turned off by someone else, or a flood destroys your workstation), it will do in a pinch. Anything that doesn't require someone to click a button on a regular basis is a win.

When adding automation, it is important to think of a notification strategy. The most basic strategy is to send an email when the process has finished – whether it has encountered issues or not. While this does potentially create some extra volume of information, it serves as a reminder that there is a process that is constantly running. This ensures that people don't forget that it exists and they continue to be conscious that their actions can potentially have an impact on whether or not the process is completed successfully. On the other hand, sending an email could simply annoy people and make them enemies of the voice pipeline. It is important to have knowledge of the team that will use the pipeline and adapt to their team culture.

It is easy to automate the tools developed specifically as part of the voice pipeline. However, there can sometimes be greater opportunities in automating third-party tools such as DAWs. Automating tasks that aren't especially complicated can be a huge win with little investment. If all files need to be normalized, trimmed, and/or resampled, automating these steps by calling a command line and providing a few parameters may cost an hour of time but could potentially save hundreds of hours—especially when dealing with 100,000 files or more.

Analytics and automation go hand in hand, where the time spent can be justified by the information that the analytics provide. No matter which system you use, keeping track of analytics to be able to identify how many man-hours are saved and the return on investment can be useful when making an analysis of potential future improvements and as a source of personal pride. One additional benefit is that reviewing the analytics can help point out problematic areas of the pipeline and provide a source of inspiration for future improvements.

5.4.4 Disaster Recovery/Revision Control

Both Disaster Recovery and Revision Control help protect people from their own mistakes. When receiving thousands of lines of recorded voice, there is always the potential for human error, no matter how solid the pipeline is. The question becomes: How to empower users to undo mistakes and recover accidentally deleted work?

One common solution is to use a revision control system such as Perforce or Plastic SCM. These systems are built to handle large volumes of data files and have fine-grained controls built-in to control the size of the repository long-term. Administrators can determine the best policy for data retention versus size-on-disk. Additionally, it is commonplace to have a disaster recovery plan specifically for the revision control system in place for any data stored on these servers (such as daily backups, replication, etc.). Whatever the choice for a revision control system, it is important to choose one that is well adapted to the type of data that you will be manipulating, as not all systems handle binary data the same.

Of course, not everyone has the benefit of having a revision control system available to them, and not everyone has the expertise to configure, deploy, and manage these types of systems in addition to all of the other tasks that are required of them. The barebones method is to have a shared folder where the different people responsible can put recorded files to be used in the pipeline. These could be stored on any cloud storage provider's platform, easily accessible to everyone (and easily deletable as well).

No matter how the data is stored, make sure it is accessible to those who need access and that you develop a plan for a worst-case scenario (someone accidentally drops a mug full of coffee on the external hard drive, destroying it) and a method to recover from it.

5.4.5 Integrating Third-Party Tools

Spending time creating a tool which duplicates the functionality of an existing third-party tool can sometimes seem wasteful but may end up being an important and essential decision to avoid being stuck reimplementing the same functionality in the middle of production. When designing a voice pipeline, integrating third-party tools can save enormous amounts of time. It is important to analyze and evaluate the tool's history and how the team responsible for supporting it responds to issues. Is there the possibility the tool will stop working if a certain server (which is in the control of the vendor) is suddenly taken offline without any notice? What will happen if the company that sells the tool suddenly stops responding to support requests and closes their doors permanently? What if the tool is open source and its development is suddenly stopped? These are not situations any developer with their own looming deadline wants to have to experience, let alone mitigate the fallout. Simply reflecting on the impact of losing one specific tool in the pipeline can be enough to push developers into planning for the worst-case scenario before it arrives.

5.5 IMPLEMENTATION

With the long list of requirements in hand and your rough design done, the next challenge is implementing everything. Most of the following sections discuss general software design principals and examples of their application in the context of a voice pipeline.

5.5.1 Deployment

Issues will happen, requirements will change, and new challenges will be introduced into the pipeline many times throughout development. It's important to try and prevent that which is preventable, but the ability to make changes and tweaks and have the result available immediately is important. Many production teams already have a plan in place to distribute new code and data, but it is not always appropriate for always-running processes that may be hard or impossible to test before deploying changes to them. Regardless of how the game editor or a game build is created, the needs for pipelines don't always align with these deployment methods. There are several different strategies for deployment, ranging from once code/data is submitted and the result executable/build is available then it is ready for use, all the way to long-term planning and infrequent releases (think middleware or game engines releasing a polished version only a few times a year). Obviously if there is a code fix that is needed for one tool used in the voice pipeline, then waiting a week for it to be deployed is going to be a bottleneck.

5.5.2 Error Handling for Non-technical People

When implementing any tool, it's always a good practice to add in validations and debugging information. One of the most basic pieces of debugging/error logging that will be familiar to anyone who has worked in C# is the following:

```
try
{
    FetchAudioFiles();
}
catch(Exception ex)
{
    Console.Error.WriteLine(ex.Message);
}
```

This is great as a first implementation or whenever you're debugging a specific action. However, it is almost always a complete failure as a useful or meaningful piece of information for non-programmers. A null reference exception or access violation exception with a callstack will mean nothing to people who aren't coders. This means that we need to output meaningful errors with actionable messages.

To empower users to address issues, even ones that they may have caused themselves, they need actionable messages. Consider the following (contrived) example:

```
class ProgramA
{
  static void Main(string[] args)
  {
    using (StreamReader reader =
            new StreamReader(
              File.Open(@"C:\RandomFile.wav",
                    FileMode.Open,
                    FileAccess.Read, FileShare.None)))
    {
      Thread.Sleep(100000);
    }
  }
}

class ProgramB
{
  static void Main(string[] args)
  {
    try
    {
      File.Delete(@"C:\RandomFile.wav");
    }
    catch (UnauthorizedAccessException ex)
    {
      Console.Error.WriteLine(ex.Message,
        "Please ensure this file isn't open in any other program");
    }
  }
}
```

Running `ProgramA` will ensure that no other program (or user) can delete the file. Executing these together will most likely result in the exception being thrown for `ProgramB`. If the error message were simply the message text of the exception (Access to the path 'C:\ RandomFile.wav' is denied), it would not be clear to the user why that is or what they can do to fix it. Adding a simple message such as Please ensure this file isn't open in any other program will help users (adding the program name goes a step further, making it even easier).

Proper messages and error handling aren't specific to voice pipeline design. However, because of the large amounts of data that voice pipelines handle, the one-in-a-thousand type of errors are more likely to appear. Without the proper actionable messages, the programmer responsible for the pipeline can become a bottleneck and/or overwhelmed with the amount of support given to users.

5.5.3 Nothing More Permanent than a Temporary Fix

One almost universal truth is that there is nothing more permanent than a temporary fix, especially in software development. This adage refers to the fact that any code or implementation that is submitted and declared as a temporary fix has a reasonable chance of becoming a permanent addition to the code base and/or pipeline.

It is important to remember this fact when deciding between spending 1–2 more days on a particular part of the pipeline and moving on to the next task. Something that is "good enough for now" will usually come back to haunt developers later on in production. Having a long-term vision rather than simply focusing on the current deliverable or production can help remind developers that they are building reusable processes and tools.

5.6 CONCLUSION

Most of the topics that were discussed were basic software engineering principles. Their importance in relation to a voice pipeline is in applying these principles well and consistently. Implementing good error logging some of the time, having a rigid set of failure principles that fail to consider edge cases that haven't happened, or monolithic designs will result in a voice pipeline that is fragile, hard to use, and sucks up debugging time. Keep in mind that the purpose of the pipeline is to be able to handle data easily and flexibly, with the ultimate goal of adding high-quality data that is important to the finished game.

While most game productions will have a limited lifetime, voice pipelines often extend past this time into future projects. Forgetting this fact can provide a source of frustration in the future because of rigid design choices that limit the ability of developers to refactor and improve the pipeline.

CHAPTER 6

A Stimulus-Driven Server Authoritative Voice System

Tomas Neumann
Blizzard Entertainment

CONTENTS

6.1 INTRODUCTION

Spoken words are often at the core of why players connect and relate to the characters within a video game. Voices can be used for tutorials, to tell the story, to create drama, or to convey gameplay information. Enemies in the original *Wolfenstein 3D* were yelling "Achtung!" and "Mein Leben!"

to telegraph their AI states; in *The Witcher*, the voice lines drive the camera cuts in most of the in-game cinematics; *Overwatch*'s heroes warn each other with a "Behind you!"; and in *The Last of Us*, we can hear the heart-wrenching death cries of a young girl.

In a single-player offline game, the client makes all of the decisions about which voice lines to play, but multiplayer games are more complex because it may be necessary that all players hear the same variation of a line. By playing the same line on all clients, all of the connected players can experience the world through a shared experience. And if some funny voice lines have a rare probability to play, all players will share their surprise and this moment with each other when they do play.

In this chapter, I present some techniques which can be used to create a voice system which is based on an authoritative server. The server directs which lines are chosen, picks who says something, and which client should play these lines.

6.2 CLARIFYING TERMINOLOGY

Game voice over (VO) is often called "dialog" or "dialogue." Historically, hardware channels on a soundcard were also called voices, often in the context of a voice limit. However, these days the term "voice" is generally used to describe spoken words in the field of game audio. The mechanism through which game characters talk, at least in this chapter, are voices, dialogue, and VO, and they are used interchangeably.

Some games like *The Sims* use an artificial language for all of their character dialog,[1] but a vast majority of games need to translate and localize their voice lines for each supported language or locale. A *locale* describes a cultural set of words out of a language and country: for instance, *es-ES* for Spanish spoken in Spain (sometimes referred to as "Castilian Spanish") or *es-MX* for Spanish in Mexico. *Localization* is the process of translating a voice line in a manner culturally appropriate for a given locale, casting voice talents appropriate to the preferences of that region, recording the audio assets, and importing the data. Many multiplayer games allow players to connect to the same server or play directly with each other even if their game clients are set to different locales.

A *stimulus* is an event that invokes a specific reaction; in the case of this voice system, it can be as simple as what a game character should talk about.

---

[1] The artificial language in *The Sims* is called *Simlish*.

6.3 THE PURPOSE OF A SERVER AUTHORITATIVE VOICE SYSTEM

Imagine a multiplayer fantasy game with a powerful raid boss who has several random variations of voice lines to say when the group of brave warriors all storm her throne room. Most likely all players are connected together via voice chat to coordinate their attacks. If every game client chooses randomly which voice line to play for the boss, there could be some confusion amongst the friends why some players heard a different voice line than their friends. If instead the game server picks the line and informs all clients to play the same line, all of the players will experience the world as more consistent and less artificial.

Additionally, imagine that the game designer had the tools to write some additional "Easter egg" lines with a dramatically low probability to play or which require some very specific criteria (e.g. all warriors are paladins). When they rush through the door, the boss suddenly says, *Is any of you fools Leeroy Jenkins?* If all of the players hear the same line, it creates a magical shared moment for all those players. They now have a story to share which would not be possible without an authoritative voice system.

6.3.1 Playing in a Multiverse

While the server helps to create a world of consistency, there might arise situations in a multiplayer game in which players who stand right next to each other might want to hear different voice lines. One simple example might be after your game character heals up to play a satisfied breath exert, which the surrounding players probably do not need to hear. Similarly, a player may hear other game characters telegraphing information to them, while the players controlling those other characters might not be aware that their character is speaking on someone else's game client. In *Overwatch*, every hero has an ultimate ability, and their voice lines each have two variants: a hostile and a friendly one. Players in the same match only hear one of them depending on what team they are on. There are also examples where stimuli, such as those to warn a specific player, are not executed on some clients. We will dive more into the details of selecting voice lines later in this chapter.

In short, each player experiences a consistent shared world through a personal lens that makes the most sense for them. In the examples below, I focus on the challenges which arise from this setup. In practice, these challenges are often the edge cases, but solving these problems early can make a dramatic difference in the capability of the voice system and the perceived quality of VO in the game.

6.4 SERVER WORKFLOW

All connected clients send their player inputs to the server with very different bandwidth and latency times. The server receives these inputs, simulates the world, and executes what the game characters might do and say. A server-based voice system collects all requests over the length of the server frame and then figures out which stimuli to send to which clients.

6.4.1 Collecting and Rating Stimuli

In a given frame, the server may have received multiple stimuli. Let's take an example of two frames and three game characters (Ana, Brigitte, and Cain) each being played by three players (A, B, and C) on different clients. Table 6.1 lists all the events.

In frame 10, the server must deal with only a single stimulus. Ana gets shot in the back by an opponent, and we want to help Player A by casting a little shout-out onto Brigitte or Cain to say: *"Behind you!"* This is really only helpful for Player A. Brigitte and Cain both witnessed Ana receiving damage, so we pick the character most relevant to what Player A sees. Let's assume Brigitte was in the field of view of Player A, so the server only sends a network message to Player A's client indicating that Brigitte should say the warning line. No other players receive this message—it would be rather confusing for Player B to hear their character to say, *"Behind you!"*

In frame 11, the server gets four requests in random order. Stimuli with a higher priority override and interrupt lines spoken on the same character. By sorting the stimuli within a frame by stimulus priority, it is easy to work off the enqueued stimuli, and each character can be assigned their most important line to say. In frame 11, the most important stimulus is a death cry of Brigitte. This message is sent to all clients.

TABLE 6.1   List of Examples of Stimuli on Server

Frame	Stimulus	Priority	Speaker	Sent To
10	Witnesses Ana takes damage	4	Brigitte or Cain	A
11	Brigitte dies	5	Brigitte	A, B, C
11	Ana uses ability	4	Ana	A, B, C
11	Brigitte uses ability	4	Brigitte	None
11	Cain uses ability	4	Cain	A, B, C

The next three stimuli with the characters all using their ability have the same priority of 4. Ana is alive and can talk, and all clients are informed about her voice request. Brigitte is dead but more importantly is already requested to say a higher-priority line within the same server frame. Her additional voice request can be dropped, and no client ever receives a request. Cain is also alive, so the server sends this request to all clients.

6.5 CLIENT WORKFLOW

Each client receives a unique set of VO information and commands, and they have some flexibility to follow the server's directives. One example of what the received stimuli might be is shown in Table 6.2. The damage-witnessed warning from frame 10 is only sent to Client A to make Brigitte say the warning to the player controlling Ana. When Client A receives the request to play a death line for Brigitte on the next frame, it needs to handle the request by interrupting her previous warning line. Player A might hear something like "*Behin ... Aaargh....*" Clients B and C can just play the death line directly, because they never received the warning request. In the end, all clients hear Brigitte's death line.

For the two remaining requests of frame 11 of Ana and Cain using their ability, all clients received the same information, but each client can determine which of the two requests makes more sense to their players. For example, there may be a mechanism in place that limits how many voice lines of a certain category or with the same stimulus priority can play at the same time.

Let's say there are already two characters who are currently saying priority 4 lines and the game has a rule to only ever play three priority 4 lines on a client. Which client should play which of Ana's and Cain's lines? Imagine now Ana and Brigitte are nearby, while Cain is on the other side of the map. Depending on the game type, it could make more sense for Clients A and B to play Ana's line, while Client C chooses to play Cain's line.

While most lines are requested by the server and played consistently on all the three clients, each client also makes specific decisions based on

TABLE 6.2 Examples of Stimuli Received by Client

Frame	Stimulus	Priority	Speaker	Sent to	A Hears	B Hears	C Hears
10	Ana takes damage	4	Brigitte	A	Brigitte	–	–
11	Brigitte dies	5	Brigitte	A, B, C	Brigitte	Brigitte	Brigitte
11	Ana uses ability	4	Ana	A, B, C	Ana	Ana	–
11	Cain uses ability	4	Cain	A, B, C	–	–	Cain

some game rules in order to improve the clarity and understanding of the game world for each player.

6.6 LINE SELECTION

Until now, we have ignored the topic of line selection in order to focus on stimulus handling. Once a server has selected which stimuli to send to which clients, it must now decide which specific voice line should be played on those clients. Voice line variants can have different probabilities or extra criteria. Depending on the state of the game, the server might pick, for instance, friendly or hostile versions of the same stimulus or special lines depending on what map is active or which team is in the lead. Once it makes the selection, the server can then send unique messages to specific clients with different voice line IDs. From the client's perspective, it just receives a line ID and executes the line according to its playback rules.

In *Overwatch*, when opponents of the hero McCree hear the line "It's high noon!" they learn quickly to take cover to avoid fatal hits. But all members of his team hear him say the less threatening friendly variant "Step right up." What variant should the player controlling McCree hear? Maybe the friendly version? After all, he is a member of his own team and cannot harm himself. But having him say the enemy line sells the fantasy of being a hero better and teaches the player in return to be very cautious if they ever hear this line from another player. Table 6.3 shows how the server would pick line variants and format packets to send to the clients accordingly. Players M, N, and O are on one team, and Players P, Q, and R are their opponents.

6.7 NETWORK CONSIDERATIONS

Sending information over the wire will always introduce issues to consider and weigh against. Speech for a character is not something that requires sending updates every frame—we mostly get away with telling the clients which character should say what line, specified by your system of identification.

TABLE 6.3   Example of Friendly and Hostile Line Selection on Server

Frame	Stimulus	Speaker	Friendly Variant	Hostile Variant
20	High Noon by M	McCree	N, O	M, P, Q, R

6.7.1 Prediction and Client-Only VO

Latency is the time that it takes messages to travel from the client to the server or vice versa. If we waited for the complete round trip from the server to the client and back again every time a player wanted to jump to verify whether the jump is legitimate, the game would not feel very responsive. Often network models use a form of prediction, and the player can jump right away, even if in some cases the server corrects the client, e.g. when the player was stunned by someone else, which the client mispredicted.

For VO, we do not want to wait for a round trip for a simple exhale sound. Because these types of voice lines are not game critical, the client can just pick a variation and play it. The server will inform bystanders who observe the other player jump about the action, and their client will also play a random jump exhale. In this case, the integrity of a consistent world is not endangered if we cheat a little and play different voice files.

The decision of which lines can be client-authoritative and which are server-driven must be made per category. For example, if your game has very distinct death callouts, that may be something you would wait for the server to authenticate. Or, alternatively, you could prime all clients with a random seed so that the same variations can be played without waiting for the server assuming that you can guarantee that the stream of random numbers remains in synch. There is plenty of detailed information available about how to reduce the perceived lag with multiplayer games, and especially VO can also benefit from these techniques.

6.7.2 Network Reliability

A chat with your friendly colleague who is in charge of network messaging will quickly reveal that it is a deep and complex topic. A server voice system can contribute to a smoother gameplay experience if the data to be sent over the wire is small and if the message reliability is chosen correctly. A reliable packet will be resent by the server if it does not receive a confirmation that the packet was accepted by the client. Contrariwise, an unreliable packet will be sent just once and never resent. The sender will never know if it was accepted.

In order to reduce network usage, some "chatter" voice lines—lines which are not meaningful to gameplay but which provide some immersive quality to the game world—can be sent in an unreliable fashion. A player with high packet-loss may experience that some characters do not say their chatter lines because the packet to inform their client to play the line never was received. Voice lines which are important to the gameplay must be sent reliably because it is more important for the player to hear the line at all, even if there is a substantial delay.

6.8 VOICE LINE TRIGGERED GAMEPLAY AND MULTI-LOCALE CLIENT CONNECTIONS

There might be situations when game designers want to time a certain event after a voice line has finished playing, perhaps for a tutorial or an impressive cinematic moment in the game. In a multiplayer game, it can be dangerous to rely on the actual playback of a voice file on the client. The client might not have a functioning sound card, or maybe a cheater could replace the voice line on disk with a shorter or longer one to get an unfair advantage.

Despite smaller timing challenges introduced by latency and packet loss, the most secure option is to store durations of these voice files on the server. The actual audio files are not needed because the server never actually plays any sounds. However, if a game event needs to happen after a voice line finishes, the server can start a timer with the duration of the chosen voice file and then inform the client of the event after the timer expires. The voice line duration can be extracted in a build process when other game data is baked.

During localization, each voice line is marked either to be translated exactly to match the original file length in the production language or to give the localization team some freedom to shorten or lengthen their file by a time or percentage. If the game allows clients with different locales to connect to the same server and the server only uses the production language timing, it is possible that the enqueued game event that is triggered after the voice line will happen at different points in the audio file for different clients. In order to avoid this inconsistency, the server can always use the maximum of all translated file variants of a voice line or only consider the lengths of the locales of the clients currently connected to the server.

Table 6.4 shows examples of how the same voice line could have different playback durations in different locales. If two players with en-US and zh-TW locales play together, the server would wait 1.4 seconds to queue up

TABLE 6.4   Examples of Different Duration Times of a Voice Line

Locale	en-US	de-DE	es-ES	zh-TW
Duration in seconds	1.2	1.6	1.1	1.4

the game event the game designer wants to invoke after the line, and the player with en-US will wait 0.2 seconds after their line has finished playing. If the same en-US player would play with someone in the es-ES locale, then they would not wait any extra time, but the es-ES player would need to wait 0.1 seconds.

6.9 CONCLUSION

For a multiplayer game, a server authoritative voice system allows for very interesting gameplay features, dramatically higher clarity and quality in VO for individual players, and hardening of anti-cheat efforts. But this feature comes with the additional cost of dealing with edge cases when looking through the player-specific lens of the game world. There are logistical hurdles to resolve and network issues and delays to be compensated for. I hope I was able to introduce you to some techniques and ideas and you have a kick start once you approach this field and consider developing a voice system yourself.

III

Audio Engines

CHAPTER 7

Building the Patch Cable

Ethan Geller

Epic Games

CONTENTS

7.1 ON PATCH CABLES

Hand me that cable / Plug into anything

"Rock and Sing" by Big Thief

In the history of electricity, there are few mechanisms more human-involved than the patch cable. Recall the first time you plugged a guitar into an amp or heard your own voice amplified through a monitor. There's a satisfying click, and with it, you are audible; a circuit is closed, and you are in it. So often we consider electricity a utility (a means to power your refrigerator) or a luxury (a means to power your television), but analog audio signals give us the chance to be *complicit* in the systems we use. When you plug an instrument into an amp or a PA, you are engaging in a century-old ritual in which your kinesics drive a current used to push demoniac amounts of air.

This is what got me into audio in the first place. There's no visual correlate for being *amplified*, nor is there one for *resonating* in a physical space. These are experiences that are unique to sound: to have every motion of your fingers along a fretboard interact with every surface of a room or to glissando upward and find sudden resonances along the way. In many cathedrals, a single sound at a single point in time will have *seconds* of consequences.

Imagine my disappointment when I realized that very little of this magic is reproducible in game audio programming. Granted, there is plenty of software that lets you design and iterate on arbitrary signal flows: MaxMSP/Pure Data, Supercollider, Reaktor Blocks, and Reason are all brilliant tools for iterating on audio systems. But these are all sandboxes: once we build the topology we want, it can't be extracted into a component of a larger piece of shipped software. Patches built in PureData must stay in PureData—you can record the results of your patch, but you can't take it with you.[1] Faust is the closest thing to what I'd like: a way to experiment with routing signals within a larger piece of compiled software. However, at the end of the day, there is still a distinct barrier between the systems I use in Faust and the systems I use in my larger C++ codebase.

What makes this such a shame is that the act of playing a game is very similar to playing an instrument. Compare the experience of playing guitar through an amplifier with the experience of playing any action game. You apply pressure to the left thumb stick; your avatar begins to run. You press A while applying that same pressure to the thumb stick, and your avatar jumps across a precipice, narrowly escaping death. You keep the right trigger held down and tap the left trigger at *just* the right time, and the tail of your car lurches out from behind you: you are *drifting*, and it is *badass*. Watch any participant's hands during a fighting game

---

[1] This is only partially correct: Enzien did create and later open-source a service called Heavy, which transcompiles PureData patches into C++.

tournament, and you will know that the best fighting games are as idiomatic as any Chopin étude.

7.2 C++ AUDIO ABSTRACTIONS

What I want is for game audio programming to be as joyful and easy as patching my telecaster into my delay pedal, and this is not something that exists in any game code base I have seen. The C++ standard is not concerned with giving me this, nor should it be. But the true forte of C++ is that you can pick and choose the abstractions you use on a case-by-case basis. Smart pointers are the apotheosis of useful abstraction in C++: a terse representation of a common pattern. What you lose in the ability to micromanage the runtime, you gain in readability and programmer efficiency. Having worked in both C and C++ codebases, I can tell you that I work multiple times faster if I can use smart pointers, which means I spend more time in C++ experimenting, testing, profiling, and iterating.

It's not hyperbole when I say this is *nearly all I care about* when I write code. Fast iteration times are the cornerstone of being good at your job: If you can implement *any* idea faster, you can discover and implement the *best* idea faster. But if it's the case that useful abstractions in C++ are vital to success, why do audio programmers suffer a dearth of abstractions for their domain? There is certainly no shortage of common patterns in real-time audio systems. In this chapter, we'll build some abstractions for these common patterns.

7.3 FIRST-PASS ABSTRACTIONS

Let's write a mono, fixed-sample-rate audio system. Here's an interface for something that generates audio:

```
class AudioInputInterface
{
public:
  AudioInputInterface();
  virtual ~AudioInputInterface();
  virtual GenerateAudio(float* OutAudio, int32_t NumSamples) = 0;
}
```

And here's an interface for something that receives audio:

```
class AudioOutputInterface
{
public:
```

```
  AudioOutputInterface();
  virtual ~AudioOutputInterface();
  virtual ReceiveAudio(const float* InAudio, int32_t NumSamples) = 0;
}
```

And here's an audio engine. It asks instances of AudioInputInterface to generate audio, mixes that audio together, and then broadcasts the resulting audio to instances of AudioOutputInterface:

```
class AudioEngine
{
private:
  std::vector<AudioInputInterface*> Inputs;
  mutable std::mutex InputListMutationLock;
  std::vector<AudioOutputInterface*> Outputs;
  mutable std::mutex OutputListMutationLock;
  std::vector<float> ScratchAudioBuffer;
  std::vector<float> MixedAudioBuffer;

public:
  void RegisterInput(AudioInputInterface* InInput)
  {
    std::lock_guard<std::mutex> ScopeLock(InputListMutationLock);
    Inputs.push_back(InInput);
  }

  void UnregisterInput(AudioInputInterface* InInput)
  {
    std::lock_guard<std::mutex> ScopeLock(InputListMutationLock);
    auto found = std::find(Inputs.begin(), Inputs.end(), InInput);
    if (found != Inputs.end())
      Inputs.erase(found);
  }

  void RegisterOutput(AudioOutputInterface* InOutput)
  {
    std::lock_guard<std::mutex> ScopeLock(OutputListMutationLock);
    Outputs.push_back(InOutput);
  }

  void UnregisterOutput(AudioOutputInterface* InOutput)
  {
    std::lock_guard<std::mutex> ScopeLock(OutputListMutationLock);
    auto found = std::find(Outputs.begin(), Outputs.end(), InOutput);
    if (found != Outputs.end())
      Outputs.erase(found);
  }
```

```
void ProcessAudio()
{
  const int32_t NumSamples = 1024;
  MixedAudioBuffer.resize(NumSamples);
  ScratchAudioBuffer.resize(NumSamples);

  memset(MixedAudioBuffer.data(), 0, NumSamples * sizeof(float));

  // Poll inputs:
  std::lock_guard<std::mutex> ScopeLock(InputListMutationLock);
  for(AudioInputInterface* Input : Inputs)
  {
    Input->GenerateAudio(ScratchAudioBuffer.data(), NumSamples);
    // Mix it in:
    for(int32_t Index = 0; Index < NumSamples; Index++)
      MixedAudioBuffer[Index] += ScratchAudioBuffer[Index];
  }

  // Push outputs:
  std::lock_guard<std::mutex> ScopeLock(OutputListMutationLock);
  for(AudioOutputInterface* Output : Outputs)
  {
    Output>ReceiveAudio(MixedAudioBuffer.data(), NumSamples);
  }
}
}
```

This simple interface provides a lot of opportunities for expansion. A DSP processor or bus could implement both `AudioInputInterface` as well as `AudioOutputInterface`. Heck, the `AudioEngine` class itself could implement the input and output interfaces and be plugged into other `AudioEngine` instances. This is starting to look an awful lot like a way to build arbitrary audio topologies in C++. The advantage of doing something like this is that it's a zero copy, zero latency solution: Every registered instance of `AudioOutputInterface` is going to get audio as soon as it is generated.

7.4 THE PATCH CABLE ABSTRACTION

This abstraction is not what I'm looking for. This sort of interface might help me build and run a new synthesizer or source manager, but it's not helping me plug anything into anything else. What thread is `AudioEngine::ProcessAudio()` getting called on? Probably not the same thread as the network socket I want to send audio over or that I'm receiving audio from. Nor is it helping me pipe audio to the gameplay capture system we're trying to use to record replays to a directory of movie files.

What if there's a codec we're trying to use that only takes 20 milliseconds of audio at a time and the number of samples per each callback of `ProcessAudio()` is not exactly 20 milliseconds of audio? What if any given call to `GenerateAudio()` or `ReceiveAudio()` takes a prohibitively long amount of time?

With this framework, we've created a good set of interfaces to build a single-threaded topology for audio signal processing. However, if anyone else wants to try patching audio from our subsystem to theirs, they will have to debug and understand our audio engine, rather than focus on theirs.

When I build an API that will allow you to send or receive an audio signal, I don't want to give you a buffer or a callback. I want to give you one end of a patch cable, and I want you to be able to plug it into *anything*. Consider the following API:

```
class AudioEngine
{
//...
public:
  PatchInput ConnectNewInput(uint32_t MaxLatencyInSamples);
  PatchOutput ConnectNewOutput(uint32_t MaxLatencyInSamples);
}
```

After calling `ConnectNewInput()`, you can pass the `PatchInput` object around freely and push audio to it from whatever thread you want.

```
AudioEngine DefaultAudioEngine;
//...
PatchInput MySynthSend = DefaultAudioEngine.ConnectNewInput(4096);

// In your synth's callback:
float* BufferOfGeneratedAudio = ...;
uint32_t NumSamplesInBuffer = 2048;
uint32_t NumSamplesPushedToEngine =
  MySynthSend.PushAudio(BufferOfGeneratedAudio, NumSamplesInBuffer);
// if NumSamplesPushedToEngine is less than NumSamplesInBuffer,
// we've maxed out our buffer.
```

In this example, `MySynthSend` is patched into `DefaultAudioEngine`, but in principle, `MySynthSend` could be connected to anything, and it would not change our core render loop. We can render as much as we want on any thread as long as our buffer is big enough. We have finally arrived at the useful abstraction we're going to be implementing in this chapter: a thread-safe patch cable composed of a circular buffer and smart pointers.

7.5 PATCH INPUTS AND OUTPUTS

7.5.1 Circular Buffer

Before we build our `PatchInput` and `PatchOutput` classes, we need to decide on a buffering mechanism. If you read *Game Audio Programming Principles and Practices Volume 2*, Chapter 3, "Multithreading for Game Audio" (Murray 2019), then you're already well informed about various buffering mechanisms for transporting audio between threads: double buffering mechanisms, lockless queues, and mutex-locked single arrays are all good solutions for specific applications.

However, we are looking for a buffering mechanism that can be used with arbitrary buffer sizes, callback rates, and preferably with as little locking as possible. Because of this, we will use a circular buffer. Consider the following implementation of a circular buffer, which is the style of circular buffer implemented in the Unreal Engine, as well as the kind of circular buffer I use personally for almost any application:

```
template <typename SampleType>
class CircularAudioBuffer
{
private:
  std::vector<SampleType> InternalBuffer;
  uint32_t Capacity;
  std::atomic<uint32_t> ReadCounter;
  std::atomic<uint32_t> WriteCounter;

public:
  CircularAudioBuffer()
  {
    SetCapacity(0);
  }

  CircularAudioBuffer(uint32_t InCapacity)
  {
    SetCapacity(InCapacity);
  }

  void SetCapacity(uint32_t InCapacity)
  {
    Capacity = InCapacity + 1;
    ReadCounter.store(0);
    WriteCounter.store(0);
    InternalBuffer.resize(Capacity);
  }
```

```
// Pushes some amount of samples into this circular buffer.
// Returns the amount of samples read
uint32_t Push(const SampleType* InBuffer, uint32_t NumSamples)
{
  SampleType* DestBuffer = InternalBuffer.data();
  const uint32_t ReadIndex = ReadCounter.load();
  const uint32_t WriteIndex = WriteCounter.load();

  uint32_t NumToCopy = std::min(NumSamples, Remainder());
  const int32_t NumToWrite =
    std::min(NumToCopy, Capacity - WriteIndex);
  memcpy(
    &DestBuffer[WriteIndex],
    InBuffer,
    NumToWrite * sizeof(SampleType));

  memcpy(
    &DestBuffer[0],
    &InBuffer[NumToWrite],
    (NumToCopy - NumToWrite) * sizeof(SampleType));

  WriteCounter.store((WriteIndex + NumToCopy) % Capacity);

  return NumToCopy;
}

// Same as Pop() but does not increment the read counter.
uint32_t Peek(SampleType* OutBuffer, uint32_t NumSamples) const
{
  SampleType* SrcBuffer = InternalBuffer.data();
  const uint32 ReadIndex = ReadCounter.load();
  const uint32 WriteIndex = WriteCounter.load();

  uint32_t NumToCopy = std::min(NumSamples, Num());

  const int32 NumRead = std::min(NumToCopy, Capacity - ReadIndex);
  memcpy(
    OutBuffer,
    &SrcBuffer[ReadIndex],
    NumRead * sizeof(SampleType));

  memcpy(
    &OutBuffer[NumRead],
    &SrcBuffer[0],
    (NumToCopy - NumRead) * sizeof(SampleType));

  return NumToCopy;
}
```

```
// Pops some amount of samples into this circular buffer.
// Returns the amount of samples read.
uint32_t Pop(SampleType* OutBuffer, uint32_t NumSamples)
{
  uint32_t NumSamplesRead = Peek(OutBuffer, NumSamples);

  ReadCounter.store(
    (ReadCounter.load() + NumSamplesRead) % Capacity);

  return NumSamplesRead;
}

// When called, seeks the read or write cursor to only
// retain either the NumSamples latest data (if
// bRetainOldestSamples is false) or the NumSamples oldest data
// (if bRetainOldestSamples is true) in the buffer. Cannot be
// used to increase the capacity of this buffer.
void SetNum(uint32_t NumSamples, bool bRetainOldestSamples = false)
{
  if (bRetainOldestSamples)
  {
    WriteCounter.store(
      (ReadCounter.GetValue() + NumSamples) % Capacity);
  }
  else
  {
    int64_t ReadCounterNum =
      ((int32)WriteCounter.load()) - ((int32) NumSamples);
    if (ReadCounterNum < 0)
    {
      ReadCounterNum = Capacity + ReadCounterNum;
    }

    ReadCounter.store(ReadCounterNum);
  }
}

// Get the number of samples that can be popped off of the buffer.
uint32_t Num() const
{
  const uint32_t ReadIndex = ReadCounter.load();
  const uint32_t WriteIndex = WriteCounter.load();

  if (WriteIndex >= ReadIndex)
  {
    return WriteIndex - ReadIndex;
  }
  else
  {
```

```
        return Capacity - ReadIndex + WriteIndex;
      }
    }

    // Get the current capacity of the buffer
    uint32_t GetCapacity() const
    {
      return Capacity;
    }

    // Get the number of samples that can be pushed onto the
    // buffer before it is full.
    uint32_t Remainder() const
    {
      const uint32_t ReadIndex = ReadCounter.load();
      const uint32_t WriteIndex = WriteCounter.load();

      return (Capacity - 1 - WriteIndex + ReadIndex) % Capacity;
    }
};
```

This structure is safe for SPSC situations. Notice how we explicitly load our read and write counters at the beginning of Peek(), Pop(), and Push() but only increment them at the very end of Pop() and Push(). We then truncate the amount of audio we push to the buffer based on our potentially stale read counter or truncate the amount of audio we peek/pop based on our potentially stale write counter. In short, if one thread is in the middle of calling Push while another thread is calling Pop, the worst thing that can happen is that we *truncate* the push and pop calls but we never lock either call. If the buffer is suitably large enough, we won't need to worry about the push and pop calls fighting each other.

7.5.2 Patch Output

So now we've got a good buffering mechanism that will let us push audio to a buffer from one thread (our patch input) and pop from that buffer on another thread (our patch output). All we need is to wrap this circular buffer in a way that abstracts away its life cycle. First, we're going to create a PatchOutput class that encapsulates our circular buffer and hides the push mechanism for anyone besides the PatchInput class:

```
struct PatchOutput
{
private:
  // Internal buffer.
  CircularAudioBuffer<float> InternalBuffer;
```

```
    // For MixInAudio, audio is popped off of InternalBuffer onto
    // here and then mixed into OutBuffer in MixInAudio.
    std::vector<float> MixingBuffer;

    // This is applied in PopAudio or MixInAudio.
    std::atomic<float> TargetGain;

    std::atomic<int32_t> NumAliveInputs;
public:
    PatchOutput(uint32_t MaxCapacity, float InGain = 1.0f)
      : InternalBuffer(MaxCapacity)
      , TargetGain(InGain)
      , NumAliveInputs(0)
    {}

    // The default constructor will result in an uninitialized
    // disconnected patch point.
    PatchOutput()
      : InternalBuffer(0)
      , TargetGain(0.0f)
      , NumAliveInputs(0)
    {}

    // Copies the minimum of NumSamples or however many samples
    // are available into OutBuffer. Returns the number of samples
    // copied or -1 if this output's corresponding input has been
    // destroyed.
    int32_t PopAudio(
       float* OutBuffer, uint32_t NumSamples, bool bUseLatestAudio)
    {
      if (IsInputStale())
      {
        return -1;
      }

      if (bUseLatestAudio
        && InternalBuffer.Num() > NumSamples)
      {
        InternalBuffer.SetNum(NumSamples);
      }

      int32 PopResult = InternalBuffer.Pop(OutBuffer, NumSamples);

      return PopResult;
    }

    // Sums the minimum of NumSamples or however many samples
    // are available into OutBuffer. Returns the number of
```

```
// samples summed into OutBuffer.
int32_t MixInAudio(
  float* OutBuffer, uint32_t NumSamples, bool bUseLatestAudio)
{
  if (IsInputStale())
  {
    return -1;
  }

  MixingBuffer.SetNumUninitialized(NumSamples, false);
  int32_t PopResult = 0;

  if (bUseLatestAudio
    && InternalBuffer.Num() > NumSamples)
  {
    InternalBuffer.SetNum(NumSamples);
    PopResult = InternalBuffer.Peek(
      MixingBuffer.GetData(), NumSamples);
  }
  else
  {
    PopResult = InternalBuffer.Pop(
      MixingBuffer.GetData(), NumSamples);
  }

  MixInBuffer(MixingBuffer.GetData(), OutBuffer, PopResult, Gain);

  return PopResult;
}

// Returns the current number of samples buffered on this output.
size_t GetNumSamplesAvailable() const
{ return InternalBuffer.size(); }

// Returns true if the input for this patch has been destroyed.
bool IsInputStale() const { return NumAliveInputs == 0; }

friend class PatchInput;
friend class PatchMixer;
friend class PatchSplitter;
};
```

I've added MixInAudio() for use with the PatchMixer class that we will
build later in this chapter. The MixInBuffer() function that it uses takes
an existing buffer and sums it into a different one[2]:

---

[2] For dynamic gain values like these, we will need to interpolate from one gain value to the next in
order to avoid significant discontinuities.

```
void MixInBuffer(
  const float* InBuffer, float* BufferToSumTo,
  uint32_t NumSamples, float Gain)
{
  for(uint32_t Index = 0; Index < NumSamples; Index++)
  {
    BufferToSumTo[Index] += InBuffer * Gain;
  }
}
```

7.5.3 Ownership Semantics

Our `PatchOutput` holds a circular buffer, and there will be a `PatchInput` class that will push audio to that circular buffer. The first concern we should have here is how we handle the `PatchInput` and `PatchOutput` life cycles: if a `PatchInput` instance is pushing audio to memory owned by the `PatchOutput` class on a separate thread, how can we guarantee that the `PatchOutput` instance won't be destroyed while the `PatchInput` is using it? We have two options:

```
using PatchOutputStrongPtr = std::shared_ptr<PatchOutput>;
using PatchOutputWeakPtr = std::weak_ptr<PatchOutput>;
```

We can have the `PatchInput` class own a strong pointer to its corresponding `PatchOutput` in order to guarantee that it is not deleted until the `PatchInput` instance is deleted as well. Alternatively, we can have the `PatchInput` class own a weak pointer to the `PatchOutput` instance, and any time we want to query or push audio to the `PatchOutput` instance, we would attempt to lock the weak pointer, converting it to a strong pointer for the scope of our work. Using a strong pointer has the advantage of avoiding the overhead of incrementing and decrementing an atomic reference count during every audio callback. Using a weak pointer has the advantage of ensuring the circular buffer is deleted as soon as the `PatchOutput` is deleted.

I've decided on the weak pointer, in order to ensure correctness.

7.5.4 Patch Input

Let's take a look at the other end of our cable, the `PatchInput` class:

```
class PatchInput
{
private:
  // Weak pointer to our destination buffer.
```

```cpp
    PatchOutputWeakPtr OutputHandle;

public:
    // Valid PatchInputs can only be created from explicit outputs.
    PatchInput(const PatchOutputStrongPtr& InOutput)
      : OutputHandle(InOutput)
      , PushCallsCounter(0)
    {
      if (InOutput)
      {
        InOutput->NumAliveInputs++;
      }
    }

    PatchInput(const PatchInput& Other)
      : PatchInput(Other.OutputHandle)
    {
      if (auto StrongOutputPtr = OutputHandle.lock())
      {
        StrongOutputPtr->NumAliveInputs++;
      }
    }


    PatchInput& operator=(const PatchInput& Other)
    {
      OutputHandle = Other.OutputHandle;
      PushCallsCounter = 0;

      if (auto StrongOutputPtr = OutputHandle.lock())
      {
        StrongOutputPtr->NumAliveInputs++;
      }

      return *this;
    }

    // Default constructed PatchInput instances will always
    // return -1 for PushAudio and false for IsOutputStillActive.
    PatchInput()
      : PushCallsCounter(0)
    {}

    ~PatchInput()
    {
      if (auto StrongOutputPtr = OutputHandle.lock())
      {
        StrongOutputPtr->NumAliveInputs--;
      }
```

```
    }

    // Pushes audio from InBuffer to the corresponding PatchOutput.
    // Returns how many samples were able to be pushed or -1 if
    // the output was disconnected.
    int32_t PushAudio(const float* InBuffer, uint32_t NumSamples)
    {
        PatchOutputStrongPtr StrongOutput = OutputHandle.lock();

        if (!StrongOutput)
        {
            return -1;
        }

        int32_t SamplesPushed =
            StrongOutput->InternalBuffer.Push(InBuffer, NumSamples);

        return SamplesPushed;
    }

    void SetGain(float InGain)
    {
        PatchOutputStrongPtr StrongOutput = OutputHandle.lock();

        if (!StrongOutput)
        {
            return;
        }

        StrongOutput ->TargetGain = InGain;
    }

    // Returns false if this output was removed, because either
    // someone called PatchMixer::RemoveTap with this PatchInput
    // or the PatchMixer was destroyed.
    bool IsOutputStillActive() const
    {
        return !OutputHandle.expired();
    }

    friend class PatchMixer;
    friend class PatchSplitter;
};
```

And just like that, we've built a thread safe SPSC cable. There are two ways we could be passing shared pointers around. The first option is to encapsulate all of the state and APIs that the PatchInput will need to use in a struct that is private to the PatchOutput class and instead give the `PatchInput` instance a shared pointer to that. The other option is to delete the copy constructor on the `PatchInput` class and only reference the `PatchOutput` with unique pointers. Under this second option, we give the `PatchInput` a raw pointer to the `PatchOutput` and then have the `PatchOutput` signal the `PatchInput` in its destructor. The `PatchOutput` destructor would then need to lock its destructor with any `PatchInput` calls that rely on it.

7.6 PATCH CABLE MIXER

The next thing we are going to need is a *mixer*, which will have an arbitrary amount of `PatchInputs` (potentially on multiple threads) and sum them down to one `PatchOutput`.

```
class PatchMixer
{
private:
  // New taps are added here in AddNewPatch, and then are moved
  // to CurrentPatches in ConnectNewPatches.
  std::vector<PatchOutputStrongPtr> PendingNewInputs;

  // Contended by AddNewPatch, ConnectNewPatches,
  // and CleanUpDisconnectedTaps.
  mutable std::mutex PendingNewInputsCriticalSection;

  // Only accessed within PopAudio. Indirect array of taps that
  // are mixed in during PopAudio.
  std::vector<PatchOutputStrongPtr> CurrentInputs;
  mutable std::mutex CurrentPatchesCriticalSection;

  // Called within PopAudio. Flushes the PendingNewPatches array
  // into CurrentPatches. During this function, AddNewPatch is
  // blocked.
  void ConnectNewPatches()
  {
    std::lock_guard<std::mutex> ScopeLock(
      PendingNewInputsCriticalSection);

    // If AddNewPatch is called in a separate thread, wait until
    // the next PopAudio call to do this work.
    for (PatchOutputStrongPtr& Patch : PendingNewInputs)
    {
      CurrentInputs.push_back(Patch);
    }

    PendingNewInputs.reset();
  }
```

```cpp
public:
  PatchMixer() {}

  // Adds a new input to the tap collector. Calling this is
  // thread safe, but individual instances of PatchInput are only
  // safe to be used from one thread.
  PatchInput AddNewInput(uint32_t MaxLatencyInSamples, float InGain)
  {
    std::lock_guard<std::mutex> ScopeLock(
      PendingNewInputsCriticalSection);

    PendingNewInputs.emplace_back(
      new PatchOutput(MaxLatencyInSamples, InGain));
    return PatchInput(PendingNewInputs.back());
  }

  // Mixes all inputs into a single buffer. This should only be
  // called from a single thread. Returns the number of non-silent
  // samples popped to OutBuffer.
  int32_t PopAudio(
    float* OutBuffer, int32_t OutNumSamples, bool bUseLatestAudio)
  {
    std::lock_guard<std::mutex> ScopeLock(
      CurrentPatchesCriticalSection);
    CleanUpDisconnectedPatches();
    ConnectNewPatches();

    memset(OutBuffer, 0, OutNumSamples * sizeof(float));
    int32_t MaxPoppedSamples = 0;

    for (int32_t Index = CurrentInputs.size() - 1; Index > 0; Index--)
    {
      PatchOutputStrongPtr& OutputPtr = CurrentInputs[Index];
      const int32_t NumPoppedSamples =
        OutputPtr->MixInAudio(
          OutBuffer, OutNumSamples, bUseLatestAudio);

      if (MaxPoppedSamples < 0)
      {
        // If MixInAudio returns -1, the PatchInput has been
        // destroyed.
        CurrentInputs.erase(CurrentInputs.begin() + Index);
      }
      else
      {
        MaxPoppedSamples =
          std::max(NumPoppedSamples, MaxPoppedSamples);
      }
```

```
  }

  return MaxPoppedSamples;
}

// This returns the number of inputs currently connected to
// this patch mixer. Thread safe, but blocks for PopAudio.
size_t Num() const
{
  std::lock_guard<std::mutex> ScopeLock(
    CurrentPatchesCriticalSection);
  return CurrentInputs.size();
}

// This function call gets the maximum number of samples that's
// safe to pop, based on the thread with the least amount of
// samples buffered. Thread safe but blocks for PopAudio.
int32_t MaxNumberOfSamplesThatCanBePopped() const
{
  std::lock_guard<std::mutex> ScopeLock(
    CurrentPatchesCriticalSection);
  ConnectNewPatches();

  // Iterate through our inputs, and see which input has the
  // least audio buffered.
  uint32 SmallestNumSamplesBuffered =
    std::numeric_limits<uint32_t>::max();

  for (PatchOutputStrongPtr& Output : CurrentInputs)
  {
    if (Output)
    {
      SmallestNumSamplesBuffered =
        std::min(SmallestNumSamplesBuffered,
          Output->InternalBuffer.Num());
    }
  }

  if (SmallestNumSamplesBuffered ==
      std::numeric_limits<uint32>::max())
  {
    return -1;
  }
  else
  {
    // If this check is hit, we need to either change this
    // function to return an int64_t or find a different way
    // to notify the caller that all outputs have been
    // disconnected.
```

```
      assert(SmallestNumSamplesBuffered <=
        ((uint32_t)std::numeric_limits<int32_t>::max()));
      return SmallestNumSamplesBuffered;
    }
  }
};
```

7.7 PATCH SPLITTER

This implementation of PatchMixer is surprisingly simple, and now that we have that in place, we'll also want a *splitter*. The PatchSplitter will have one PatchInput and distribute it to multiple PatchOutputs (also potentially on different threads). Once again, the implementation using the patch cable abstraction is straightforward.

```
class PatchSplitter
{
private:
  std::vector<PatchInput> PendingOutputs;
  mutable std::mutex PendingOutputsCriticalSection;

  std::vector<PatchInput> ConnectedOutputs;
  mutable std::mutex ConnectedOutputsCriticalSection;

  // Called from PushAudio().
  void AddPendingPatches()
  {
    std::lock_guard<std::mutex> ScopeLock(
      PendingOutputsCriticalSection);
    // Append PendingOutputs to ConnectedOutputs.
    ConnectedOutputs.insert(
      ConnectedOutputs.begin(),
      PendingOutputs.begin(), PendingOutputs.end());
    PendingOutputs.clear();
  }

public:
  PatchSplitter() {}

  // The destructor will mark every still connected PatchOutput
  // as stale.
  ~PatchSplitter() {}

  // Adds a new output. Calling this is thread safe, but
  // individual instances of PatchOutput are only safe to be
  // used from one thread. The returned PatchOutputStrongPtr
  // can be safely destroyed at any point.
  PatchOutputStrongPtr AddNewPatch(
```

```
    uint32_t MaxLatencyInSamples, float InGain)
{
  PatchOutputStrongPtr StrongOutputPtr =
    std::make_shared(new PatchOutput(
      MaxLatencyInSamples * 2, InGain));

  {
    std::lock_guard ScopeLock(PendingOutputsCriticalSection);
    PendingOutputs.push_back(StrongOutputPtr);
  }

  return StrongOutputPtr;
}

// This call pushes audio to all outputs connected to this
// splitter. Only should be called from one thread.
int32_t PushAudio(const float* InBuffer, int32_t InNumSamples)
{
  AddPendingPatches();

  std::lock_guard<std::mutex> ScopeLock(
    ConnectedOutputsCriticalSection);

  int32_t MinimumSamplesPushed =
    std::numeric_limits<int32_t>::Max();

  // Iterate through our array of connected outputs from the end,
  // removing destroyed outputs as we go.
  for (int32_t Index = ConnectedOutputs.size() - 1;
       Index >= 0;
       Index--)
  {
    int32_t NumSamplesPushed =
      ConnectedOutputs[Index].PushAudio(InBuffer, InNumSamples);
    if (NumSamplesPushed >= 0)
    {
      MinimumSamplesPushed =
        std::min(MinimumSamplesPushed, NumSamplesPushed);
    }
    else
    {
      // If this output has been destroyed, remove it from our
      // array of connected outputs.
      ConnectedOutputs.erase(ConnectedOutputs.begin() + Index);
    }
  }

  // If we weren't able to push audio to any of our outputs,
  // return -1.
```

```cpp
  if (MinimumSamplesPushed == std::numeric_limits<int32_t>::max())
  {
    MinimumSamplesPushed = -1;
  }


  return MinimumSamplesPushed;
}

// This returns the number of outputs currently connected to
// this patch splitter. Thread safe but blocks for PushAudio.
size_t Num() const
{
  std::lock_guard<std::mutex> ScopeLock(
    ConnectedOutputsCriticalSection);
  return ConnectedOutputs.size();
}

// This function call gets the maximum number of samples that's
// safe to push. Thread safe but blocks for PushAudio.
int32_t MaxNumberOfSamplesThatCanBePushed() const
{
  std::lock_guard<std::mutex> ScopeLock(
    ConnectedOutputsCriticalSection);

  // Iterate over our outputs, and get the smallest remainder of
  // all of our circular buffers.
  uint32_t SmallestRemainder = std::numeric_limits<uint32_t>::max();

  for (PatchInput& Input : ConnectedOutputs)
  {
    if (auto OutputHandlePtr = Input.OutputHandle.lock())
    {
      SmallestRemainder =
        std::min(SmallestRemainder,
          OutputHandlePtr->InternalBuffer.Remainder());
    }
  }

  if (SmallestRemainder == std::numeric_limits<uint32_t>::max())
  {
    return -1;
  }
  else
  {
    // If we hit this check, we need to either return an int64_t
    // or use some other method to notify the caller that all
    // outputs are disconnected.
    assert(SmallestRemainder <=
      ((uint32_t)std::numeric_limits<int32_t>::Max()));
```

```
        return SmallestRemainder;
    }
  }
};
```

7.8 PATCH MIXER SPLITTER

Besides managing our array of inputs for `PatchMixer` and our array of outputs for `PatchSplitter`, we didn't really need to do much to create a very robust SPMC and MPSC data structure.

In general, producer/consumers can be built using these two principles:

1. MPSC behavior can be obtained by consuming from multiple SPSC structures.

2. SPMC behavior can be obtained by producing to multiple SPSC structures.

`PatchMixer` follows from the first, and `PatchSplitter` follows from the second. Given this, we can effectively create an MPMC data structure by connecting an MPSC structure to an SPMC structure, as long as there is some worker thread or fiber that can consume from the MPSC structure and produce to the SPMC structure. That MPMC structure for us will be `PatchMixerSplitter`: a class that will mix down inputs from multiple threads and send the result to outputs on multiple threads.

```
class PatchMixerSplitter
{
private:
  PatchMixer Mixer;
  PatchSplitter Splitter;

  // This buffer is used to pop audio from our Mixer and push it to
  // our splitter.
  std::vector<float> IntermediateBuffer;

protected:
  // This class can be subclassed with OnProcessAudio overridden.
  virtual void OnProcessAudio(std::span<float> InAudio) {}
public:
  PatchMixerSplitter() {}

  // The destructor will mark every PatchOutput
  // and PatchInput which is still connected as stale.
  virtual ~PatchMixerSplitter() {}
```

```cpp
// Adds a new output. Calling this is thread safe, but
// individual instances of PatchOutput are only safe to
// be used from one thread. The returned PatchOutputPtr
// can be safely destroyed at any point.
PatchOutputStrongPtr AddNewOutput(
  uint32_t MaxLatencyInSamples, float InGain)
{
  return Splitter.AddNewPatch(MaxLatencyInSamples, InGain);
}

// Adds a new input to the tap collector. Calling this is
// thread safe, but individual instances of PatchInput are
// only safe to be used from one thread.
PatchInput AddNewInput(uint32_t MaxLatencyInSamples, float InGain)
{
  return Mixer.AddNewInput(MaxLatencyInSamples, InGain);
}

// Mixes audio from all inputs and pushes it to all outputs.
// Should be called regularly.
void ProcessAudio()
{
  int32_t NumSamplesToForward =
    std::min(Mixer.MaxNumberOfSamplesThatCanBePopped(),
      Splitter.MaxNumberOfSamplesThatCanBePushed());

  if (NumSamplesToForward <= 0)
  {
    // Likely there are either no inputs or no outputs connected,
    // or one of the inputs has not pushed any audio yet.
    return;
  }

  IntermediateBuffer.reset();
  IntermediateBuffer.insert(
    IntermediateBuffer.begin(), NumSamplesToForward, 0);

  // Mix down inputs:
  int32_t PopResult =
    Mixer.PopAudio(
      IntermediateBuffer.GetData(), NumSamplesToForward, false);
  assert(PopResult == NumSamplesToForward);

  OnProcessAudio(
    std::span<float>(IntermediateBuffer.data(),
      IntermediateBuffer.size()));

  // Push audio to outputs:
```

```
   int32_t PushResult =
     Splitter.PushAudio(
       IntermediateBuffer.GetData(), NumSamplesToForward);
   assert(PushResult == NumSamplesToForward);
  }
};
```

Note the virtual function OnProcessAudio(), which will allow
PatchMixerSplitter to be subclassed and used as a thread safe, consolidated processing unit. Imagine that your reverb algorithm is too
expensive to run on your main audio render thread. You could run that
algorithm in a PatchMixerSplitter subclass and move the actual work
for your reverb to an arbitrary thread. It doesn't have to stop there: you
can run any graph-based processing in an arbitrary thread using the
PatchMixerSplitter.

When task-based programming was becoming popular, we lamented
cases like audio rendering or VFX compositing pipelines which
involve sequential processing on large buffers of data. But by wrapping
PatchMixerSplitter::ProcessAudio() in a task, we could run our *entire
rendering graph* in parallel. Alternatively, you could also decide that the
drawbacks of this approach (giving up sample accuracy, allocating a circular buffer for every connection) are not worth it.

7.9 PATCH CABLE ABSTRACTION APPLICATIONS

Thanks to the five classes we've created, we can describe in just a few
words the process of *parallelizing your entire DSP graph*. If that isn't proof
of the usefulness of an abstraction, I don't know what is. There are other
tasks that are much easier to try out with our patching classes: dynamic
oversampling for better distortion processing, dynamically routed acoustic processing for nearby rooms in interior spaces, and runtime-configu-
rable audio analysis and instrumentation just to name a few.

I have briefly alluded to the drawbacks of our patching classes, but
there are some mitigation strategies for those drawbacks. The first and
most important of these drawbacks is that it's much more difficult to
have *strongly timed* audio processing between components connected
with these patching classes, for example, making sure a wah filter on one
thread is sample accurate with one on a different thread. Strongly timed
systems are not impossible here, though. If you've used a modern DAW,
you can see that it is able to run DSP processing on multiple threads while
guaranteeing strong timing.

You may notice that this is already implemented in the `PatchMixerSplitter`. When we pop from the `PatchMixer`, we only pop as much as the minimum amount buffered to any input. When we push to the `PatchSplitter`, we only push as much as the minimum amount we can push to any output. By doing this, we are able to keep our inputs synchronized for our `PatchMixer` and keep our outputs synchronized for our `PatchSplitter`. This gives us the option of having fully deterministic, strongly timed signal processing, as long as every input is patched and starts from the same timestamp.

This may seem like something that is only possible in the realm of linear media, but all you need is a little bit of premonition: start your system well before you need to output the rendered audio. Finding a good place to *start* your system may seem like a hard problem at first, but it gets easier over time to spot the points where you can begin priming audio for playback.

7.10 CONCLUSION

Recently, a programmer reached out to me because they wanted to be able to send Unreal's native VOIP output to any arbitrary playback device on Linux. While I did not have a Linux machine handy, I exposed an API from our VOIP engine class:

```
Audio::FPatchOutputStrongPtr GetMicrophoneOutput();
Audio::FPatchOutputStrongPtr GetRemoteTalkerOutput();
```

I had also created an `FVoiceEndpoint` class that takes an `FPatchOutputStrongPtr` and a device ID as constructor arguments. After I told him about this API and that class, he was able to get the feature up and running in an hour. When he told me it worked, I was overjoyed. I finally felt like I was working with patch cables.

It was a fantasy of my 20s to become a game audio equivalent to David Smith or Roger Linn. David Smith tweaked and redesigned a polyphonic synthesizer *endlessly* before he came to the Prophet-5. To me, that synth feels so much more *material* than anything I have worked on. The warmth of the key-tracked filters, the aggression of their sawtooth VCO, and so on: there are thousands of details that were added, removed, and changed before arriving at the sheer *physicality* of that instrument.

The hard realization I made about software audio programming is that the product of your work is inherently immaterial: a litany of instructions for some weary processor out there in the world, collecting dust under the veneer of a frail plastic fan. And yet our work *does* have a material impact in one important place: labor. When you write difficult code, it has consequences for the people that need to finish using it before they can go home and have dinner with their families.

I've been the victim of this in some cases and the perpetrator in others. These are consequences much worse to me than any bug I could try and introduce in a codebase. There's one very effective cure I've found for this, and it is this: build useful abstractions and APIs, make sure they are readable, document them, test them, and share them. Build something that will let someone route VOIP audio to an external device within an hour rather than within a 6-hour, energy-drink-fueled panic. At the very least, take this abstraction, use it, and share it. The next time you see someone panicking over the specifics of multithreaded audio, give them a patch cable. The rest is intuition.

REFERENCES

Murray, Dan. "Multithreading for Game Audio." *Game Audio Programming Principles and Practices Volume 2*, edited by Guy Somberg. CRC Press, 2019, pp. 33–62.

CHAPTER 8

Split Screen and Audio Engines

Aaron McLeran

Epic Games

CONTENTS

8.1 INTRODUCTION

Split screen is a technique whereby a game engine provides multiple views into the same game instance with separate controls given to multiple local (non-networked) players. Each local player can control their own view, and each view is independent. Exactly where and how the splits are displayed on the screen is up to the game engine and often provided as player settings preference. For example, a player may choose to split a screen between top and bottom or between left and right. The number of splits supported is also up to the game and the game engine. Most games which support split screen usually limit it to two screens, but there are many notable examples that support up to four splits. Figure 8.1 shows some of the possible arrangements.

In the early days of video gaming, when the Internet was less common, split screen was a commonly supported feature. For multiplayer games without a network connection, it was a requirement. As networked multiplayer became more widely adopted in the early 2000s by gaming consoles, split screen began to fall out of favor. However, it has seen somewhat of a resurgence in recent years, especially with local split screen in combination with networked multiplayer. In other words, multiple players can play on one game console client while also playing along with other players connected to the same game on remote clients.

Split screen support is fundamentally challenging from a CPU and GPU resource point of view, as displaying multiple views requires rendering and processing more objects. Furthermore, many optimization techniques that depend on frustum culling or distance-based culling are less effective when multiple views in multiple locations can be rendered.

While graphical quality is reduced and rendering multiple views for split screen can be confusing for players, the audio experience of split

FIGURE 8.1 From left to right, the most common split screen arrangements. Vertical split, horizontal split, and four-way split.

screen in particular suffers from a fundamental limit of human biology: *ears can't be split*. As a result, a number of things which might conceptually make sense for audio and split screen simply don't work as you might expect in practice.

This chapter will describe the technical issues involved with implementing split screen for an audio engine and provide a reasonable solution which compromises computational requirements, architectural simplicity, and audio quality.

8.2 3D GEOMETRY

To understand the details of split screen for audio, it's important to first review the basic mathematics of 3D geometry.

8.2.1 Frames of Reference

3D geometry in a game engine is always defined relative to a *frame of reference*. A frame of reference is conceptually simple: it means the location from which a given coordinate is based. A coordinate can also be considered to be a *transformation* from a point at the origin to some other location translated through space.

As a concrete example of a frame of reference, consider a simple point plotted on an *X–Y* graph, as shown in Figure 8.2.

Typically, the origin of the *X–Y* graph is defined to be at (0, 0). A point in the graph can be thought of as a transformation of a point at the origin to a translation off the origin. The point at (4, 3) could be thought of as a point at the origin transformed through a translation, relative to the origin, to the right 4 and up 5.

However, the origin of the graph could itself be relative to yet a different origin, whereby the entire *X–Y* graph we drew can be considered

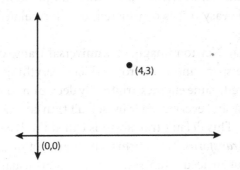

FIGURE 8.2 Simple *X–Y* plot of a point relative to an origin (0, 0).

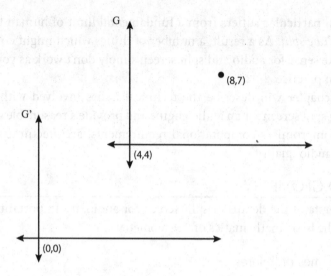

FIGURE 8.3 The original point, in the frame of reference of G, could also be considered relative to a different arbitrary frame of reference, G'.

to be a transform relative to a different origin. Each point, including the origin, would translate relative to this other origin. This setup is shown in Figure 8.3.

This change in representation is made relative to a frame of reference. In the frame of reference G (Figure 8.2), the point is (4, 3). In the frame of reference of G' (Figure 8.3), the point is (8, 7).

It is important to emphasize that the absolute, non-relative, nature of the points in the graph remain unchanged between the different frames of reference. The only things that change are the numbers we use to describe the geometry of those points. This is a powerful mathematical technique that can be used to solve difficult problems. Often, a hard problem is made easy if it is considered, or reformulated, in a different frame of reference.

Although Isaac Newton imagined a universal frame of reference as a kind of absolute space and time from which everything in the universe could be measured, game engines arbitrarily decide on some origin (called the world origin), and everything is by default transformed relative to that reference frame. This default transform is called the *World Transform* or a *World Space Transform*. Transforms which are not measured from this World origin but instead from some other point (usually some object) are called *Object Transform*, *Object Space Transform*, or *Local Space Transform*. In Figure 8.3, if G' was a world origin, the point plotted relative to G' would be a world-space transform, and the point plotted relative to G would be an object-space, or local-space transform.

8.2.2 The Math of Transforms

The three operations which are used to describe 3D geometry relative to a frame of reference are translation (T), scale (S), and rotation (R). In a 3D game engine, to fully describe the geometry of an object, all three transformations are combined into a single matrix called a transform matrix (M).

$$M = TRS$$

Applying the transform matrix, M, on a point in space, p, we get p', which is that point transformed according to the matrix M:

$$p' = Mp$$

$$p' = TRSp$$

$$p' = T\left(R\left(Sp\right)\right)$$

Note that the application of the transforms follows right to left. First, S, then R, then T are applied to the point, p. The order in which these transformations are applied does change the outcome, as shown in Figure 8.4.

Combining these matrices in any order results in a technically valid transformation matrix. However, the standard convention is to first apply scale, then rotation, then translation. This convention is used primarily because it's easier to conceptualize the results of these operations in this order than other orders.

8.2.3 Reversibility

One important property of the linear transformations we use in 3D game engines is that they are reversible. To undo the operation of a scale (S), we multiply by its inverse (S^{-1}):

$$I = S^{-1}S$$

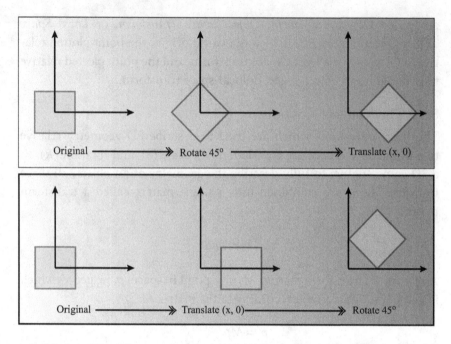

FIGURE 8.4 The order in which rotation and translation transformations are applied in a given coordinate system (frame of reference) has an effect on the resulting output.

where I is the identity matrix—a matrix with ones in the diagonals and zeroes everywhere else. A 3×3 identity matrix looks like this:

$$\begin{bmatrix} 1 & 0 & 0 \\ 0 & 1 & 0 \\ 0 & 0 & 1 \end{bmatrix}$$

In the case of a simple scalar transformation, this is identical to dividing a scalar value by itself. This reversibility is true of the other transformations, and dividing by a rotation or translation doesn't have the same conceptual analog. However, matrix inversions can be calculated for transformation matrices used in 3D game engines. Thus, generally speaking, to reverse a transformation matrix M, multiply by the inverse of the transform matrix, M^{-1}.

Since a transform M is a composite of underlying transforms of scale (S), rotation (R), and translation (T), the inverse of M is as follows:

$$M = TRS$$

$$M^{-1} = S^{-1} R^{-1} T^{-1}$$

The inverse transformations are applied in reverse order that they were applied to begin with – that is, first inverse scale, then inverse rotation, then inverse translation. This makes sense if you imagine the steps needed to precisely undo scaling, rotating, and translating an object in a 3D scene. You'd need to first move it back to the origin (undoing translation), reverse the rotation, and then multiply the scaling by its inverse.

8.2.4 Changing Frames of Reference Using Transforms

If you have a local space (or object space) transform for object P_{local} which is relative to another object which has a world-space transform V_{world}, you can derive the world-space transform of P_{world} by multiplying them together:

$$P_{world} = V_{world} \times P_{local}$$

If you consider only the translation operation, this formula is identical to our first example of frames of reference of a point in an X–Y graph in Figures 8.1 and 8.2.

This idea of "chaining" transforms and inverse transforms to go to and from various frames of references (or spaces) is a key concept in 3D games and specifically a key concept to understand how to deal with split screen for audio engines.

8.3 LISTENER GEOMETRY

Audio engines typically have an object which contains properties which represent information about a virtual listener. You can think of a virtual listener as a pair of ears (or, more generally, a microphone) in a game world. Audio is rendered from the perspective of this listener, and many significant CPU optimizations are made based on the location and orientation of this listener relative to sound sources. For VR games and first-person games, listeners are almost invariably hooked up to head-tracking mechanisms and represent the orientation of the player's head in the game.

Much like a camera and its transform, listeners usually have their 3D orientation represented by a matrix transform of translation, orientation, and scale—although the scale transform is almost always ignored. The listener transform is often set by the same code which sets up the camera transform but not always. There are many cases where you may want to render audio relative to a virtual listener even though there is no camera transform available (e.g. tools which preview spatialization or game features which allow listener traversal without changing a game's camera position).

3D sounds in games are panned and distance-attenuated relative to this listener transform, though there are some notable exceptions. For example, third-person games often have a hybrid listener setup where an optional position vector is used to determine distance-attenuation vs the translation of the listener transform.[1] This decoupling is usually to compensate for the fact that game cameras are often far above a controllable game character, and attenuating from the camera position would result in nearly all audio sounding far away, which is likely not the desired effect.

8.4 LISTENERS AS A FRAME OF REFERENCE

3D sound in a game is usually represented in an efficient manner from gameplay code as a world-space transform. Like listener transforms, only the transform translation and rotation are relevant. Because of this, it's intuitive to think that an audio renderer would need to take into account both the listener and the source transforms to be able to render 3D audio of the source (i.e. build speaker maps for panning, render HRT, perform distance attenuation, etc.). However, given the fact that we can compute a transform of the sound that is relative to the listener transform, it's possible to entirely ignore the geometry of the listener in an audio engine renderer and essentially render audio *from the perspective of the listener*. This trick greatly simplifies audio renderers and, it turns out, is a key concept to supporting split screen.

Given a sound's world-space transform, $Sound_{world}$, and given the world-space listener transform, $Listener_{world}$, it's simple to compute the listener-space sound transform, $Sound_{listener}$.

First, given the earlier discussion about composite transforms, the $Sound_{world}$ transform, which is set by the game engine, is composed of the following chained transform equation:

$$Listener_{world} \times Sound_{listener} = Sound_{world}$$

---

[1] For more details about how third-person camera attenuation works, see Somberg (2017).

To derive the $Sound_{listener}$ transform used by the audio renderer, multiply both sides of this equation by the inverse world-space listener transform, $Listener_{world}^{-1}$, as follows:

$$Listener_{world}^{-1} \times Listener_{world} \times Sound_{listener} = Listener_{world}^{-1} \times Sound_{world}$$

Note that the order of operations here does matter, so only multiply the inverse transform from the left on both sides to keep it simple. On the right is a computable transform using any 3D math library which deals with affine transform. (You can also work it out by hand to prove it.) On the left, the inverse listener transform multiplied by the listener transform cancel out, creating an identity transform (i.e. essentially multiply by 1.0). This leaves the desired answer for the $Sound_{listener}$ transform since an identity matrix multiplied by any other matrix is just the matrix itself:

$$I \times Sound_{listener} = Listener_{world}^{-1} \times Sound_{world}$$

$$Sound_{listener} = Listener_{world}^{-1} \times Sound_{world}$$

If the audio engine always uses listener-relative transforms for sounds, the audio renderer (the low-level DSP mixing code required to actually generate audio from the parameters derived from higher level features) only ever needs to deal with listener-relative sound spatialization and attenuation. In fact, no representation of the listener is required to accurately render audio; many details are consequently simplified, and there is a significant reduction in code complexity.

8.5 MULTIPLE LISTENERS

From the perspective of the audio engine, the key difference with split screen games is the addition of extra listeners. Each split screen view has its own camera transform and a corresponding listener transform.

On first impulse, you might expect that an audio engine would have to deal with many additional complexities and details to render audio from multiple perspectives. However, if the audio engine uses listener-space sound transforms, it becomes surprisingly easy to support any number of additional listeners. The only additional step required before computing a given sound's listener-relative transform is to determine that sound's closest listener.

As a result, an audio renderer already ignoring listener transforms can continue to ignore listener transforms even in a multilistener game. Essentially, once all sounds have been transformed relative to their closest listener, all listeners can conceptually be superposed on top of each other, each using the same conceptual identity matrix. All the panning, spatialization, attenuation, and other 3D information and features are computed correctly for each source relative to their closest listener, including occlusion, attenuation, angular listener-based focus, reverb sends, and so on.

8.6 COUNTERINTUITION: PLAYING ONCE

Importantly, each sound is only ever rendered once in an audio engine with this technique: from the perspective of the closest listener. It may be counter-intuitive that this singular rendering would be preferred over other more complex schemes. One such scheme could be that if a sound is played that is in range to a listener, then it should be played from the perspective of that listener: if a sound is in the audible range of two listeners, the sound should be played once for each listener. After all, this is exactly what a graphics engine does in split screen rendering: the same object in view to both screens will indeed be rendered twice.

There are several reasons why a multiple-playback scheme like that doesn't work well in practice for audio.

8.6.1 Multiple Triggering

Playing a sound multiple times for each listener in range would result in a large percentage of 3D sounds in a game getting triggered multiple times. Every gun shot, every footstep, every line of 3D dialogue…—everything would be played multiple times. It would sound confusing in a two-player split screen. In a four-player split screen, it would be total sonic chaos. Players will not be able to distinguish which camera/listener any given sound is coming from.

8.6.2 Clipping and Phasing

As of this writing, most audio engines still employ sample-based audio playback techniques: i.e., every sound heard in a game is essentially audio file playback. Although every modern audio engine uses a variety of techniques to maximize sample variations during playback, with so many sounds playing multiple times at the same time, there is a high probability of sounds playing back which are of the exact same variation at the exact same time (or possibly with slight timing differences). This situation will likely result in clipping: audio sources summing together to create audio amplitudes larger than can be represented in the renderer (e.g. over 1.0). In addition to clipping, identical sample file playback that is offset by a small amount of time usually results in a comb-filter effect, what is often referred to as "phasing." When not intended for a special effect, this sound is universally undesirable in games.

8.6.3 Significantly Extra CPU Costs

Rendering every sound multiple times will result in a correspondingly larger CPU cost, often increasing linearly with the number of played sounds. Rendering audio for a four-way split screen experience could result in four times the CPU rendering cost.

8.7 DRAWBACKS AND EDGE CASES

8.7.1 Boundary Flipping

Sounds which are on the boundary between two listeners can suddenly flip when the sound needs to be rendered suddenly to a different (closer) listener. This switch can be particularly jarring if the two listeners are facing away from each other. A sound will be rendered, for example, behind one listener and then suddenly be rendered in front of another. While this is a real problem, it is usually not an issue for the majority of sounds in practice. The situations where it would be potentially noticeable are rare (they are literally boundary conditions), and usually there is enough sonic complexity going on in the rest of the game that the artifacts are less noticeable.

8.7.2 Singleton Systems

One drawback of the technique of playing each sound only on the closest listener (and, in fact, split screen in general) for audio engines is that a variety of audio engine features are often implemented assuming a singleton listener.

For example, the majority of audio engines traditionally implement a listener-based reverb. In other words, what reverb settings to use (or which convolution impulse response chosen) are based on where the listener is. Running multiple reverbs, one for each listener, would be computationally expensive as reverb is often one of the more expensive DSP effects in games. For systems that assume a singleton listener (e.g. ambient zones, dynamic ambient systems, global effects processing like underwater DSP effects), usually the first (primary) listener is nominated to be one used to determine such settings and features. Though, strictly speaking, an audio engine could run multiple instances of any of these features, it's a matter of taste for how to apply them for split screen.

8.7.3 CPU Costs

Although rendering a 3D sound once relative to the closest listener is computationally less expensive than rendering it for each listener, there is still an additional CPU cost for split screen audio rendering. The additional cost is usually a result of playing more sounds than would otherwise be played—with multiple listener locations, more audio is simply in range. Thus, doing CPU performance analysis between split screen and non-split-screen games will usually result in some ratio of additional cost somewhere between one and two times as expensive. This factor may not seem like that much for an optimized audio renderer, but split screen usually has CPU overhead across the board. To compensate, it's possible to reduce audio rendering quality or disable certain features when in split screen mode in order to maintain a more constant CPU profile.

8.7.4 Competitive Multiplayer

For competitive multiplayer games, rendering audio only from the perspective of the closest listener may have gameplay implications. A player who can hear all audio from their perspective (even if far away) will have a significant competitive advantage over a player who is always hearing audio that is far from them but close to their split screen partner. This may seem like a good argument for rendering the audio multiple times, but that will not resolve this issue. Split screen audio (and graphics) will fundamentally make a player have inferior information to be competitive, so it's not a reasonable constraint for split screen audio.

8.8 ADDITIONAL AUDIO CONSIDERATIONS

Besides 3D audio rendering techniques and singleton audio engine systems, there are other audio problems involved in split screen which need to be considered.

8.8.1 Music

Music in split screen should always be a singleton—otherwise it will be cacophony. It is up to the music system designer as to how each player in a split screen interacts with the music. For example, an interactive music system which plays different music states based off stealth modes or action modes will need take into account the actions and state of all players. Such a system should largely operate identically between single screen and split screen modes.

8.8.2 Local-Player-Only Audio

Often in multiplayer games, there is a portion of audio that is intended to only play on the local player and not be heard by other players, such as quest queues or health warnings. However, there are multiple local players for split screen audio, and—in most cases—local-player-only sounds will need to be played for each split screen player, even though many gameplay systems are often written to assume there is only one listener.

8.8.3 User Interface Audio

Like local player audio, audio for interface feedback will need to always be played regardless of the split screen mode. This should go without saying, but again, there are sometimes complexities involved with making sure UI and gameplay systems are written to support multiple listeners, especially if the audio is 3D.

8.9 RENDERING TWICE: DUAL OUTPUT

Although not widely done, it is possible to create separate audio rendering instances and render audio uniquely for each listener in a split screen context. If each of these instances plays back on the same output audio device endpoint heard by all players of a split screen game, this will suffer from the exact same drawbacks as described earlier: CPU cost, chaos, confusion, phasing, and clipping. However, if the instances are rendered to different audio device endpoints and the players are using headphones, it's possible to allow players to hear audio only from their unique perspective. This would be analogous to rendering to a different display for each player (or to a VR headset for each player). And, like graphics, it would exactly double the CPU cost for two-player split screen, quadruple for four-player split screen, and so on.

8.10 CONCLUSION

If reasonable compromises are accepted, split screen support for audio engines is surprisingly straightforward to implement. The key insight is to convert world-space sound transforms to the listener-space transform of the sound's closest listener. Usually, the experience of playing the same game with your friend (or enemy) on the couch locally is compelling enough to overcome any of the side effects of the technique. In general, if players are playing a split-screen game, the overall experience should be optimizing the social experience.

REFERENCES

Somberg, Guy. "Listeners for Third-Person Cameras." *Game Audio Programming Principles and Practices*, edited by Guy Somberg. CRC Press, 2017, pp. 197–208.

CHAPTER 9

Voice Management and Virtualization

Robert Gay

Epic Games

CONTENTS

9.1 THE NEED FOR VOICE MANAGEMENT

In its most basic form, voice management is to games and game engines what polyphony is to traditional hardware synthesizers. It is the feature set responsible for dealing with scenarios when a system or collection of systems attempts to play more sounds that the hardware can or should sonify. Voice management encompasses multiple features and design patterns which can be implemented to some level or another as your engine or game requires. Regardless of scale and complexity, every project needs to consider voice management—preferably as early in development as possible.

Building an audio engine that caters to various types of games with sonically complex scenarios requires complex systems of voice management. From this perspective, it is easier to scale features and functionality down than up. Therefore, it is preferable to provide voice management features in the hands of the sound designers which can be enabled or disabled at will. Even if it is only the programmer that is to be fiddling with voice management parameters, providing such a toolset remains useful for flexibility and iterative development. Breaking out voices into well-organized data structures that are configurable in editor or development builds allows for rapid iteration and scalability, which is paramount in dialing in the final game's experience. This is crucial, particularly when time becomes scarce and the development cycle is nearing completion.

This chapter does not intend to indoctrinate a particular methodology to manage voices, nor does it aim to hyperfocus on a particular aspect. An entire textbook could be written on this topic in much further detail. Rather, this chapter serves as an introduction to what voice management is, an overview of the typical feature set it entails, and how a programmer can begin building a system from the ground up that is readily extensible and scalable.

9.2 SONIFYING A FOREST

Sonification is the process of determining which sounds to play. In this sense, voice management dances with the age-old philosophical question: "If a tree falls in the forest and no one is around to hear it, does it make a sound?"

As sounds play, the decision whether to sonify them is determined by prioritizing the playing sounds against other playing sounds and comparing their various properties. These properties may be simple, like attenuation falloff—preferring to play closer (and therefore louder) sounds over those further and quieter. Or they may be complex, such as evaluating a rule that a sound designer has specified what should be considered more aesthetically more important.

Furthermore, we must define what we mean when we refer to a "sound" in an audio engine. For the purposes of this chapter, a sound will be considered as an *asset*, a *real voice*, or a *virtual voice*. An *asset* is any contiguous body of audio data, compressed or uncompressed, to be processed and rendered at runtime. A *real voice* refers to the voice that is to be actually rendered and processed in the final mixed output buffer sent to hardware. A *virtual voice* refers to any requested voice from a higher gameplay layer that is logically playing but not necessarily being rendered. As a general rule, a real voice is more expensive, both in processing power required and memory than a virtual voice, as it requires an asset to be loaded into memory and potentially decompressed at runtime.

9.3 THE SINGLE CAP TRAP

A single cap on permissible voices to play at once is rarely—if ever—a valid full voice management solution, yet it is a good place to start the conversation of managing voices. Having a final cap can be a good idea as a last line of defense from total voice saturation and producing performance bottlenecks on other systems, but other systems should be in place to keep that limit from being hit. In general, an engine requires two types of grouping mechanisms that work.in tandem to control performance and mix voice requirements independently, which we will refer to as *real* and *virtual* voice pools. These two concepts are too often conflated, which can over-complicate or hinder the system's design. When a single object combines aspects of both, the number of states that it can be in are too numerous, and it can be challenging to keep them straight.

The term *pool* here is being used in an abstract fashion. While it may make sense to allocate real and virtual voice data up front in a traditional memory pool, the term *pool* used here is referring to a group of voice references that maintains a maximum number of allotted items that can be played at once. In both the cases of real and virtual pools, a single rendered voice may subscribe to multiple pools. In a way, a final cap could be considered a form of a real voice pool in which all playing real voices are members.

9.4 REAL VOICE POOLS

Real voice pools are responsible for restricting the number of concurrent sounds played at a particular time that may share similar static asset or performance characteristics. For example, such a pool may manage streaming sounds that may be extremely large like music or ambience and require similar behavior to load and unload chunks of audio from disk. Another type of pool may be made for sounds that are compressed using a certain format that may have hardware restrictions on the number available to be decompressed at one time. Yet another could be a reserved number of real voices that are allowed to stop gracefully, fading over a quick time period to avoid pops in audio. If a maximum single cap has been instigated, best practice is to ensure the maximum number of voices for each type of real voice pool is at or below the maximum single cap.

Because real voice pools deal with hardware-level rendering, they are typically managed on a dedicated audio render thread. They may be software imposed to avoid performance overage stressing other critical engine systems or may be hardware imposed.

The real voice pool is performance-critical, so when a real voice pool reaches its maximum, we assume that resources are starved. This situation may manifest as undesired audible behavior such as sounds immediately stopping or starting delayed. We can mitigate abrupt interruptions, avoiding pops by applying fast transitions at the buffer level. Regardless, these pools are generally a last line of defense for avoiding resource starvation and constraining your audio system's runtime performance and memory characteristics. Therefore, it is recommended to stress test your game or audio engine in many voice-heavy scenarios to determine what these pool limits should be set at in order to avoid sudden, perceptible interruption. When a real voice pool reaches its limits, it is crucial to include adequate logging and other debug information in order to be able to determine how best to tune the voice pools and their respective maximum distributions.

9.5 VIRTUAL VOICE POOLS

Whereas real voice pools manage resource limitations, virtual voice pools manage perceptual limitations. Virtual voice pools limit sounds of a particular sonic category from flooding a sound mix. For example, a designer may instigate a virtual pool limit on music by having at most two tracks playing at once, one fading in and another fading out. Another pool may exist to throttle ambience using a similar restriction for sounds tagged as ambience. Yet another may be created to avoid having too many weapon sounds. These are relatively simple examples, and more typically the virtual voice pools are further divided to better control the maximum number of similar events that can be processed at any given time.

This pooling architecture helps to solve the perceptual problem that humans can only process a limited number of sound events at once, and playing more can lead to sonic confusion, while conveniently and consequently culling sounds from stressing the real voice pool system. Virtual pool voices may be tagged as a member of a single pool or multiple pools within the engine's content management system. By tuning the virtual pool limits, sound designers have the indirect power to avoid real voice pool saturation and sonic artifacts therein.

9.6 REVIVING THE DEAD

Enforcing a healthy virtual pool voice count is only half of the battle for programmers and designers alike. Sounds that stop due to virtual pool saturation often need to resume later once other higher priority voices finish. There are two broad categories of sounds that need to be handled differently: looping sounds that play continuously until a gameplay event requests the sound to stop and "fire-and-forget" or "one-shot" sounds, where a gameplay system requests a sound to be played without managing the sound's lifetime. Generally, one does not need to resume one-shot sounds that are short and transient, which have been terminated early to enforce a pool's voice limit. However, looping sounds and longer-tailed one-shots typically require a virtualization mechanism in order to resume playback.

There are many situations where virtual voices need to be resumed. The classic example is when a player exits and re-enters the audible range of a particular in-world asset such as a waterfall or fire. It may be tempting to despawn ambient attenuated sounds when their associated model becomes visually occluded or culled, but an object's visibility does not necessarily coincide with the sound source's audibility. Another example may be when a scene requires a dense sonic landscape with many sources that are persistent and the sound designer wants to dynamically prioritize sounds closer to the listener. Virtualization can help manage both of these examples.

9.7 REAL TREES IN A VIRTUAL FOREST

When a virtual voice pool is found to contain a number of active voices that is greater than its limit, it must evict a sound from the pool, whether that be a newly added sound or one of lower priority that has been playing. Evicted sounds may be either *killed*, resulting in destruction of both the virtual and real counterparts, or *virtualized*, resulting in the real voice being stopped but the virtual counterpart persisting. When a voice stops playing and space becomes available once again in the virtual voice pool, a real voice can then be recreated and played, a process called *realization*. A real voice is typically comprised of an active object that is rendering output to the hardware. A virtual voice is, ideally, a minimal set of data required to determine whether or not a real voice should be created. In the event that there is not enough space in one of the pools that a virtual voice subscribes to when playback is requested, it should be virtualized immediately without ever initiating a request to start a real voice.

In order to determine whether a virtual voice is eligible to play back as a real voice when its subscribed virtual pools are saturated, this minimal set of data is evaluated against a ruleset. This virtualization data is a combination of runtime and static information about the sound asset. Static virtualization data can be extracted when the assets are serialized or compressed. If a sound's virtualization ruleset requires volume data, one common technique is to store a coarse array of root mean square volumes and a corresponding seek table in order to allow for seeking and resuming based on the elapsed time of the virtual voice.

As the game starts and stops sounds, space will be used up and freed, respectively, in the virtual voice pools, requiring a mechanism to evaluate virtualization logic. Typically, this logic happens on an audio logic thread, which can run at a slower rate than the audio rendering thread. Depending on the platform architecture, the audio logic can be evaluated on the main game thread or on a dedicated thread. In situations where there is a dedicated thread that needs to poll the gameplay state, the update rate of the audio logic thread should be both configurable and independent of the gameplay update rate.

9.8 RULE BUILDING

Each virtual pool has a set of rules that are evaluated when the pool becomes saturated from the advent of a new playback request. These rules determine whether a voice should continue playing as a real and virtual voice (an active voice), as just a virtual voice (said to be *virtualized*), or stopped entirely. Designing and applying these rules allows sound designers to walk a balance between performance and aesthetics and to avoid flooding virtual voice pools (and by extension real voice pools). A good set of rules will have a minimal impact on the listening experience while managing its actual performance.

The most basic rule is a Boolean value that determines whether a virtual pool is active or not, which is a useful tool for both debugging and isolation. This rule can help determine if sounds are stopping or cutting out due to this system or another independent gameplay mechanism. Using this basic rule effectively disables the pool: all playback requests create a virtual voice in a single pool unrestricted by any rules or voice limit.

Rule design should be as flexible as possible, since the rulesets will undergo many iterations throughout the development lifecycle. Different classes of sounds will need different rules, and the rules may even change based on gameplay state. It is best to design the rule system in a way that can be parameterized easily.

9.9 VIRTUAL POOL RULES

Rules can be broken down into the following three stages of evaluation:

Individual Voice Rules → Voice Stealing Rules → Virtualization Rule

The first stage of evaluating individual voice rules falls into three basic classes: time-based rules, distance-based rules, and volume-based rules.

9.9.1 Time-Based Rules

Time-based rules compare how much time remains for a voice and a pre-scribed value. For instance, a gunshot sound has a quiet tail, and its virtual pool is saturated. The sound has been playing as a real voice for 5 seconds, while only having a remaining playtime of 0.2 seconds. A time-based rule may declare that beyond this limit, it is no longer a candidate for virtualization and should be killed. Correspondingly, if the same sound has been virtualized for 0.2 seconds and has 5 seconds of playtime remaining when a slot then becomes available in the pool permitting it to play, it may or may not make more sense to eject the sound from the virtual pool and no longer process it as a virtual voice. In this case, it defers to the realization settings (see Section 9.9.5) in order to determine whether to realize or kill the voice.

9.9.2 Distance-Based Rules

Distance-based rules control whether a voice should be real based on the sound source's max distance (the distance at which its attenuation curve reaches a terminally zero volume) plus an optional distance buffer. This buffer avoids abrupt stopping and starting of the sound if the listener is quickly moving in and out of range. If a sound is close to being inaudible due to its distance attenuation and a saturated voice pool, it does not need to occupy a real voice. Even though distance-based rules bear some similarity to volume-based rules (see Section 9.9.3), distance should be evaluated separately because distance does not necessarily correspond linearly with volume. Distance-based rules can prevent thrashing the virtualization system with nearly inaudible sounds by preventing them from playing when the sound is close to or beyond its max distance.

9.9.3 Volume-Based Rules

Volume-based rules evaluate whether a sound is a candidate for virtualization or eviction based on whether its final output volume is below a certain threshold. For example, a sound could be considered for virtualization when its volume drops below a threshold of −40 dB. Each volume rule may be evaluated pre attenuation or post attenuation. Post attenuation, rules combine the distance attenuation and volume attenuation together, which can simplify the rulesets. However, if the sound designers desire more fine-grained control, they can select pre-attenuation and then add a separate distance rule if required.

9.9.4 Voice Stealing

After all of the rules have been applied to all of the sounds in a virtual pool, there may still be more real sounds than the virtual pool has allotted. In such a case, the virtual pool needs to virtualize or stop a playing sound, ideally one that is low priority and which will not adversely affect the mix if it is stopped.

The most common technique to determine which sounds to virtualize is to sort the list of currently playing sounds by one or more predicates and virtualize or stop the lowest-priority sounds until the voice pool limit is reached. The sorting predicates are usually fairly simple: how long the sound has been playing, its current audibility, or a priority value that the sound designers can set.

9.9.5 Realization

When a virtual voice is no longer able to play due to its pool being saturated, it can be either stopped or virtualized. Correspondingly, when a virtual voice is realized, there are a few potential ways in which it can continue playback. Table 9.1 summarizes the various realization settings that sound designers can choose from.

TABLE 9.1   Virtualization Rules

Value	Description
Disabled	Stops virtual and corresponding real voice
Restart	Restarts the real voice
Resume (Real Time)	Resumes the real voice from elapsed time the real voice has played
Resume (Virtual Time)	Resumes the real voice from elapsed time the virtual voice has played

Each of these settings is useful in different contexts:

- **Disabled**—Short one-shot sounds. This is the cheapest option because the sound can be simply stopped and there is no further logic required.

- **Restart**—Looping beds where the user has no discernable way to tell the beginning of the sound from any other part of the loop. This is the cheapest replay option, since it does not require a seek.

- **Resume (Real Time)**—Objects in game that emit a distinctive sound such as music which can be interrupted, such as a music box or a record player.

- **Resume (Virtual Time)**—Long-tailed one-shots such as reverberant tails that decay over time and other sounds that have distinct, temporally identifiable audible qualities.

9.10 RUNTIME ASSET CACHING

The voice management system is in a position to coordinate closely with the asset loading system by providing hints for stream chunk loading and unloading. For sounds that are fully loaded into memory (usually on level load but potentially at runtime), no coordination is necessary since all of the audio data is already resident. However, streamed sounds can resume playback with reduced latency by ensuring that the next chunk of stream data is always resident in memory. The appropriate stream chunk to load depends on the realization settings for the sound:

- **Disabled** or **Restart**—Always keep the first chunk of the stream resident in memory while any instance of the voice is playing.

- **Resume (Real Time)**—Keep the most recently played chunk in memory until the voice is stopped or realized.

- **Resume (Virtual Time)**—Provide a periodic callback (or poll elapsed time) to trigger prior to the time the next chunk is required, which unloads the current chunk and loads the next chunk.

9.11 DYNAMIC POOL ALLOCATION

As a game's play session changes context, it may be necessary to change the limits on the virtual pools dynamically. For example, when the player is interacting with a lobby or menu system, the limits can favor UI sounds, whereas during a match or in-game the limits can be geared toward actions, voices, and music. Throughout each context, different types of sounds will take priority, so having the ability to change voice pool limits will account for large stateful transitions.

In addition to game context, hardware and platform restrictions may affect pool sizes as well: consoles, PCs, and mobile devices all have different characteristics that will affect how many real voices can be played at once. Architectural differences among the platforms may also affect the real voice limit or limits: threading models, CPU architecture, caching mechanisms, and supported compression formats all are factors in the number of real voices. Another consideration for virtual voice pool limits is a client's listening environment. For example, designers may want to adjust pool limits based on the final output being sent to a TV, 5.1 surround, phone speakers, or headphones.

9.12 CONCLUSION

Approaching voice management as a collection of real and virtual voices assigned to real and virtual pools allows the rendered sound to be split from the voice's gameplay lifetime. Splitting the logic into individual voice rules, voice stealing rules, and a voice's virtualization rule makes the whole process of determining playback priority manageable and scalable.

CHAPTER 10

Screen-Space Distance Attenuation

Guy Somberg

Echtra Games

CONTENTS

10.1 INTRODUCTION

Action RPGs like *Torchlight, Diablo, and Path of Exile* have many distinctive challenges in their audio. One of the most fundamental challenges is that of panning and attenuation, which are shared with many other games that have a third-person perspective on the action. The problem is that the distance to the camera is not a meaningful measurement at all in these games—rather, it is the distance to the player that matters.

The problem of using the distance to the player for attenuation has already been solved, and the solution is taken as a given in this chapter. The thing that we're going to do is take a step back and ask what we mean by "distance."

10.2 DISTANCE ATTENUATION REVIEW

The classical model of audio distance attenuation and panning has been in use for decades. The listener is placed at the camera, and the distance from each sound source to the listener position is passed into an attenuation function. These attenuation functions may encode a realistic sound falloff curve, some generic nonrealistic but game-targeted function, or a custom curve that is designed per event. Regardless of the actual function, the attenuation is parameterized by the distance from the sound source to the listener.

This model is simple, but it works for many categories of games—particularly well for first-person shooters. Unfortunately, it breaks down when the camera and the player are not one and the same, which will be the case in any game with a third-person camera. For a third-person camera, we must separate the concept of the *attenuation position* from that of the *panning position*. The attenuation position must be placed at the player's location, and the panning position must be placed at the camera. This is the only way in which the attenuation and the panning of all sounds will sound right.

Decoupling the attenuation and panning positions from the listener requires a bit of vector math if your middleware doesn't implement it for you. Figure 10.1 shows how to go about this. The attenuation position (A) is placed in the player's head, and the panning position (L) is in the camera. We calculate the distance from each of the three sound sources (A, B, and C) to the attenuation position and then reposition each of the sounds along the vector from the panning position to the sound source at the distance from the sound source to the attenuation position giving positions A′, B′, and C′. For more details on this algorithm, see Somberg (2017).

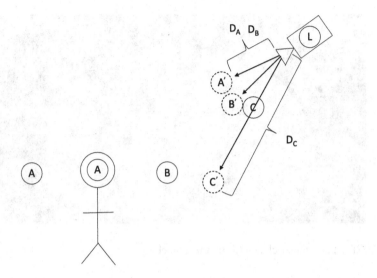

FIGURE 10.1 Third-person camera setup with separated attenuation position. Sound sources A, B, and C are repositioned to positions A′, B′, and C′.

10.3 THE PROBLEM WITH ACTION RPGs

In ARPGs, the player character is in the center of the screen, and the camera is placed in the sky above the player at an angle. This setup is perfect for the attenuation/panning split because without it, audio distance becomes meaningless. If the listener is in the camera, and a sound has a max distance of 10 meters, at what point does it become audible? There is no right answer when the distance is measured to the camera. Decoupling attenuation and panning solves this problem by providing a real, in-world meaning to distance. A sound which is configured to have a max distance of 10 meters equates exactly to 10 meters in world space from the sound source to the player character.

But let's take a look at what the player sees in the world. Figure 10.2 shows a player character in a test level standing in the center of concentric rings at 10 and 20 meters. If a sound designer wants a sound to be audible only while it's on the screen, what value should she choose for the max distance? Let's try a few different values in Table 10.1 and see what happens.

Once again, we have a problem: there is no meaningful value that our sound designer can choose that will give her the attenuation that she wants. We are back to square one: our audio distance values have an intuitive meaning that matches the game world, but the values themselves are

FIGURE 10.2   Player character in a test level.

TABLE 10.1   A Selection of Max Distances and Whether They Succeed in Matching the Sound Designer's Intention

Max Distance	Audible Onscreen	Inaudible Offscreen
10 meters	True at the bottom of the screen but only covers half the screen or less on the sides and the top	True everywhere except at the bottom of the screen
15 meters	True for roughly the bottom half of the screen	True for roughly the top half of the screen
20 meters	True everywhere except the upper corners	Only true in the upper corners
25 meters	True everywhere	False everywhere

useless for mixing and tuning. This is particularly true in ARPGs because in general, the things on the screen are the ones that matter.

10.4 THE MEANING OF DISTANCE

Taking a step back, we must question some of our fundamental assumptions. Our intuition leads us to state that the distances passed into our audio engine must, perforce, be the straight-line distances from the sound source to the attenuation position. However, there is nothing that says that the measured distance must be the 3D distance.

One thing to note from Table 10.1 is that in every cell, we refer to sections of the *screen* where the attenuation matches or doesn't match the sound designer's intent. More particularly, we do not refer to sections of the *world*.

This observation leads us to the solution to our distance conundrum: what if we measure distance in screen space instead of world space? All of a sudden, our concept of distance no longer has an in-world analog, but it does have an on-screen analog. And, particularly, our sound designer can now select a value that describes exactly what she wants: that a sound is only audible while it is on the screen and that it attenuates smoothly to every point. She can now mix the entire game because she has an understanding of when a sound will actually play.

We will come back to the problem of the lack of an in-world analog later in this chapter, but for now, let's examine how to accomplish our screen-space distance projection.

10.5 CONVERTING TO SCREEN-SPACE

The first thing we must do is write a function that will convert our world space coordinates to screen space. In principle, this is fairly simple, given the point, the camera's view and projection matrices, and the viewport size. We need to multiply the point by the view matrix and then the projection matrix, which will give us a 4D vector in "clip space." Sometimes the view and projection matrices are premultiplied by the graphics engine as an optimization. We normalize the result into device coordinate space, which gives us a vector in the range [−1...+1]. We rescale the values into the range [0...1] and then multiply by the viewport size in order to get the resulting position:

```cpp
std::optional<Vector2> WorldSpaceToScreenSpace(
  const Vector3& Point,
  const Matrix4& View, const Matrix4& Projection,
  const Vector2& ViewportSize)
{
  auto ClipSpacePosition =
    Projection * View * Vector4(Point, 1.0f);
  if (ClipSpacePosition.W == 0.0f)
    return std::nullopt;
  ClipSpacePosition /= ClipSpacePosition.W;
  ClipSpacePosition.X = (ClipSpacePosition.X / 2.0f) + 0.5f;
  ClipSpacePosition.Y = 1.0f - (ClipSpacePosition.Y / 2.0f) - 0.5f;
  return Vector2{
    ClipSpacePosition.X * ViewportSize.X,
    ClipSpacePosition.Y * ViewportSize.Y };
}
```

Figure 10.3 shows the resulting coordinate space. Most 3D engines already have such a function built in. In Unreal, this function is

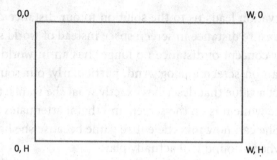

FIGURE 10.3   Screen-space coordinate system used for graphics.

in UGameplayStatics::ProjectWorldToScreen(). In Unity, it is Camera.WorldToScreenPoint(). As handy as these functions are, we cannot use them with their default inputs (that is, the player's active camera) and in their default form—at least not directly. We'll take a look at why this is true in the next section.

10.6 SCREEN-SPACE DISTANCE ALGORITHM

It seems as though we ought to be able to use this as our algorithm:

1. Convert attenuation position to screen space.

2. Convert sound position to screen space.

3. Find the 2D distance between the two points $\left(\sqrt{\Delta X^2 + \Delta Y^2} \right)$.

Unfortunately, this won't work for a few reasons.

10.6.1 Pixels Are Not Meaningful

Screen space is in pixels, and the number of pixels is not consistent from computer to computer or even from moment to moment within a play session (e.g. if the player changes resolution while running). What we need is a coordinate in device coordinate space. Fortunately, we already have that value as an intermediate result in our previous code, so we can just omit the viewport size and renormalization from the code:

```
std::optional<Vector2> WorldSpaceToClipSpace(
    const Vector3& Point,
    const Matrix4& View, const Matrix4& Projection)
{
    auto ClipSpacePosition =
```

```
    Projection * View * Vector4(Point, 1.0f);
  if (ClipSpacePosition.W == 0.0f)
    return std::nullopt;
  ClipSpacePosition /= ClipSpacePosition.W;
  return Vector2{
    ClipSpacePosition.X, ClipSpacePosition.Y };
}
```

Figure 10.4 shows how this code has affected the coordinate space.

10.6.2 The Range Is Too Small

The code that we just described provides values for each axis in the range [−1...+1]. What this means is that values at the edge of the screen have a magnitude of 1 and the center of the screen has a magnitude of 0. Since the attenuation position in an ARPG is either at or close to the center of the screen, this means that the max distance for most sounds will be at a value of 1.0. Technically, we could leave this alone, but the problem is that we now have to hand these values off to two interested parties: the sound designers and the audio middleware.

Let's take a look at the audio middleware first. In general, off-the-shelf audio middleware is not expecting to be operating in a scale where max distance is 1. Figure 10.5 shows a Spatializer DSP in FMOD Studio with a minimum distance of 0.6 and a maximum distance of 1.0. This is a practically unusable user experience. The min and max points on the slider are practically touching, and the right 90% of the control is completely unused. Other audio middleware has similar issues.

The second customer that will have problems with this scale is the sound designers. The range of 0...1, although morally equivalent to any other scale, will feel constricting to sound designers. At that scale,

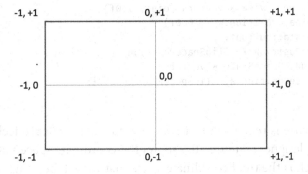

FIGURE 10.4   Screen-space coordinate system centered at the center of the screen.

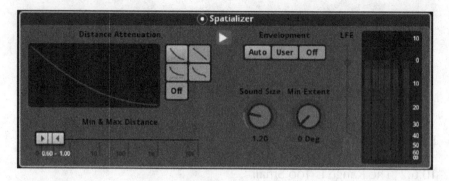

FIGURE 10.5   FMOD Studio Spatializer with minimum distance of 0.6 and maximum distance of 1.0.

miniscule changes can have meaningful effects on the distance, which will make it difficult for the sound designers to come up with an intuition for what the numbers mean. Recall that the whole point of this exercise is to provide a meaningful value for distance that the sound designers can use intuitively.

These statements about sound designers are all purely subjective and patently false. Sound designers are supremely adaptable, and they will be able to come up with an intuition for what the various values mean, no matter what the range is. However, it is also true that a larger range is easier for sound designers to work with, and the cost of doing so is a single multiplication:

```
std::optional<Vector2> WorldSpaceToAudioSpace(
  const Vector3& Point,
  const Matrix4& View, const Matrix4& Projection)
{
  auto ClipSpacePosition =
    Projection * View * Vector4(Point, 1.0f);
  if (ClipSpacePosition.W == 0.0f)
    return std::nullopt;
  ClipSpacePosition /= ClipSpacePosition.W;
  return AudioSpaceScale * Vector2{
    ClipSpacePosition.X, ClipSpacePosition.Y };
}
```

My experience is that a value of 20.0f for AudioSpaceScale feels natural for sound designers. Figure 10.6 shows the coordinate space with a scale of 20, which is the final coordinate space that we will be using. However, we are still not quite finished.

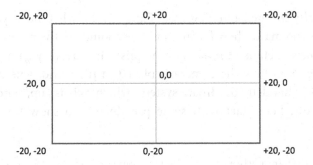

FIGURE 10.6 Screen-space coordinate system centered at the center of the screen and scaled to 20 units.

10.6.3 Using the Wrong Camera

The last problem with our algorithm is that it is using the wrong camera. Or, more precisely, it is using the player's camera, which is correct only some of the time. The problem comes about when the game supports zooming. Compare the viewport from Figure 10.2, which shows the camera fully zoomed out with the viewport from Figure 10.7, where the camera is fully zoomed in. In Figure 10.7, the top of the screen cuts off at less than 20 meters away, and the bottom of the screen is just a meter or two away from the player. While Figure 10.2 also cuts off at the top around 20 meters, the sides and the bottom are much further away, providing the player with a broader view of the action.

Depending on the game, it may be desirable for the audioscape to match the viewport exactly. However, it is more likely that the desired effect is

FIGURE 10.7 Player character in a test level with the camera zoomed in.

that the **fully zoomed-out view** from Figure 10.2 is what the player should be hearing, no matter how far in they have zoomed in their camera.

The precise details of how to accomplish this are very game-specific. They depend on how the camera is placed in the world, whether it is a right- or left-handed coordinate system, which axis is "up," and various other details. Let's start with some pseudocode to show the shape of the code:

```
// Return either a view and projection matrix separately or a
// premultiplied view/projection matrix
ViewProjectionMatrix GetAudioViewProjectionMatrix()
{
  auto Transform = CalculateCameraLocationAndOrientation();
  auto ViewMatrix = GetViewMatrix(Transform);
  auto ProjectionMatrix = GetProjectionMatrix(Transform);
  return ViewMatrix * ProjectionMatrix;
}
```

Real code is rarely so pithy. If you're using Unreal, then the code will look something like this (with error checking and some game-specific code elided for brevity):

```
FMatrix GetAudioViewProjectionMatrix(
  const TOptional<FVector3>& OverridePosition,
  FIntRect* OutViewRect)
{
  // Find the camera component.  Details are game-specific, so
  // this is a fakey placeholder.
  UCameraComponent* CameraComponent = GetCameraComponent();

  // Grab the camera view info from the camera.  We will presume
  // that the camera's view info does not
  // change meaningfully as the camera moves around.
  constexpr float UnusedDeltaTime = 0.0f;
  FMinimalViewInfo ViewInfo;
  CameraComponent->GetCameraView(UnusedDeltaTime, ViewInfo);

  // Make sure that we don't get black bars
  ViewInfo.bConstrainAspectRatio = false;

  // Another fakey placeholder.  This function should use game-
  // specific logic to calculate ViewInfo.Location and
  // ViewInfo.Rotation.  If the OverridePosition is set, then
  // it should use that instead.
  CalculateViewInfoTransform(ViewInfo, OverridePosition);
```

```
// This section of code is adapted from
// ULocalPlayer::GetProjectionData().
// We need to build a structure that has all of the appropriate
// matrices in order to be able to do the world->screen projection.
// Details of getting and error-checking ViewPort are omitted
// for brevity.  It is accessible from the PlayerController's
// LocalPlayer.
auto X = Viewport->GetInitialPositionXY().X;
auto Y = Viewport->GetInitialPositionXY().Y;
auto SizeX = Viewport->GetSizeXY().X;
auto SizeY = Viewport->GetSizeXY().Y;
auto UnconstrainedRectangle =
    FIntRect{ X, Y, X + SizeX, Y + SizeY };
if (OutViewRect != nullptr)
    *OutViewRect = UnconstrainedRectangle;

FSceneViewProjectionData ProjectionData;
ProjectionData.SetViewRectangle(UnconstrainedRectangle);
ProjectionData.ViewOrigin = ViewInfo.Location;
ProjectionData.ViewRotationMatrix =
    FInverseRotationMatrix{ ViewInfo.Rotation } * FMatrix{
        FPlane{0, 0, 1, 0},
        FPlane{1, 0, 0, 0},
        FPlane{0, 1, 0, 0},
        FPlane{0, 0, 0, 1} };
FMinimalViewInfo::CalculateProjectionMatrixGivenView(
    ViewInfo, AspectRatio_MajorAxisFOV, nullptr, ProjectionData);

return ProjectionData.ComputeViewProjectionMatrix();
}
```

We have sneaked ahead and added a couple of features to this function that we will need later on: an override position and an output parameter that fills in the view rectangle. We will be using these for debug visualization later on.

10.7 NEXT STEPS

With all of these details taken into account, our algorithm is now subtly but importantly modified:

1. Convert attenuation position to scaled clip space using the view projection from the fully zoomed-out camera.

2. Convert sound position to scaled clip space using the view projection from the fully zoomed-out camera.

3. Find the 2D distance between the two points $\left(\sqrt{\Delta X^2 + \Delta Y^2} \right)$.

With this algorithm hooked up, sound designers can now start to assign minimum and maximum distances to their sounds that are in screen space. If there is already a pre-existing set of sounds, then they will have to go through all of their existing assets and rebalance their ranges.

But even this algorithm is a little bit off. By taking the 2D distance between the points, we are describing a circle in screen space around which our sound is audible, rather than actually describing whether or not the sound source is on the screen. We will need one more tweak in order to fully describe our screen-space distance attenuation.

10.8 RECTANGULAR DISTANCES

Our coordinate system has a value of 20 units at the edges. If the listener position is in the center of the screen, then the positions at the centers along the edges of the screen will all have a distance of 20 units, and the corners will all be $20\sqrt{2}$ units away. In order for a sound to be audible while it's on the screen, the sound designers will have to set maximum distances of over 28, which is far larger than intended.

What we actually want is a setup such that every point along the edge of the screen is 20 units away from the attenuation position, no matter where it is. Note that this is subtly different from having it be 20 units away from the center of the screen—we still want to take the attenuation position into account. Figure 10.8 shows how the distances need to work: we break the screen into quadrants, and each quadrant's axes are scaled to 20 units away from the attenuation position.

In order to create this projection, we project our point and the attenuation position into screen space, scale each axis of the projected point by the size of the quadrant, and then return the maximum of the x and y coordinates. We can express this in code thus:

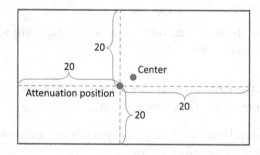

FIGURE 10.8 Screen broken up into quadrants by the attenuation position, rather than the center, with each quadrant having a logical size of 20 units.

```
float GetDistanceSquared(
  const Vector2& ProjectedPosition,
  const Vector2& ProjectedAttenuationPosition)
{
  auto XDistance =
    ProjectedPosition.X - ProjectedAttenuationPosition.X;
  auto YDistance =
    ProjectedPosition.Y - ProjectedAttenuationPosition.Y;

  Vector2 RescaledPosition = ProjectedPosition;
  if (XDistance >= 0.0f)
  {
    RescaledPosition.X *=
      (20.0f - ProjectedAttenuationPosition.X) / 20.0f;
  }
  else
  {
    RescaledPosition.X *=
      (20.0f + ProjectedAttenuationPosition.X) / 20.0f;
  }
  if (YDistance >= 0.0f)
  {
    RescaledPosition.Y *=
      (20.0f - ProjectedAttenuationPosition.Y) / 20.0f;
  }
  else
  {
    RescaledPosition.Y *=
      (20.0f + ProjectedAttenuationPosition.Y) / 20.0f;
  }

  return std::max(RescaledPosition.X * RescaledPosition.X,
                  RescaledPosition.Y * RescaledPosition.Y);
}
```

Working with rectangular coordinates may feel a bit foreign to sound designers. It may be worthwhile to implement both circular and rectangular coordinates and see which one the sound designers like better. Implementing a debug toggle that can switch at runtime is an effective mechanism to help the sound designers hear and visualize the difference.

If you choose to use rectangular distances instead of circular distances, then the final algorithm only changes in step 3:

1. Convert attenuation position to scaled clip space using the view projection from the fully zoomed-out camera.

2. Convert sound position to scaled clip space using the view projection from the fully zoomed-out camera.

3. Find the rectangular distance between the two points.

But once again, we are faced with a dilemma whether we use circular or rectangular coordinates, because while the sound designers have a meaningful value that they can understand for any given sound, they have no way to visualize it in the world.

10.9 ON-SCREEN DEBUG VISUALIZATION

When our distance model was based on world coordinates, the natural model for representing minimum and maximum distances on the screen was a sphere. We could simply draw two spheres and call it a day. However, we have to do a bit more work now that we have changed our distance model. There is no standard off-the-shelf shape that we can draw that will precisely describe the distance at which a sound will be audible. We will have to construct our own shape.

10.9.1 Describing the Shape

Ultimately, for the max distance, we want to draw on the screen a shape such that the sound is audible when the player character walks into that shape and is inaudible when the player character leaves the shape.

10.9.1.1 Circular Shape

If the sound is at the center of the screen, then the shape that it will draw on the screen is a circle centered about the origin, stretched out to an oval at the aspect ratio of the rendered viewport. Figure 10.9 shows how we build our shape in screen space. The nice thing is that, because our coordinate system is resolution-independent, we can operate on the circle from Figure 10.9b, and it will come out looking like an oval. We want to take this oval and project it into the world such that the shape will still look like an oval when projected back into screen space.

10.9.1.2 Rectangular Shape

If the sound is at the center of the screen, then the shape that it will draw on the screen is a square centered about the origin, stretched out to a rectangle at the aspect ratio of the rendered viewport. Figure 10.10 shows how we build our shape in screen space. As with the circular shape, we

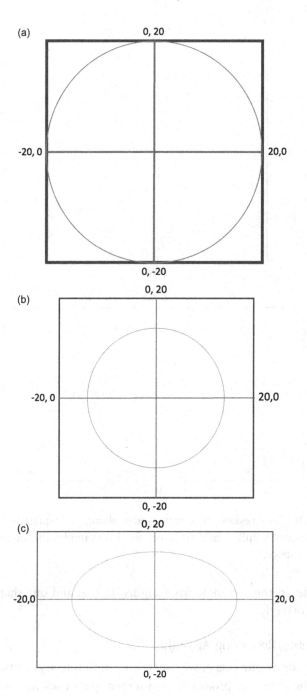

FIGURE 10.9 Progression of circular shape. (a) Starting circle. (b) Circle scaled to the desired radius (10 units = half the screen for this example). (c) Circle stretched out to screen space.

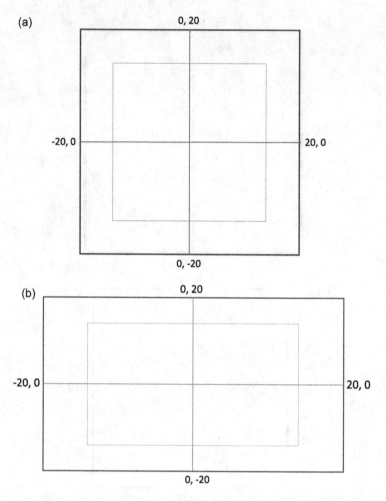

(a)

0, 20

-20, 0   20, 0

0, -20

(b)

0, 20

-20, 0   20, 0

0, -20

FIGURE 10.10 Progression of a rectangular shape. (a) Square scaled to the desired distance (10 units = half the screen for this example). (b) Square stretched out to screen space.

can operate on the rectangle from Figure 10.10a, and our shape will be rendered correctly.

10.9.2 Debug Rendering Algorithm

In order to draw our shape, we break it up into line segments. For each point on the shape, we project it from screen space back into world space at the plane of the attenuation position. By connecting all of these points together, we get the shape that we're interested in. Let's take a look at the algorithm in pseudocode as we have described it so far:

```
void DrawDebug()
{
  // [Detail 1]

  std::vector<Vector3> Points;
  Plane PlayerPlane{ AtenuationPosition, UpVector };

  for (auto& ScreenSpacePoint : GetShape())
  {
    // Projecting from screen space to world space will return
    // a point at the near field and a ray into the scene.
    auto [WorldPosition, Direction] = ScreenToWorld(ScreenSpacePoint);

    // We intersect the ray with the player's plane
    auto Point =
      LinePlaneIntersect(
        WorldPosition,
        WorldPosition + Direction,
        PlayerPlane));

    // [Detail 2]
    // [Detail 3]

    // Add the point to the list
    Points.push_back(Point);
  }

  // Draw line segments for each adjoining pair of points
  for (size_t i=0; i<Points.size(); i++)
  {
    DrawLine(Points[i], Points[i+1], Color);
  }

  // Draw one last line segment connecting the end of the circle
  // to the beginning
  DrawLine(Points.back(), Points.front(), Color);
}
```

There are three extra details that we have not yet covered that are marked in comments in the pseudocode. Let's fill those pieces in.

First, all of this so far has been ignoring the sound's position and just using the origin. In order to determine where to center our circle, we must take our sound's source position and project it into screen space—but at the elevation of the attenuation position. If we do not adjust the elevation, then the circle that we are drawing will not look correct if the player is not at the same elevation as the sound. We will use our GetAudioViewProjectionMatrix() function from Section 10.6.3, with the overridden position. This allows us to fill in our [Detail 1] with the following:

```
auto SoundLocationOnGround = GetPosition();
SoundLocationOnGround.Z = AttenuationPosition.Z;
auto ScreenSpaceOffset =
  ProjectPointToScreenSpace(SoundLocationOnGround);
```

Let us skip the second detail for a moment and jump to the third detail. If you implement this debug drawing function unmodified, your debug draw circles will likely be invisible because they will be at the same Z position as the ground. They will either be "Z fighting" and end up flickering, or they will be completely invisible. In order to avoid this, we push the debug draw circle up slightly in [Detail 3]:

```
Point.Z += VisibilityAdjustment;
```

Finally, we can get to the second detail. Now that we can actually see our shape, it is close to but doesn't actually match up with where the sound is audible. The reason for the discrepancy is that this point is where the sound would have to be if the attenuation position were at the sound's location, but what we want is where the attenuation position should be given the sound's location—the exact opposite. Fortunately, this is easy to rectify by flipping the X and Y axes around the sound's position. We can now finish our algorithm by filling in [Detail 2]:

```
Point.X = SoundLocationOnGround.X -
           (TargetLocation.X - SoundLocationOnGround.X);
Point.Y = SoundLocationOnGround.Y -
           (TargetLocation.Y - SoundLocationOnGround.Y);
```

Finally, with all of these details filled in, we can draw our shape. When using circular distance, the shape looks like an oval when viewed from the camera's default angle (Figure 10.11) but appears to be a strange, oblong, off-center egg shape when viewed from above (Figure 10.12). When using rectangular distance, the shape looks like a trapezoid when viewed from the camera's default angle (Figure 10.13) and is a slightly oblong trapezoid when viewed from above (Figure 10.14).

10.9.3 Example Code for Unreal Engine

As before, the real code is never quite so terse as the equivalent pseudocode. In this section, we present one possible implementation using Unreal

FIGURE 10.11   Circular min and max distance debug display from the game camera.

FIGURE 10.12   Circular min and max distance debug display from above.

FIGURE 10.13   Rectangular min and max distance debug display from the game camera.

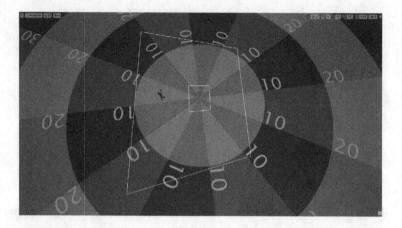

FIGURE 10.14   Rectangular min and max distance debug display from above.

Engine. Note that we take advantage of the extra parameters that we added into GetAudioViewProjectionMatrix() earlier in order to override the position and exfiltrate the view rectangle.

```
void DrawDebug(bool bUseCircleShape)
{
  // Get the sound's position on the ground
  auto OriginalSoundLocation = GetLocation();
  auto SoundLocationOnGround = OriginalSoundLocation;
  SoundLocationOnGround.Z = AttenuationPosition.Z;

  // Find the view projection matrix given the sound's location
  FIntRect ViewRect;
  auto ViewProjectionMatrix =
    GetAudioViewProjectionMatrix(SoundLocationOnGround, &ViewRect);
  if (!ViewProjectionMatrix.IsSet())
    return;

  // Now transform the original world location into -1..+1
  // screen space.
  FPlane TransformedPoint =
    ViewProjectionMatrix->TransformFVector4(
      FVector4{ OriginalSoundLocation, 1.f });
  if (TransformedPoint.W == 0.0f)
    return;

  const float RHW = 1.0f / TransformedPoint.W;
  FVector2D ScreenSpaceOffset{
    TransformedPoint.X * RHW, TransformedPoint.Y * RHW };

  auto InverseMatrix = ViewProjectionMatrix->InverseFast();
  FPlane PlayerPlane{ AttenuationPosition, FVector::UpVector };
```

```
auto DrawShape = [&](float Distance, const FColor& Color)
{
  // Make a circle in screen space at the max distance.
  // For each point in the circle:
  const float DistanceScale = Distance / 20.0f;
  TArray<FVector> Points;
  auto AddPoint = [&](FVector2D ScreenSpacePosition)
  {
    // Scale it to the max distance of the sound source
    ScreenSpacePosition *= DistanceScale;

    // Center our circle on the projected screen space location
    ScreenSpacePosition -= ScreenSpaceOffset;

    // Convert it to 0..1.  Note that Y coordinates are from
    // the top of the screen, so we need to flip Y.
    ScreenSpacePosition.X = (ScreenSpacePosition.X + 1.0f) / 2.0f;
    ScreenSpacePosition.Y =
      1.0f - ((ScreenSpacePosition.Y + 1.0f) / 2.0f);

    // Finally, skew the position into view space.
    ScreenSpacePosition.X *= ViewRect.Width();
    ScreenSpacePosition.Y *= ViewRect.Height();

    // Get a world origin and direction from the screen coordinate
    FVector WorldOrigin;
    FVector WorldDirection;
    FSceneView::DeprojectScreenToWorld(
      ScreenSpacePosition, ViewRect, InverseMatrix,
      WorldOrigin, WorldDirection);

    // Intersect our line with the player's plane
    auto TargetLocation =
      FMath::LinePlaneIntersection(
        WorldOrigin, WorldOrigin + WorldDirection, PlayerPlane);

    // Here's the problem, though: our projected point is where
    // the sound would have to be located if the player's
    // attenuation position were at the sound's location.  In
    // order to make this a real point, we have to flip it
    // around the X and Y axes, which is what is happening here.
    TargetLocation.X =
      SoundLocationOnGround.X -
        (TargetLocation.X - SoundLocationOnGround.X);
    TargetLocation.Y =
      SoundLocationOnGround.Y -
        (TargetLocation.Y - SoundLocationOnGround.Y);

    // Finally, we add a few centimeters to the Z axis in order
```

```
      // to make sure that the line that we draw doesn't intersect
      // with the ground geometry.
      TargetLocation.Z += 10.0f;
      Points.Add(TargetLocation);
    };

    int PointCount;
    if (bDrawCircle)
    {
      PointCount = 16;
      const float RadiansPerPoint =
        2.0f * PI / static_cast<float>(PointCount);
      Points.Reserve(PointCount);
      for (int i = 0; i < PointCount; i++)
      {
        auto Angle = static_cast<float>(i) * RadiansPerPoint;
        // Start with a circle in -1..+1 space
        AddPoint(FVector2D{ FMath::Cos(Angle), FMath::Sin(Angle) });
      }
    }
    else
    {
      PointCount = 4;
      Points.Reserve(PointCount);
      AddPoint(FVector2D{ -1.0f, -1.0f });
      AddPoint(FVector2D{ -1.0f, 1.0f });
      AddPoint(FVector2D{ 1.0f, 1.0f });
      AddPoint(FVector2D{ 1.0f, -1.0f });
    }

    // Finally, draw the shape by connecting lines among all of
    // the points
    for (int i = 0; i < (PointCount - 1); i++)
    {
      // Just in case...
      if (!Points.IsValidIndex(i)
          || !Points.IsValidIndex(i + 1))
        continue;

      DrawDebugLine(World, Points[i], Points[i + 1], Color);
    }

    // Close the circle by connecting the last point to the first one.
    DrawDebugLine(World, Points.Last(), Points[0], Color);
  };

  DrawShape(MinDistance, MinDistanceColor);
  DrawShape(MaxDistance, MaxDistanceColor);
}
```

10.10 CONCLUSION

Attenuating sounds by screen-space distance is a powerful and effective technique. At a fundamental level, the algorithm for calculating panning and attenuation is unchanged: we calculate the distance and reposition the sound and the appropriate panning position based on the distance to the attenuation position. What we have done in this chapter is take a step back and redefine the concept of *distance* to be calculated in screen space. By calculating the distance in screen space, we are able to provide sound designers with a way to understand when a sound will be audible that translates particularly well for ARPGs, so long as our debug display is robust.

REFERENCES

Somberg, Guy. "Listeners for Third-Person Cameras." *Game Audio Programming Principles and Practices*, edited by Guy Somberg. CRC Press, 2017, pp. 197–208.

Under the Influence

Using Influence Maps for Audio

Jon Mitchell

Blackbird Interactive

CONTENTS

11.1 INTRODUCTION

Influence maps (IMs) are a well-established game AI technique, originating in RTS games. RTS AI needs to make high-level strategic decisions about its goals, as well as low-level tactical decisions about how individual units should react and navigate the game's landscape. AI players and units can't see the game in the way the human player does, so all their knowledge comes from inspecting the state of the game directly. An AI unit may need to make hundreds of checks per second, such as the following:

- What is the nearest enemy unit to me?

- How dangerous is the nearest enemy unit?

- How many friendly units are nearby?

- Do my nearby friendly units have the firepower to defeat nearby enemies?

IMs can make the code to answer questions like this simpler. The game map is divided into a grid, and grid cells are populated using an IM function representing a feature of the game data. For example:

- **Combat level**—Total damage inflicted on units in the last 10 seconds.

- **Enemy threat level**—Summed power of enemy weapons within range of the cell.

- **Balance of power**—Enemy threat level – Friendly threat level.

Rather than complex code which needs to make direct queries of game entity data, we can make simple mathematical checks:

```
bool isUnitInDanger =
  EnemyThreatMap.SumValuesInRadius(position, radius) <
    PlayerThreatMap.SumValuesInRadius(position,radius);
```

Figure 11.1 shows an overview of the stages of creating and using an influence map.

11.2 HOW ARE IMs USEFUL FOR AUDIO?

Generally, audio programmers and designers aren't too concerned about the details of game AI implementation, but there can be a substantial amount of overlap in some areas, especially gameplay code. We use much the same sort of queries as AI to help determine things like the following:

- What stems of interactive music should we play next?

- What line of dialog is the most appropriate to play in response to a game event?

- What sound should we play knowing the sounds that have played recently in this area of the game?

Just like AI decisions, these queries require that the game gather a context-specific state from the game objects, evaluates conditions on that state, and chooses an appropriate response. Gameplay audio code already frequently makes use of game AI techniques like finite state machines, behavior trees, blackboards, and stimulus-response systems, and IMs work extremely well in tandem with them.

11.3 STORING INFLUENCE MAPS

11.3.1 Grid

The simplest implementation of an IM is a 2D array—a contiguous block of memory, with each cell in the grid having a permanently allocated, directly addressable area of memory. This is the easiest to write, and with densely populated grids, it can sometimes be the most performant from a CPU perspective. Most likely, this is the best approach to start with until it no longer works for your game. The main disadvantage is memory consumption: if you have an enormous game world, then even a coarse grid

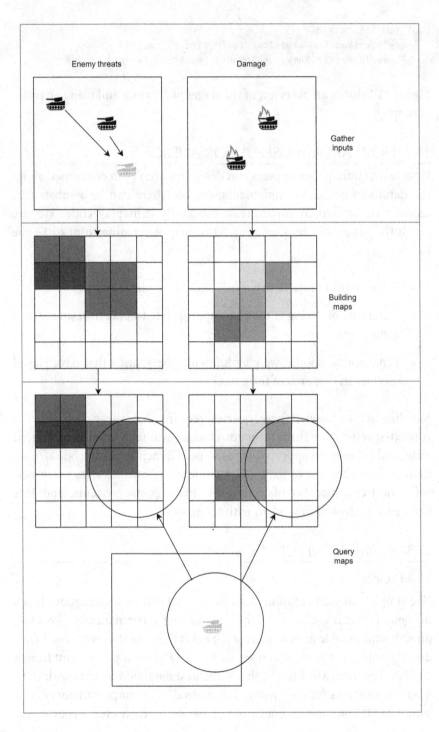

FIGURE 11.1 An overview of the stages of creating and using an IM.

can use a significant amount of memory, especially if you have many IMs for different game contexts. Also, when the grid is sparse (that is, it has very few active entries relative to its size), then not only are large sections of memory sitting idle, but any queries that operate on large areas of the grid will be needlessly performing operations as they traverse the mostly empty array.

11.3.2 Sparse Grids

Rather than directly allocating the whole grid, a sparse grid keeps track of which cells are active, and all cell accesses are indirect. With an empty grid, the memory overhead is only the size of the tracking structures, and summing the values of a mostly empty map will be fast. The downsides come as the density of the grid increases. The cost of the accesses can add up, and by the time the grid is full, the memory and CPU consumption are much worse than a plain 2D array.

11.3.3 "Infinite" Influence Maps

Mike Lewis (2015) discusses "Infinite" IMs in an article published at GameAIPro. This article is well worth reading and has a good discussion of the pros and cons of various discrete, grid-based IM implementations. Infinite IMs essentially reject this approach in favor of using a set of influence sources with a known position, radius, and differentiable falloff function. This lets you determine influence at an arbitrary point and solves the problem of handling very large regions, as well as the performance problems you can have where influence needs to be propagated across large regions touching large numbers of cells. However, it adds complexity to building and querying. In a way, the Control Sources system used in our RTS (described in Mitchell 2019) could be considered a system of this type. It also consists of a set of influences with points and radii, where the exact falloff value of each source is calculated at the point of query rather than being continuously evaluated. This approach has a lot in common with how game engines handle physics entities and other object/object interactions, and many of the same spatial partitioning and broad-phase optimizations can be applied. For simplicity, I'll only be discussing discrete IMs, but if you need large areas of influence and high query resolution over a large gameplay area, this may be your only realistic option.

11.3.4 Combining Different Representations

As with most game data, the final choice of data structure for a given map will depend on how it's populated and how frequently it is accessed, but there's no reason your game has to use a single data representation for each of its maps. So long as you have a shared interface to query the maps, the under-the-hood representation for each needn't be important to client code.

11.4 BUILDING THE MAPS

11.4.1 Adding Points

If you've written any low-level 2D drawing code, writing to an IM will seem very familiar to you. Writing a point value to a single cell is just the same as writing a pixel!

11.4.2 Adding Points Across Cell Boundaries

When writing to an IM cell, we initially placed the full influence value in a single cell, so if the value depended on an object's position, the IM value would snap from one cell to another as the object moved across the map. For some of our queries, this gave inaccurate results, so we added the option to blend the influence value across adjoining cells. The blend amount for each cell is computed as the ratio of the size of a single cell to the amount of overlap a cell placed at an object's position would have. An object placed exactly at the cell center overlaps exactly, and so that cell receives 100% influence, whereas an object at the corner of four cells should receive 25% of the total influence in each cell. This is essentially like drawing an anti-aliased pixel, except we're not concerned with how the result looks but preserving the property that 100% of the influence value is stored in the grid—this is important to ensure that queries where we sum the values in a region give us the results we expect. Figure 11.2 shows several examples of blending a point influence value across neighboring cells.

11.4.3 Adding Radii

Adding a point of influence with a center, a radius, and a falloff function is essentially the same problem as rasterizing a filled, shaded 2D circle. Especially for larger radii or high-resolution maps, computing these values every time can be expensive. In many cases, the radius and falloff

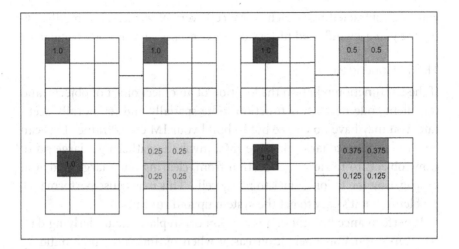

FIGURE 11.2   Blending a point influence value across neighboring cells.

functions are known ahead of time and remain constant for each game entity, so these can be computed once and then cached. Continuing the 2D graphics analogy even further, using these pre-computed values is basically the same as software sprite rendering.

11.4.4 GPU Accelerated IMs

Given the heavy overlap between 2D rendering, textures, and simple grid-based IMs, leveraging the GPU to provide the drawing, blitting, and blending operations that can be slow on a CPU seems like a natural fit. You then have the problem of getting the results of the GPU operations back to the CPU for use in the game itself, but audio responses don't always have the extremely tight latency requirements of code that needs to respond directly to player input. If only the results of the queries are needed, rather than the maps in their entirety, then the amount of data to move should be relatively small.

11.5 UPDATING

11.5.1 Event-Based

Game events like impact damage, deaths, and collisions are transient, and unless we track them somehow, this knowledge can't be used by our audio systems. We use IMs to track deaths, damage, and targeting changes, updating the map every time an event happens. Maps have a fade-out value which is subtracted from each active cell every N seconds, essentially giving the game a windowed history of where events have recently occurred.

11.5.2 Continuous

If the IM function relies on the location of an object or set of objects, and the client code needs this function to be spatially and temporally accurate, you may have no choice but to build your IM every frame. This can be a worst-case scenario for large IMs, involving gathering a large set of game objects to retrieve the location from, clearing out a large grid, and propagating the falloff values to many cells. This may cause performance problems, but it's easy to get the system up and running.

If performance becomes an issue, you can replace the underlying data structures and implementation easily when optimizing. Since building maps based on continuously updating values has the distinct stages of gathering game state and writing the cells, this makes them good candidates for implementation via job systems or other parallel approaches. If the map is also double-buffered, then the current version of the map can be used for querying while the next version is built over as many frames as needed to maintain performance.

11.5.3 Static

IMs aren't only useful for monitoring the history of game events or watching dynamic game state—there are lots of potential uses for a map that is built once when the game starts, and is only queried (never updated) subsequently:

- **Ground surface type**—Map cells contain an integer switch value to select a game object's footstep sounds or tire tread sounds.

- **FX send amount**—Map cells contain a floating-point parameter value to control the amount of an entity's audio FX, such as reverb wet/dry and early reflections.

- **Ambient volume control**—Map cells contain a set of floating-point parameters used to drive the volume levels of background ambient sounds.

Static maps of this sort can also be built offline from a game's splat maps or other level data or hand authored.

11.6 QUERYING

Our maps implement a simple querying interface, allowing us to either retrieve a single cell value or return the aggregate value of a given area. This interface can be backed by any of the described storage structures.

```
public interface IQueryInfluenceMap<T>
where T : struct, IEquatable<T>
{
  Number<T> GetCellValue(GridCell cell);
  Number<T> SumValuesInRect(Rect rect);
  Number<T> MaxValueInRect(Rect rect);
  Number<T> MinValueInRect(Rect rect);
  Number<T> SumValuesInRadius(Vector2 point, Real radius);
  Number<T> MaxValueInRadius(Vector2 point, Real radius);
  Number<T> MinValueInRadius(Vector2 point, Real radius);
  Number<T> SumOfAllValues();
  Number<T> MaxOfAllValues();
  Number<T> MinOfAllValues();
}
```

11.7 DEBUGGING AND VISUALIZING

Since they are just 2D grids with a numerical value, IMs can be easily rendered to a texture and projected onto your game world or displayed in 2D in another window. Many uses of IM rely on the aggregation of multiple IMs by taking their sum, minimum, maximum, or by logical operations like AND/OR/XOR. These operations can be performed by texture blend modes or shader code, giving you a direct visualization of the results the game works with. Figure 11.3 is a screenshot of our IM visualizer.

11.8 FEATURE CASE STUDY: GRID ACTIVITY REPORT (GAR)

11.8.1 Feature Design

One use we made of IMs in our most recent RTS project was to drive some of our commander speech. The game map is divided into nine sectors corresponding to the compass directions and a "central" sector, as shown in Figure 11.4.

Dialog lines were written to inform the player about the state of play in these sectors, to alert them to events they should pay attention to. Some example situations are as follows.

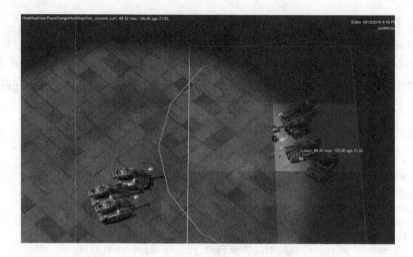

FIGURE 11.3   Screenshot of IM visualizer showing enemy threat values and the clusters extracted from those values.

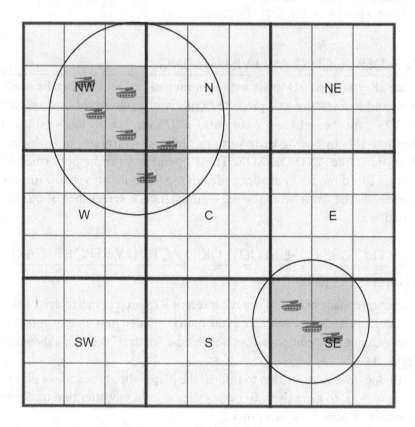

FIGURE 11.4   GAR sectors and clustered IM values.

Event Name	Context	Example Lines
combat_start	The enemy is engaging you. You will be told the strength of the attacking force and the location	*Enemy engaged! Medium force in southwest sector!* *Contact with medium enemy force!*
combat_casualties	Your units are being damaged	*Units in north-east sector taking heavy losses!* *Battle review needed—heavy damage in central sector*

11.8.2 Feature Implementation

To help implement these contexts, we created maps for the following:

- **Enemy danger**—The map contains the threat levels of each enemy unit currently aiming at or firing at a friendly unit, if they are in firing range of the targeted unit. Since the points of influence are game object locations, this map is constantly updated. For performance reasons, it is not updated every frame.

- **Friendly damage**—The map contains the locations where friendly units have taken damage. This map is event-driven, updating when we receive OnHit events on friendly units. Every few seconds, the map is updated to reduce the cell values, so the values fall off over time.

11.8.2.1 Region Thresholds

The values in our maps are constantly changing and are monitored to determine when it's most appropriate to play the speech events. The first approach we tried was tracking the sum of the values in the GAR sectors. This worked well for triggering our combat_casualties events. We specified different thresholds for *low, medium*, and *heavy* casualties and queued the appropriate speech requests whenever the thresholds were crossed. It didn't work nearly as well for determining when to play combat_start events, largely because the unit locations were continuously moving. We'd hear dialog like the following:

> Enemy engaged! Small force in northeast sector! Enemy Engaged! Small force in north sector!

What was really happening, of course, is that a single, medium-sized group of units was attacking from two sectors simultaneously. What we

needed to be able to do was identify clusters of activity to be able to treat
them as a single entity.

11.8.2.2 Cluster Analysis

Finding clusters, at least in a grid of values, isn't too hard—for all active
cells in a grid, a cluster is the set of cells that can reach each other via
a path through the other active cells. This is very similar to cliques in
a graph. For each active cell in our map, we can recursively check the
active neighbor cells to see if they're already used in a cluster, adding if
not. This essentially flood-fills the grid of active cells, stopping when we
hit inactive cells.

```
void FindClusters(IMap map, Collection<Cluster> clusters)
{
  foreach(GridCell cell in map.ActiveCells)
  {
    if(IsActiveAndFree(cell))
    {
      continue;
    }

    Cluster newCluster = new Cluster();
    Cluster.Add(cell);
    Clusters.Add(newCluster);

    SearchNeighbours(cell,map,newCluster);
  }
}
bool IsActiveAndFree(IMap map, Cell cell)
{
  if (mAssignedCells.Contains(cell))
  {
    return false;
  }

  if (!map.ActiveCells.Contains(cell))
  {
    return false;
  }

  return true;
}

void SearchNeighbors(Cell firstCell, IMap map, Cluster cluster)
{
```

```
// For simplicity, the "self" cell is considered a Neighbor.
foreach(NeighborCell neighbor in Neighbours)
{
  GridCell curCell= map.GetCell(firstCell, neighbor);

  if(!IsActiveAndFree(map,curCell)
  {
    continue;
  }

  cluster.Add(curCell);
  mAssignedCells.Add(curCell);

  SearchNeighbors(curCell,map,cluster);
  }
}
```

11.8.2.3 Cluster Tracking and Thresholding

Just as with regions, we have events when the summed value of our clustered cells crosses a tunable threshold value. Unlike static regions, clusters change shape and location over time, so to see if a cluster was considered the same from one update to the next, we calculate the centroid of the cluster. If a cluster centroid on one frame is within a small distance from a cluster centroid on a previous frame, we assume it's an evolution of the previous cluster, not a brand new one. We used an event triggered when a cluster crossed a tunable age threshold to trigger combat_start and used the cluster centroid and summed value to select the appropriate dialog line for position and size of the attacking force.

11.9 CONCLUSION

IMs are a feature from the game AI world, and it's not immediately obvious that they will be useful in a game audio context. However, by connecting an AI feature to audio, we are able to implement features that would not otherwise have been possible. Hopefully this gives you some ways to think about implementing features you may not have considered—it's always worth looking at techniques in use in other areas of programming and thinking about how they can be applied to audio features.

REFERENCES

Lewis, Mike. "Escaping the Grid: Infinite-Resolution Influence Mapping." *Game AI Pro 2*, edited by Steve Rabin. CRC Press, 2015, pp. 327–342. http://www.gameaipro.com/GameAIPro2/GameAIPro2_Chapter29_Escaping_the_Grid_Infinite-Resolution_Influence_Mapping.pdf.

Mitchell, Jon. "Techniques for Improving Data Drivability of Gameplay Audio Code." *Game Audio Programming Principles and Practices Volume 2*, edited by Guy Somberg. CRC Press, 2019, pp. 227–236.

CHAPTER 12

An Importance-Based Mixing System

Guy Somberg

Echtra Games

CONTENTS

12.1 MANAGING THE CHAOS

In any game with more than a trivial degree of complexity, it is inevitable that the mix will get muddy if you don't do anything to prevent it. In fact, much of our job as audio programmers involves implementing tools and techniques to manage complex mixes and make them understandable. We have many tools at our disposal right out of the box: mixer snapshots used to be exotic but are now commonplace and come with most audio middleware systems, culling systems prevent less important sounds from playing in the first place, and we can use techniques like HDR audio to tag each sound with a dB range.

All of these techniques are valuable and useful tools in our fight to provide a coherent aural experience. However, they are all missing one fundamental concept: context. That is, they all presume that we can decide offline, at authoring time, which sounds should be heard over others. However, in the context of a game's actual play session, any offline mixing decision that we make will be upended. If we have decided that *this* sound should be louder than or have a higher priority than *that* sound, then we can always come up with a situation in which that decision should be reversed.

We were struggling with this very problem during the development of *Torchlight 3*, so we reached out to our friends at Blizzard Entertainment on the *Overwatch* team, Tomas Neumann and Paul Lackey. They told us about the Importance system that they implemented in *Overwatch*, which we were able to adapt for use in *Torchlight 3* [1]. Our implementation in the game (and therefore this chapter!) would not have been possible without their help, so I want to give a huge thank you to both of them for taking the time to explain the system to us so thoroughly.

12.2 THE IMPORTANCE OF CONTEXT

Let us examine the situation from *Torchlight 3* shown in Figure 12.1. In this screenshot, we see a scene in the forest with several goblin warriors, a couple of goblin brutes, a goblin chanter, two players each with their own train and pet, and any number of environmental sounds. Common sense says that the brutes and the shamans are more important than the warriors. But is that always the case? If there is a goblin brute attacking another player, isn't it less important than a goblin warrior that is attacking me? What about the other player? Even if they are the same character class as my player character, are their skills as important as my player's skills?

FIGURE 12.1 Gameplay from *Torchlight 3*.

The answer to all of these questions very much depends upon the context of what's going on in the game. A goblin brute attacking another player is probably less important than the goblin warrior that is attacking my player because of who it is targeting. The other player's skills are probably less important than my player's skills, but if it's a buff that is targeting my player, perhaps it is equally important.

Every game will have a different set of rules for what properties of the context will make a sound more or less important than another. The first step in creating an Importance system, therefore, is to determine what makes a particular game entity more or less important in your game's context.

12.3 IMPORTANCE SYSTEM ALGORITHM

The basic algorithm for the Importance system is very simple, bordering on trivial:

- Assign each object an importance score.

- Sort all of the objects in the game by importance score.

- Place the sorted objects into buckets.

- Apply the appropriate effect to the sounds in each bucket.

Let's dive deeper into the details of this algorithm.

12.3.1 Assign Each Object an Importance Score

The first task in the algorithm is to assign every object in the game an importance score. But we cannot (or should not) actually do this, because there will usually be far too many objects in the game world, and most of them are not relevant to the importance system. The ground plane, for example, probably does not need an importance score. Instead, tag the objects that can make sound with a component or other marker that indicates that they are relevant to the Importance system. Doing this offline will catch most of the situations, but often scripts or other runtime systems can trigger sounds on objects that aren't tagged, so make sure that the system is capable of tagging objects after they have already been created. In *Torchlight 3*, for example, where we are building on top of the Unreal Engine, we have an Audio Importance Component that we can add dynamically to any actor in the game.

The next issue is how frequently to run this scoring. The more frequently we run it, the faster our game can respond to changes. However, iterating over these lists too frequently can get expensive, which can be a limiting factor. We need to iterate over the entire list of objects every time, so measure the performance, and be cognizant of the potential cost of the iteration.

Now that we have our list of objects to score and a frequency of scoring them, the time has come to actually assign the score. Each game will have its own inputs into what makes a particular entity more or less important at any given moment in time. Here are some ideas for inputs:

- Proximity to the player.

- Identity (monster, friendly player, enemy player, etc.).

- Class (healer, tank, etc.).

- Is currently targeting player.

- Is performing an "important" skill (like an ultimate ability).

- Size of player on the other person's screen.

- "Drama" score relative to other nearby entities.

- Distance to nearest enemy unit.

A first-person shooter is going to have very different requirements than an action RPG. Discuss with your sound designers and come up with a set of criteria. The only requirements are that each criterion should be measurable efficiently and that it should be expressible as a floating-point number. Be wary of selecting too many inputs to the system. Four or five inputs are usually enough to describe a very complex system.

The last piece of the puzzle in assigning an importance score is to allow your sound designers to place a relative weight on each score. Perhaps identity is more important than drama score. In that case, identity can get a scaling factor of 1.0, and the drama score can get a scaling factor of 0.5. (Or, alternatively, identity can be 2.0 and drama can be 1.0.)

Once we have assigned a value to each individual criterion and weight, then the total identity score is the sum of each score times its relative weight:

$$I = \sum_c s_c w_c$$

12.3.2 Sort All Objects by Score

This procedure is as simple as it sounds. Use your standard library's built-in sorting routines to sort the list by score, descending. Let us go back to the situation from *Torchlight 3* from Figure 12.1. We assign each entity on the screen a score, which are shown in Figure 12.2 and Table 12.1.

12.3.3 Place Sorted Objects into Importance Buckets

The next piece of the puzzle that we will need to do is to dole out the entities into importance buckets. An importance bucket is a collection of entities that all have the same effects applied, and we assign them out from top to bottom. The number of available buckets and the number of sounds that can be in each bucket are determined by the game, although a reasonable number is four or five buckets. Any less than that and we won't have fine granularity in our mix, and any more than that will not provide meaningful differentiation among the different importance levels.

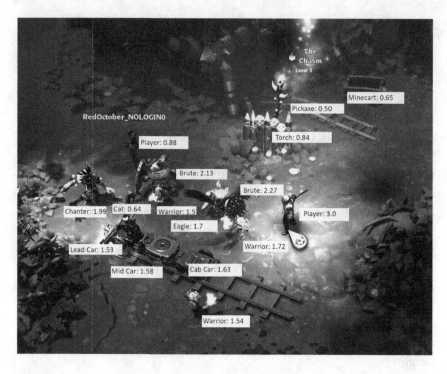

FIGURE 12.2 Gameplay from *Torchlight 3* with importance scores assigned for relevant entities.

TABLE 12.1 Sorted List of Entities with Their Matching Importance Scores

Entity	Importance
Player	3.0
Goblin Brute	2.27
Goblin Brute	2.13
Goblin Shaman	1.99
Goblin Warrior	1.72
Player Pet Eagle	1.70
Player Train Caboose Car	1.63
Player Train Middle Car	1.58
Goblin Warrior	1.55
Goblin Warrior	1.54
Player Train Lead Car	1.53
Other Player	0.88
Torch	0.84
Hammer	0.71
Minecart	0.65
Other Player Pet Cat	0.64

In our example situation, we will have four importance buckets, which we can use to assign buckets to each of the entities in our example (Tables 12.2 and 12.3).

12.3.4 Apply Effects to Sounds by Bucket

Now that we know which entities are in which buckets, we can assign effects to each bucket. Whenever a sound is played that is associated with an entity in a particular bucket, we modify its playback by attaching some effects. The effects to use are game-specific, but in general, they should be selected such that sounds at higher importance buckets are highlighted and sounds at lower importance buckets are dampened. In *Torchlight 3*, we used the effects described in Table 12.4, but each game is different and will have different needs, so coordinate with your sound designers.

TABLE 12.2 Objects per Bucket

Bucket	Count
1	2
2	4
3	5
4	Unlimited

TABLE 12.3 Game Objects with Their Importance Scores and Assigned Buckets

Entity	Importance	Bucket
Player	3.0	1
Goblin Brute	2.27	1
Goblin Brute	2.13	2
Goblin Shaman	1.99	2
Goblin Warrior	1.72	2
Player Pet Eagle	1.70	2
Player Train Caboose Car	1.63	3
Player Train Middle Car	1.58	3
Goblin Warrior	1.54	3
Player Train Lead Car	1.53	3
Goblin Warrior	1.50	3
Other Player	0.88	4
Torch	0.84	4
Hammer	0.71	4
Minecart	0.65	4
Other Player Pet Cat	0.64	4

TABLE 12.4 Bucket Effects Used in *Torchlight 3*

Bucket	Effects
1	Peaking filter
2	No change (sound plays unmodified)
3	Volume reduction
4	Volume reduction, high-shelf filter

12.3.5 Importance Changes Over Time

As our game plays and the situation around the player character changes, the entities in our game are very likely to switch their importance bucket over time. Once we have defeated the monster that is standing next to us, another monster that is further away that may have been less important will now increase in importance. In order to handle these changes, we need to implement the importance bucket effects in such a way that we can quickly fade them to a new value. We'll see how that's done in the next section.

12.4 EXAMPLE IMPLEMENTATION

This example implementation will use FMOD Studio as a back end. We will hook into the playback of Events and attach some DSPs and then manipulate the DSPs as the Event changes importance over time. Other audio middleware may have different mechanisms describing this data, but the principles are the same.

In this example code, we will be presuming a straw-man entity component system containing Actors and Components, with reasonable accessors, iterators, and weak pointers to them. This system does not actually exist in this form and would need to be adapted to whatever game systems you have. Furthermore, we will be using C++ standard library components and algorithms.

12.4.1 Calculating Importance Scores

We will not be exploring the code that calculates importance scores because it is so game-specific. Any code that we could show would not be meaningful for most games. Each AudioImportanceComponent should be able to query the game state and make a decision about its own score. Whether this is on a Tick() function on the AudioImportanceComponent or part of the AudioEngine update is up to you.

12.4.2 Data Setup

First, we need somewhere in static configuration the number of importance buckets, their max counts, and their respective audio parameters.
This might look something like this:

```
struct AudioImportanceBucketParameters
{
    // How many sounds are allowed in this bucket
    int MaxCount;
    // When displaying on-screen debug information, what color to use
    Color DebugDisplayColor;

    // In this example, we are applying a volume change, as well
    // as using a multiband EQ effect to implement a peaking filter
    // and a high-shelf filter.

    // The volume to set for this audio importance bucket.
    // Note: can be greater than 0 to increase gain
    float VolumeDecibels;

    // Settings for the peaking filter
    float PeakingFilterGainDecibels;
    float PeakingFilterFrequencyHz;
    float PeakingFilterQ;

    // Settings for the high-shelf filter
    float HighShelfFilterGainDecibels;
    float HighShelfFilterFrequencyHz;
};

// Straw-man settings structure
struct GameSettings
{
    static GameSettings& Get();
    vector<AudioImportanceBucketParameters> ImportanceBuckets;
};
```

12.4.3 Importance Bucket Assignment

Now that we have our configuration set up, we need our run-time descrip-
tion of the importance buckets:

```
class AudioEngine
{
public:
    //...
```

```
private:
  // other stuff...

  void CalculateImportance();
  int GetImportanceBucket(const Actor& Actor);

  // Each bucket is a vector, and the contents of the bucket
  // are a vector of actors.
  vector<vector<weak_ptr<Actor>>> ImportanceBuckets;
};
```

Let's see how the importance algorithm looks:

```
void AudioEngine::CalculateImportance()
{
  auto& Settings = GameSettings::Get();
  if (Settings.ImportanceBuckets.empty())
    return;

  // Collect all of the importance contexts.
  vector<AudioImportanceComponent*> ImportanceComponents;
  for (auto& ImportanceComponent : AllImportanceComponents)
  {
    // Dead monsters, for example, do not contribute to
    // importance, even though they have an importance
    // component
    if (!ImportanceComponent.ContributesToImportance())
      continue;

    ImportanceComponents.push_back(&ImportanceComponent);
  }

  // Sort by importance descending so that the most important
  // entries are at the beginning of the list
  // Note that we are not updating the actual importance scores
  // here, just sorting by the cached score.
  sort(begin(ImportanceComponents), end(ImportanceComponents),
      [](const AudioImportanceComponent* Left,
         const AudioImportanceComponent* Right)
      {
        return Left->GetImportance() > Right->GetImportance();
      });

  ImportanceBuckets.clear();
  ImportanceBuckets.resize(Settings.ImportanceBuckets.Num());

  // Helper lambda to get the max number of entries in the given
  // bucket.
```

```cpp
auto GetMaxCountInBucket = [&Settings](int Bucket)
{
  auto MaxCount = Settings.ImportanceBuckets[Bucket].MaxCount;
  if (MaxCount <= 0)
    return numeric_limits<int>::max();

  return MaxCount;
};

// Fill in each importance bucket until it is full and then
// move on to the next importance bucket.
size_t CurrentBucket = 0;
int NumberLeftInBucket = GetMaxCountInBucket(CurrentBucket);
size_t ComponentIndex = 0;
while (ComponentIndex < ImportanceComponent.size())
{
  // Grab the owner of this component
  auto Owner = ImportanceComponents[ComponentIndex]->GetOwner();
  ++ComponentIndex;

  // If the owner is already gone, then there's no need to
  // do anything.
  if (Owner.expired())
    continue;

  // Add the owner to the current bucket and decrement the
  // count of available entries left in the bucket.
  ImportanceBuckets[CurrentBucket].push_back(Owner);
  --NumberLeftInBucket;

  // Our bucket is empty; move on to the next bucket.
  if (NumberLeftInBucket <= 0)
  {
    ++CurrentBucket;

    // If the current bucket is valid, then we get the size
    // of the bucket.
    if (CurrentBucket < ImportanceBuckets.size())
    {
      NumberLeftInBucket = GetMaxCountInBucket(CurrentBucket);
    }
    else
    {
      // In general, your buckets should be configured such
      // that the last bucket has an unlimited size.
      // However, if there is some user error in setting
      // the buckets up, then this code makes it such that
      // the remainder of the entries all end up in the last
      // bucket.
```

```
        // In a properly configured system, this code will
        // never execute.  It is reasonable to declare that
        // it is an error for this to happen and to remove
        // this code entirely.
        CurrentBucket = ImportanceBuckets.size() - 1;
        NumberLeftInBucket = number_limits<int>::max();
      }
    }
  }
}
```

One important item to note (which is not reflected in the above code) is that sometimes actors can have relationships that would affect their importance. For example, if one actor is attached to another actor, then the attached actor should probably be getting its importance score from the actor that it is attached to.

12.4.4 Querying the Importance Bucket

Now that we've got our importance buckets assigned, we need to be able to query which bucket an actor is in. We'll do a linear search to find our actor:

```
int AudioEngine::GetImportanceBucket(const Actor& Actor)
{
  auto FoundBucket =
    find(begin(ImportanceBuckets), end(ImportanceBuckets),
      [&](const vector<weak_ptr<Actor>>& ActorsInBucket)
      {
        auto FoundActor =
          find(begin(ActorsInBucket), end(ActorsInBucket),
          [&](const weak_ptr<Actor>& WeakActor)
          { return WeakActor.lock().get() == &Actor });
        return FoundActor != end(ActorsInBucket);
      });
  if (FoundBucket == end(ImportanceBuckets))
    return INVALID_BUCKET;

  return distance(begin(ImportanceBuckets), FoundBucket);
}
```

If this algorithm needs to be optimized, then there are plenty of techniques such as storing the data in an unordered_set or some other easily searchable data structure, performing a binary search (which would require sorting the vector after calculating its contents), caching the results of the .lock().get() operation for the duration of a frame, caching the results of GetImportanceBucket() so that it's only called a maximum of once per frame per actor, etc. As with all optimizations, the advice is to measure first whether this lookup is expensive and perform a targeted optimization if it is.

12.4.5 Importance State

As we are tracking the lifetime of our playing sound in a state machine [2], we can store the state of which importance bucket this particular sound is in, as well as any parameters useful for fading. Note that in this code, we are using an Initialize()/Shutdown() pattern so that we can include the object directly into the memory of our playing sound, but that could be replaced with a constructor/destructor pair if we're willing to place the tracking information into the heap or use some other mechanism for late initialization such as std::optional.

```
struct ImportanceDSPFader
{
  // The actual DSPs that we will be attaching to the DSP graph
  FMOD::DSP* MultiBandEQ = nullptr;
  FMOD::DSP* Fader = nullptr;

  // Bucket fading parameters
  AudioImportanceBucketParameters From;
  AudioImportanceBucketParameters To;
  AudioImportanceBucketParameters Current;
  float RemainingFadeTimeSeconds;

  int CurrentBucket = INVALID_BUCKET;

  // We are using init/shutdown rather than constructors
  // and destructors because we need to delay initialization
  // of the DSPs until the Event is ready.
  bool Initialize(FMOD::System* FMODSystem);
  void Shutdown();
  void Tick(float DeltaTimeSeconds);

  // Whenever the sound is initially played or when the
  // buckets are updated, we should call this to effect a
  // fading of the parameters to the new bucket if necessary
  void SetImportanceBucket(int NewBucket);

private:
  void SetDSPParameters();
  void UpdateImportanceBucket(int NewBucket);
};
```

Now we just need one of those for each playing Event. The implementation of the various functions of this structure is fairly straightforward, so let's start with initialization and shutdown, where we will be creating and destroying the DSPs:

```
bool ImportanceDSPFader::Initialize(FMOD::System* FMODSystem)
{
  if (FMODSystem == nullptr)
    return false;

  // Create the multiband EQ and Fader DSP effects
  FMODSystem->createDSPByType(
    FMOD_DSP_TYPE_MULTIBAND_EQ, &MultiBandEQ);
  if (MultiBandEQ == nullptr)
    return false;

  FMODSystem->createDSPByType(FMOD_DSP_TYPE_FADER, &Fader);
  if (Fader == nullptr)
    return false;

  // Initialize the multiband EQ to implement a peaking filter
  // and a high-shelf filter
  MultiBandEQ->setParameterInt(
    FMOD_DSP_MULTIBAND_EQ_A_FILTER,
    FMOD_DSP_MULTIBAND_EQ_FILTER_PEAKING);
  MultiBandEQ->setParameterInt(
    FMOD_DSP_MULTIBAND_EQ_B_FILTER,
    FMOD_DSP_MULTIBAND_EQ_FILTER_HIGHSHELF);
  MultiBandEQ->setParameterFloat(
    FMOD_DSP_MULTIBAND_EQ_A_GAIN, 0.0f);
  MultiBandEQ->setParameterFloat(
    FMOD_DSP_MULTIBAND_EQ_B_GAIN, 0.0f);

  // Initialize the parameters based on the current bucket
  UpdateImportanceBucket(CurrentBucket);
  RemainingFadeTimeSeconds = 0.0f;
  Current = To;

  // Initialize the DSPs with the initial settings
  SetDSPParameters();
  return true;
}

void ImportanceDSPFader::Shutdown()
{
  if (MultiBandEQ != nullptr)
  {
    MultiBandEQ->release();
```

```
    MultiBandEQ = nullptr;
  }
  if (Fader != nullptr)
  {
    Fader->release();
    Fader = nullptr;
  }
  RemainingFadeTimeSeconds = 0.0f;
}
```

During the tick or update function, we will need to fade across buckets. In this example, we will be fading parameters by hand, but middleware or game engine libraries may provide either an automated way to perform these fades or a different metaphor for implementing the effects.

```
void ImportanceDSPFader::Tick(float DeltaTime)
{
  // Nothing to do if we're not changing buckets
  if (RemainingFadeTimeSeconds <= 0.0f)
    return;

  // Figure out how far through our Lerp these parameters are
  RemainingFadeTimeSeconds -= DeltaTime;
  RemainingFadeTimeSeconds = max(RemainingFadeTimeSeconds, 0.0f);

  auto& Settings = GameSettings::Get();
  auto FadeTime = Settings.GetImportanceFadeTimeSeconds();

  float LerpAmount = 1.0f - (RemainingFadeTimeSeconds / FadeTime);
  LerpAmount = clamp(LerpAmount, 0.0f, 1.0f);

  // Perform a Lerp of all the parameters.  If we care to, we
  // can perform a more complex interpolation here instead for
  // one or more of these parameters.
  Current.VolumeDecibels =
    Lerp(From.VolumeDecibels, To.VolumeDecibels, LerpAmount);
  Current.PeakingFilterGainDecibels =
    Lerp(From.PeakingFilterGainDecibels,
      To.PeakingFilterGainDecibels,
      LerpAmount);
  Current.PeakingFilterFrequencyHz =
    Lerp(From.PeakingFilterFrequencyHz,
      To.PeakingFilterFrequencyHz,
      LerpAmount);
  Current.PeakingFilterQ =
    Lerp(From.PeakingFilterQ, To.PeakingFilterQ, LerpAmount);
  Current.HighShelfFilterGainDecibels =
    Lerp(From.HighShelfFilterGainDecibels,
```

```
      To.HighShelfFilterGainDecibels,
      LerpAmount);
  Current.HighShelfFilterFrequencyHz =
    Lerp(From.HighShelfFilterFrequencyHz,
      To.HighShelfFilterFrequencyHz,
      LerpAmount);

  // Apply the updated values to the DSPs
  SetDSPParameters();
}
```

The above functions make use of the `SetDSPParameters()` and `UpdateImportanceBucket()` helper functions, which are relatively simple but included here for exposition:

```
void ImportanceDSPFader::SetDSPParameters()
{
  if (Fader == nullptr || MultiBandEQ == nullptr)
    return;

  // Set all of the individual DSP parameters according to
  // the current settings
  Fader->setParameterFloat(
    FMOD_DSP_FADER_GAIN, Current.VolumeDecibels);
  MultiBandEQ->setParameterFloat(
    FMOD_DSP_MULTIBAND_EQ_A_GAIN,
    Current.PeakingFilterGainDecibels);
  MultiBandEQ->setParameterFloat(
    FMOD_DSP_MULTIBAND_EQ_A_FREQUENCY,
    Current.PeakingFilterFrequencyHz);
  MultiBandEQ->setParameterFloat(
    FMOD_DSP_MULTIBAND_EQ_A_Q, Current.PeakingFilterQ);
  MultiBandEQ->setParameterFloat(
    FMOD_DSP_MULTIBAND_EQ_B_GAIN,
    Current.HighShelfFilterGainDecibels);
  MultiBandEQ->setParameterFloat(
    FMOD_DSP_MULTIBAND_EQ_B_FREQUENCY,
    Current.HighShelfFilterFrequencyHz);
}

void ImportanceDSPFader::UpdateImportanceBucket(int NewBucket)
{
  // Set the current bucket
  CurrentBucket = NewBucket;

  auto& Settings = GameSettings::Get();
  if (NewBucket != INVALID_BUCKET)
```

```
{
  // If we have a valid bucket, then start a fade to
  // the destination bucket
  To = Settings.ImportanceBuckets[NewBucket];
}
else
{
  // We have an invalid bucket, which likely means that this
  // is a sound that is attached to an actor that is not
  // participating in the importance system, or that this
  // sound was played before the importance score and bucket
  // were calculated for the attached actor.

  // We will set the default values for these controls
  // according to the FMOD documentation, which will cause
  // them to play unmodified.
  To.VolumeDecibels = 0.0f;
  To.PeakingFilterGainDecibels = 0.0f;
  To.PeakingFilterFrequencyHz = 8000.0f;
  To.PeakingFilterQ = 0.707f;
  To.HighShelfFilterGainDecibels = 0.0f;
  To.HighShelfFilterFrequencyHz = 8000.0f;
}

From = Current;
RemainingFadeTimeSeconds =
  Settings.GetImportanceFadeTimeSeconds();
}
```

Finally, the only part of the public interface that isn't related to lifetime or update is a function to assign the current importance bucket:

```
void ImportanceDSPFader::SetImportanceBucket(int NewBucket)
{
  // Do nothing if there is no change in bucket
  if (CurrentBucket == NewBucket)
    return;

  // Trigger a fade to the new bucket
  UpdateImportanceBucket(NewBucket);
}
```

12.4.6 Applying Filters Based on Importance

Now that we have our structure for managing the importance DSPs, we must hook it up to the playing Event. In order to make sure that we only create the DSPs when they're actually needed and that they stick around

for as long as the event is playing, we need to hook into the Event's call-
backs that trigger when the event has actually started and stopped playing:

```cpp
FMOD_RESULT F_CALLBACK PlayingEvent::EventCallback(
  FMOD_STUDIO_EVENT_CALLBACK_TYPE type,
  FMOD_STUDIO_EVENTINSTANCE *event,
  void *parameters)
{
  // In order to make callbacks work in both C and C++, FMOD
  // passes in a C structure which must be casted to its C++
  // counterpart when using the C++ API.
  auto* EventInstance =
    reinterpret_cast<FMOD::Studio::EventInstance*>(event);
  if (EventInstance == nullptr)
    return FMOD_ERR_INVALID_PARAM;

  void* UserData = nullptr;
  EventInstance->getUserData(&UserData);

  // Insert whatever mechanism you have for mapping the userdata
  // to the structure managing the playing event here.
  auto PlayingEvent = GetEventById(UserData);
  if (!PlayingEvent.IsValid())
    return FMOD_OK;

  switch (type)
  {
  case FMOD_STUDIO_EVENT_CALLBACK_STARTED:
  {
    // Helper lambda for initializing the fader context
    // and attaching the effects to the DSP chain.  We use
    // a helper lambda in order to keep the tabs under control.
    auto CreateDSPEffects = [&]()
    {
      // Get the master channel group for the event.  We will be
      // attaching our DSPs to its head
      FMOD::ChannelGroup* EventInstanceChannelGroup = nullptr;
      EventInstance->getChannelGroup(&EventInstanceChannelGroup);
      if (EventInstanceChannelGroup == nullptr)
        return;

      // Initialize the ImportanceFader structure
      FMOD::System* FMODSystem = nullptr;
      EventInstanceChannelGroup->getSystemObject(&FMODSystem);
      bool bInitSuccess =
        PlayingEvent->ImportanceFader.Initialize(FMODSystem);
      if (!bInitSuccess)
        return;
```

```
    // Attach the DSPs to the effect chain
    EventInstanceChannelGroup->addDSP(
        FMOD_CHANNELCONTROL_DSP_HEAD,
        PlayingEvent->ImportanceFader.ImportanceFader);
    EventInstanceChannelGroup->addDSP(
        FMOD_CHANNELCONTROL_DSP_HEAD,
        PlayingEvent->ImportanceFader.ImportanceEQ);
};

    // Call our helper lambda. You can avoid giving this lambda
    // a name and calling it by using an immediately invoked
    // expression: [](){}(). For clarity, this code prefers to
    // give it a name and call it.
    CreateDSPEffects();

    // In order to ensure that we don't get a pop by starting to
    // play audio data before we're ready, we set the EventInstance
    // to be paused before starting it, and then we can unpause it
    // here.
    EventInstance->setPaused(PlayingEvent->bPaused);
}
break;
case FMOD_STUDIO_EVENT_CALLBACK_STOPPED:
{
    PlayingEvent->ImportanceFader.Shutdown();
}
break;
}

    return FMOD_OK;
}
```

12.4.7 Assigning Importance Buckets

Our setup is nearly complete. We still have to initialize the bucket when the sound is first played or devirtualized, and we have to update the bucket for looped sounds only during playback. Let's start with the initialization, which we will do in the `ToPlay/Devirtualize` state of our state machine. We just have to initialize the bucket:

```
ImportanceFader.CurrentBucket =
    AudioEngine.GetImportanceBucket(Instigator);
```

Next, during the `Playing`, `Virtualizing`, and `Stopping` states (that is, all of the states where the sound is playing), we need to update the sound's bucket but only for looped sounds. One-shot sounds will be finishing soon anyway, so there is no need to update their importance bucket as they are playing.

```
bool IsOneShot = false;
EventDescription->isOneshot(&IsOneShot);
if (!IsOneShot)
{
  FMOD_STUDIO_PLAYBACK_STATE PlaybackState =
    FMOD_STUDIO_PLAYBACK_STARTING;
  EventInstance->getPlaybackState(&PlaybackState);

  // To avoid threading issues, we must wait for the playback
  // state to change from STARTING.  STARTING means that it's
  // waiting for the audio data to load, so it has not created
  // the DSPs.  All of the other states (PLAYING, SUSTAINING,
  // STOPPING, STOPPED) are safe, because either the event has
  // started and we are not in danger of reading the DSPs while
  // they're being written (because the DSPs have already been
  // written) or they are already null (either because they
  // were never written or because they have already been
  // cleared).
  if (PlaybackState != FMOD_STUDIO_PLAYBACK_STARTING)
  {
    auto NewBucket =
      AudioEngine.GetImportanceBucket(Instigator);
    ImportanceFader.UpdateImportanceBucket(NewBucket);
  }

  ImportanceFader.Tick(DeltaTime);
}
```

12.4.8 Debug Display

With this system in place, it is important for the sound designers to be able to visualize which sounds are important and why. There are three variations that are useful for this debug display:

1. A listing of actors grouped into their buckets, with each group assigned a color. Figure 12.3 shows an example of this type of debug display. This display is very noisy and coarse, so while it is important, it is likely not going to be the primary debug display chosen by the sound designers.

2. A tag on each actor that participates in the importance system, colored to match the importance bucket, and with the importance score displayed. Figure 12.4 shows this type of debug display. This is likely to be the primary debugging tool used by the sound designers.

```
[CATEGORY: AudioImportance]
PRIORITY 1
rm_f_player_C_0 - 3.00
gobchanter_b_C_2 - 1.99
goblin_brute_b_C_2 - 2.13
goblin_brute_b_C_3 - 2.27
gobgeneric_stabby_b_C_4 - 1.72

PRIORITY 2
gobgeneric_stabby_b_C_7 - 1.55
Railman_Turret_Actor1a_C_0 - 1.53
gobgeneric_stabby_b_C_5 - 1.54
Railman_FreightCar_Actor_C_0 - 1.58
Railman_CabooseCar_Actor_C_0 - 1.63
peteagle_body_03_harpy_bp_C_0 - 1.70

PRIORITY 3
dm_m_player_C_0 - 0.88
petcat_tuxedo_bp_C_0 - 0.64
gob_prop_torch_02_bp4 - 0.84
gcave_break_minecart_03_bp_C_0 - 0.65
gob_prop_tool_hammer_01_bp_C_0 - 0.71

PRIORITY 4
gob_prop_torch_02_bp_2 - 0.00
gob_prop_torch_02_bp2 - 0.00
gob_prop_torch_02_bp3 - 0.00
gob_prop_torch_02_bp4 - 0.00
gob_prop_torch_02_bp_2 - 0.00
gob_prop_torch_02_bp2_5 - 0.00
gob_prop_torch_02_bp3_8 - 0.00
gob_lootable_cauldron_01_bp_2 - 0.00
gob_prop_tool_axe_01_bp_C_0 - 0.46
gob_prop_tool_pickaxe_01_bp_C_0 - 0.50
```

FIGURE 12.3 Categorized actor list debug display.

FIGURE 12.4   Per-actor overlay debug display showing the actor name and its importance score.

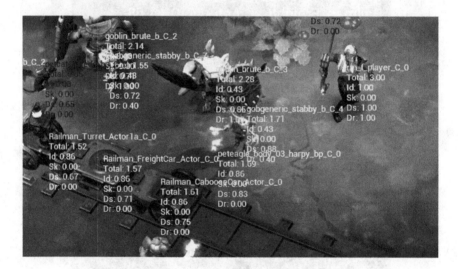

FIGURE 12.5   Per-actor overlay debug display showing the actor name, its importance score, and the individual score contributions.

- A detailed tag on each actor that shows the component scores that add up to the final score, as shown in Figure 12.5. This debug display will be useful in helping the sound designers figure out why a particular actor is more or less important than they were expecting.

12.5 CONCLUSION

With a little bit of data management, DSP wrangling, and a very simple algorithm, an importance system can revolutionize how your mix works. Importance is so fundamental, in fact, that it is now a part of my own personal "starter kit" that I will implement when starting a new audio engine project.

The concept of what is most important to hear at any given point in time is different for each game and each moment. Start by sitting down with your sound designers for an afternoon and figuring out a set of rules for your game. Once you have those rules in place, hooking up an importance system is a quick and easy mechanism for making your game's audio shine.

REFERENCES

1. Neumann, Tomas. "Realtime Audio Mixing." *Game Audio Programming Principles and Practices Volume 2*, edited by Guy Somberg. CRC Press, 2019, pp. 247–259.
2. Somberg, Guy. "Sound Engine State Machine." *Game Audio Programming Principles and Practices*, edited by Guy Somberg. CRC Press, 2017, pp. 13–30.

CHAPTER 13

Voxel-Based Emitters

Approximating the Position of Ambient Sounds

Nic Taylor

CONTENTS

13.1 INTRODUCTION

In *Game Audio Programming Principles and Practices Volume 2*, Chapter 12, "Approximate Position of Ambient Sounds of Multiple Sources" [1], I discussed how ambient sounds are designed to represent an area or volume as opposed to a point emitter. For example, a loop of a riverbed does not represent a single point in space but a volume or area representing the cumulative sounds of a section of river. From there, this chapter covered different approaches to approximate the position for an ambient sound using a point emitter that would move in real-time relative to the listener's position. In particular, the focus was on methods that computed the emitter's properties of direction, magnitude, and spread separately.

The method in Section 12.15—verbosely titled "Average Direction and Spread Using a Uniform Grid or Set of Points"—has two useful applications: approximating the position of ambient beds as the listener approaches and visual effects with area such as a beam weapon or a wall of fire. But this chapter left several implementation details for the reader to work out on their own. This chapter will revisit the implementation in more detail, add advice on debugging, explain edge cases, and discuss some extensions to the basic algorithm.

The encapsulation of the position, spread, and algorithm will be more succinctly called a "voxel emitter" or "grid emitter" for 2D.

13.2 PRELIMINARY

Before getting to the revised implementation, here is a quick review of the theory used by the algorithm. The voxel emitter takes the listener (or receiver) position $\hat{r}$ and a collection of points, the voxel centers, and returns a direction and spread value to approximate the position relative to receiver.[1]

The direction is the sum of each voxel relative to the receiver scaled by a weight function. Voxels farther from the receiver have less influence on the final emitter position and behave as if each voxel were its own emitter where the distance attenuates the volume or gain. The sum of all voxel directions is called the total attenuated direction or $\hat{\sigma}$.

Let total attenuated direction be defined as

$$\hat{\sigma} = \sum_{i \in V} \hat{v}_i \frac{W(\hat{v}_i)}{\|\hat{v}_i\|} \tag{13.1}$$

where V is the set of voxel center positions relative to the receiver position $\hat{r}$, $\hat{v}_i$ is each voxel center position in V, $\|\hat{v}_i\|$ is the magnitude or Euclidean distance from the receiver position to $\hat{v}_i$, and W is the weight function. Figure 13.1 shows the voxel emitter components for an example V.

The weight function should be zero outside of the attenuation range of the sound. Inside the attenuation range, the weight function can be a

---

[1] The hat symbol ˆ is used to differentiate vector variables from scalar variables.

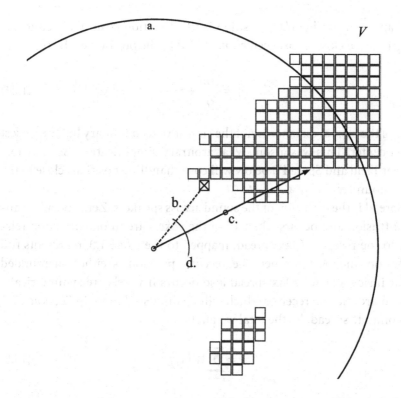

FIGURE 13.1 Voxel emitter V represented by (a) the attenuation range α from the receiver $\hat{r}$, (b) the closest voxel used to compute the magnitude m, (c) the position $\hat{p}$ along total attenuated direction $\hat{\sigma}$, and (d) an arc showing the spread amount μ which is about 0.25 in this example.

number of continuous or piecewise functions, but a reasonable start would be a linear ramp from one to zero based on the attenuation α:

$$W(\hat{v}_i) = \begin{cases} 1 - \dfrac{\|\hat{v}_i\|}{\alpha}, & \text{if } \|\hat{v}_i\| < \alpha \\ 0, & \text{if } \|\hat{v}_i\| \geq \alpha \end{cases} \qquad (13.2)$$

The magnitude m for the approximated emitter position is separate from the magnitude of the total attenuated direction. For the magnitude, the distance to the closest voxel center is used and can be defined as

$$m = \min_{i \in V}\left(\|\hat{v}_i\|\right) = \min_{i \in V}\left(W(\hat{v}_i)\right) \qquad (13.3)$$

The approximated emitter position is the direction $\hat{\sigma}$ normalized to the length of the closest voxel center, m, added to the position of the receiver:

$$\hat{p} = \frac{\hat{\sigma}m}{\hat{\sigma}} + \hat{r} \qquad (13.4)$$

Notice the closest distance is not the closest voxel boundary but the closest voxel center. This was a somewhat arbitrary simplification. Section 13.7 ("Near Field and Spread") below will cover handling positions close to the voxel boundary.

Spread is the diffusion of the sound across speakers. Zero spread means no diffusion and occurs when all of the voxels are in one direction relative to the receiver. Max spread, mapped to the value 1.0, represents full diffusion and occurs when the receiver position is either surrounded by or inside a voxel. Max spread also occurs if voxels are symmetrically spaced around the receiver which will be discussed more in Section 13.6. To compute spread, let the total weight be

$$w = \sum_{i \in V} W(\hat{v}_i) \qquad (13.5)$$

and spread

$$\mu = 1 - \mu_\theta = 1 - \frac{\|\hat{\sigma}\|}{w} \qquad (13.6)$$

Spread, μ_θ, is based on the cosine of the angle between each position $\hat{v}_i$ and the total attenuated direction $\hat{\sigma}$ scaled by the weight function and normalized by the total weight w. A larger angle formed from a voxel center and $\hat{\sigma}$ results in larger spread.[2]

The purpose of spread is to hide discontinuous jumps. As the receiver moves around the voxel emitter, spread and magnitude should update continuously relative to the movement. The total direction $\hat{\sigma}$ can flip/invert directions or change rapidly when $\|\hat{\sigma}\|$ approaches zero. These discontinuities should not be audible if spread is at the maximum value.

---

[2] Refer to Taylor [1] to see how the sum of weighted cosines reduces to $\|\hat{\sigma}\|$.

13.3 VOXEL EMITTER IMPLEMENTATION

Below is an example implementation of the voxel emitter which takes the following as inputs:

- **voxels**—A data structure which can retrieve voxel centers in an iterator fashion.

- **receiver**—The sphere to intersect with the voxel data representing the listener position and the attenuation range of the sound to approximate:

```
struct Sphere {
  Vector center;
  float radius;
};
```

- **voxel extent**—The half dimension of the voxel (or grid cell) size.

The output is the position $\hat{p}$ from Equation 13.4 and spread μ as well as additional state information such as true/false if the sound was audible and optional debugging information. The closest voxel center which is used to compute the distance m from Equation 13.3 is tracked for debugging.

```
struct AttenuatedPosition {
  bool audible;
  Vector position;
  float spread;
  int voxels_processed; // for debugging
  Vector closest_voxel_center; // for debugging
};
```

To complete the code before getting into the algorithm, `PointInsideVoxel()` is a small helper function that returns `true` if a vector relative to a voxel center is inside:

```
// Input is the direction to any voxel center.
bool PointInsideVoxel(const Vector& direction,
  const float cell_extent) {
  return fabsf(direction.x) < cell_extent &&
         fabsf(direction.y) < cell_extent &&
         fabsf(direction.z) < cell_extent;
}
```

The main function is `VoxelsToAttenuatedPosition()` which aggregates the total attenuated direction and the total weight used to compute spread. The loop will early out if the receiver position is inside a voxel.

```
template<typename VoxelContainer>
AttenuatedPosition VoxelsToAttenuatedPosition(
  const VoxelContainer& voxels,
  const Sphere& receiver, const float voxel_extent) {

  const float attenuation_range = receiver.radius;

  float total_weight = 0.f;
  Vector total_direction = { 0.f, 0.f, 0.f };
  float closest_distance = attenuation_range;
  Vector closest_voxel_direction, closest_voxel_center =
    { 0.f, 0.f, 0.f };

  int voxels_processed = 0;
  for (const Vector voxel_center : voxels) {
    const Vector direction = voxel_center - receiver.center;
    // Early out if receiver is inside a voxel.
    if (PointInsideVoxel(direction, voxel_extent)) {
      total_direction = { 0.f, 0.f, 0.f };
      closest_distance = 0.f;
      closest_voxel_center = voxel_center;
      ++voxels_processed;
      break;
    }
    const float distance = Length(direction);
    if (distance < attenuation_range) {
      if (distance < closest_distance) {
        closest_distance = distance;
        closest_voxel_direction = direction;
        closest_voxel_center = voxel_center;
      }
      const float weight = attenuation_range - distance;
      total_direction += (weight / distance) * direction;
      total_weight += weight;
      ++voxels_processed;
    }
  }

  Vector emitter_position = receiver.center;
  float spread = 0.f;
  const float total_dir_length = Length(total_direction);
  if (total_dir_length <= FLT_EPSILON) {
    // Either inside or equally surrounded by voxel(s).
    spread = 1.f;
    emitter_position += closest_voxel_center;
```

```
  } else if (total_weight > FLT_EPSILON) {
    spread = 1.f - total_dir_length / total_weight;
    const float near_field_lerp =
      GetNearFieldInterpolation(closest_voxel_direction,
        voxel_extent);
    if (near_field_lerp > 0.f) {
      spread += (1.f - spread) * near_field_lerp;
    }
    emitter_position +=
      closest_distance * total_direction / total_dir_length;
  }
  AttenuatedPosition result;
  result.audible = closest_distance < attenuation_range;
  result.position = emitter_position;
  result.spread = spread;
  result.closest_voxel_center = closest_voxel_center;
  return result;
}
```

The next sections will cover details and alternate approaches to VoxelsToAttenuatedPosition().

13.4 THE ITERATOR

In the example implementation, a container is used as the input and expected to provide the voxels with the capabilities of a forward iterator:

```
for (const Vector voxel_center : voxels) {...}
```

If the voxel emitter is being used to approximate a spell or beam weapon with a few voxels, the container might just be a vector of pre-computed positions. But more likely the iterator is a simplification hiding the implementation details of the container which depends on the context and specifics of the game.

For approximating large ambient beds, the iterator could be the most complicated and computationally expensive part of the algorithm. For example, imagine your open world game is saved in chunks as in Figure 13.2.

The iterator would require some pre-computation using the sphere to find the set of all overlapping chunks. Then assume the voxel data is stored in a 2D grid in the world chunk data. For each world chunk, iterate x and y positions[3] in the grid to test if there is an active voxel. Since the grid is

---

[3] I am using a coordinate system where x, y, and z correspond to left, forward, and up.

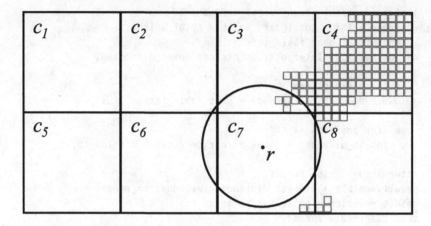

FIGURE 13.2   Game world broken into chunks $c_1, \ldots, c_n$ with overlapping attenuation range for a receiver $\hat{r}$.

2D and the game is 3D, the z axis position might need to be computed in real-time.[4]

Pseudocode for the iterator might be something like:

```
for (chunk in overlapping world chunks) {
  translate sphere to chunk coordinates
  find min and max overlap between sphere and chunk
  for (x in overlapping range) {
    for (y in overlapping range) {
      lookup voxel data from x and y
      if (voxel is active) {
        convert x and y to world coordinates
        find z position
        save iterator state
        return voxel center {x, y, z}
      }
    }
  }
}
```

This is just one example of how the iterator might work. Another option is to use a flood fill algorithm starting from the receiver position. Other

[4] Trade-offs between doing the voxel look-up in real-time and baking the data into a custom data representation stored with the world data requires experimenting. For example, the aforementioned 2D grid might store per voxel 1 bit for active/inactive state and use a few bits to specify a discrete value to approximate the z axis offset. If your world is large, the storage size for a single voxel emitter can become non-trivial in this uncompressed format.

data structures for space partitioning can also improve performance and size requirements. A full discussion of all of these options depends on the context of the game and goes beyond the scope of this chapter. But I can describe the approach I use to make algorithm decisions for voxel emitters.

When evaluating a voxel emitter in context, I start with the simple implementation, which is a nested loop like the above pseudocode, computing positions in real-time. Storage in the world or game data is also handled naively. This allows for rapid iteration on tuning variables such as voxel size and attenuation with the sound designer.

Once the sound designer and others agree, the voxel emitter sounds decent; then the storage requirements can be estimated from the tuned variables. By making a worst-case example in the test world, CPU usage can be estimated deterministically and used to find the specific code that is expensive via profiling.[5] With an understanding of the memory and CPU, decisions about the effort and complexity of optimizations can be made objectively.

13.5 ATTENUATION RANGE AND VOXEL SIZE

The input sphere's radius or attenuation range is used to set the voxel emitter's audible and inaudible state. It seems natural to use the same attenuation range as specified by the authored sound. In other words, make the attenuation range data driven from the sound designer's authoring tool. But unlike a typical emitter, small increases in the attenuation range can have a significant performance impact. For example, if the voxel search is iterating over a grid, the growth will scale quadratically.

If the attenuation range is specified by the engineer or by some other data driven number, two issues can come up. First if the authored sound has a much larger attenuation, then audio may stop abruptly as the receiver moves beyond the range. To solve this, the stop command of the sound could have a moderately long fade-out time.

If the authored attenuation range is smaller than the voxel emitter's configuration, there will be a ring between the authored range and the algorithm's range where unnecessary computation is done. If the game

---

[5] Changes to the algorithm can change the worst-case scenario setup. For example, switching from a row by column search at the attenuation boundary to a flood fill from the receiver's position would early out on the first voxel if the receiver is inside.

engine assumes the sound should be active in this ring, every other frame will attempt to turn the sound on.[6]

One solution for both cases is to attempt to use the authored attenuation range clamped to some maximum range. Then communicate this with the sound designer or have a notification as part of the data pipeline if the sound designer commits an attenuation range that is larger.

The voxel size also has a major impact on performance. Smaller voxel sizes give better granularity, but at a certain size, the difference is not audible (especially if the sound designer added their own spread). Small voxel sizes require more memory and CPU both for the running game and serialized data. Voxels which are too large cause the emitter direction to not be as precise at closer distances. Larger voxels are suitable if the listener cannot get close to the source. A balance can be found by factoring in the sound's attenuation range and how close the receiver can get. What I found is 1.0–1.5 meters seems to work well (or a voxel extent between 0.5 and 0.75) for voxel emitters where the receiver can approach such as an ocean or a river.

13.6 CLOSE TO ZERO

There are voxel arrangements relative to the receiver position where the total attenuated direction, $\hat{\sigma}$, aggregates to the zero vector[7] as seen in Figure 13.3.

This scenario is handled by the following condition in the algorithm:

```
if (total_dir_length <= FLT_EPSILON) {
    // Either inside or equally surrounded by voxel(s).
    spread = 1.f;
    emitter_position += closest_voxel_center;
}
```

Spread, which was defined as $1 - $ total dir_length/total_weight in Equation 13.6, approaches one as the magnitude of $\hat{\sigma}$ approaches zero. Because spread is at the maximum value, large changes of the direction from frame to frame should not be audible. When the total direction vector $\hat{\sigma}$ is exactly zero or too small to assign a direction, using the closest voxel center is a natural fallback for the direction to attenuated position $\hat{p}$.

---

[6] If the game engine expects the voxel emitter sound to be active and the sound is not active in the audio engine, it might be worth logging a warning and stopping the voxel emitter calculation.

[7] To get the magnitude of total direction to sum to a value less than FLT_EPSILON in game is quite rare, but I have caught it happening naturally a couple of times.

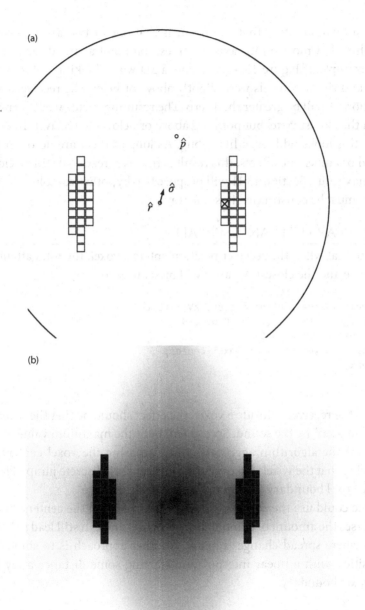

FIGURE 13.3 A voxel configuration that is symmetric relative to the receiver. (a) The magnitude of the total attenuated direction $\|\hat{\sigma}\|$ approaches zero. (b) Spread, represented by darker regions, approaches one in areas where $\|\hat{\sigma}\|$ approaches zero.

A similar situation that can occur is that one or two axes cancel and the third but most minor axis becomes dominant as the direction of $\hat{p}$. For example, if Figure 13.3 represents a 3D world looking at the x and y axes and the two voxels were slightly above or below the receiver's z axis position, $\hat{\sigma}$ will be greater than zero. The resulting vector will be length m from the closest voxel but pointing above or below the receiver. In debugging, this looks odd, even like a bug. As long as there are no other positional or ambisonic effects, this result is fine as spread will still be close to the max value. Section 13.11 will propose two hypothetical solutions if the z axis must be constrained in some way.

13.7 NEAR FIELD AND SPREAD

Notice that when the receiver position enters a voxel, the total attenuated distance and the closest distance will be set to zero:

```
if (PointInsideVoxel(direction, kVoxelExtent)) {
  total_direction = { 0.0, 0.0, 0.0 };
  closest_distance = 0.f;
  closest_voxel_center = voxel_center;
  break;
}
```

When the receiver is inside a voxel, the effect should be that the listener is "surrounded" by the sound. Spread will be at the maximum value of one.[8] Because the algorithm aggregates distance using the voxel centers, and ignoring that the voxels have volume, this causes a discrete jump of spread at the voxel boundary as seen in Figure 13.4a.

One could use the corners of each voxel instead of the centers, but this increases the amount of computation per voxel and can still lead to boundaries where spread changes rapidly. Another approach is to smooth the transition with a linear interpolation starting some distance away from the voxel boundary.

```
// Use the distance to the axis-aligned voxel to interpolate from
// 0 to 1.
float GetNearFieldInterpolation(const Vector& direction,
```

---

[8] Note that closest voxel center is set to the voxel center which will still have some distance. Using closest voxel center keeps debugging consistent. Ideally the authored sound's attenuation does not change within this distance. Otherwise a small vector in the forward direction of the receiver would also work. Using a forward vector has the advantage that in stereo configurations, the sound should be guaranteed to be spread to both speakers due to the audio engine's pan rules.

(a)   (b)

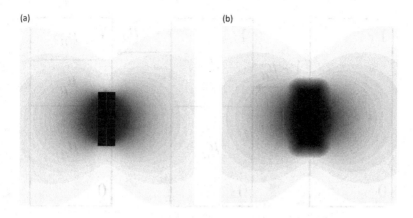

FIGURE 13.4   (a) The spread of a group of 1 m voxels. (b) The spread of a group of voxels using a 1.5 m near field.

```
const float voxel_extent) {
const float near_field_range = 1.5f;
const Vector point_on_voxel = {
  Max(0.f, fabsf(direction.x) - voxel_extent),
  Max(0.f, fabsf(direction.y) - voxel_extent),
  Max(0.f, fabsf(direction.z) - voxel_extent)
};
const float dist_to_voxel = Length(point_on_voxel);
if (dist_to_voxel >= near_field_range) {
  return 0.f;
}
return (near_field_range - dist_to_voxel) / near_field_range;
}
```

This near field[9] value ranges from zero to one and is used to interpolate the remaining spread available after removing the computed spread, μ (Equation 13.6), from the total available spread value:

```
const float near_field_lerp =
  GetNearFieldInterpolation(closest_voxel_direction, voxel_extent);
if (near_field_lerp > 0.f) {
  spread += (1.f - spread) * near_field_lerp;
}
```

The discussion so far has assumed that spread is the entire range from zero to one. It is more likely that the sound designer will want to control

---

[9] I call this the near-field range after the volume of area in a sound field close to the emitter where the relationship between distance and sound level does not observe the inverse square law.

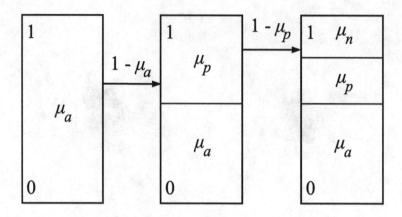

FIGURE 13.5 Representation of the spread priorities in the range zero to one for the authored μ_a, attenuated position μ_p, and near-field μ_n spread values.

spread from the authoring tool too. The priority of spreads is shown in Figure 13.5. In the same way, the near-field interpolation amount is scaled by the remaining spread after subtracting the attenuated position spread; this sum is scaled by the remaining spread after subtracting the authored spread. Let the attenuated position spread be μ_p, near-field spread be μ_n, and the authored spread be μ_a:

$$final\ spread = \mu_a + \left(1 - \mu_a\right)\left(\mu_p + \left(1 - \mu_p\right)\mu_n\right) \qquad (13.7)$$

Wwise implementation: At the time of writing this, still using Wwise 2017, the spread for a game object could be modified in Wwise from registering the AK_SpeakerVolumeMatrix during PostEvent(). The callback uses AkSpeakerVolumeMatrixCallbackInfo and an interface IAkMixerPluginContext pContext to access spread via GetSpread(). The spread is updated with the function Compute3DPositioning(). Two additional details to note:

1. Spread in Wwise ranges from 0 to 100, so μ needs to be multiplied by 100.
2. Since this callback will occur on a thread different from that on which the spread is computed, some thread safety is needed.[10]

---

[10] In my case, the game object data was guaranteed to never move in memory for the lifetime of the sound, so I wrapped the spread value as an atomic.

13.8 DEBUGGING

Various components of the voxel emitter are helpful to visualize with debugging both to identify bugs and for making the system transparent to the sound designer. The voxel emitter can be broken into these debugging components: the set of voxels, the attenuated position used as the emitter for the audio engine, and the spread.

The set of voxels can be visualized in the game world by rendering a circle or dot at the center of each voxel.[11] It is useful to see both voxels actively contributing to a playing sound and the inactive voxels. Also useful is knowing which voxel is being used as the closest voxel center. The voxel state can be visualized by color coding. For example, gray, yellow, and green for inactive, active, and closest.

When there are multiple active voxel emitters, it is not easy to differentiate which debug circles in game correspond to which voxel emitter. But it is also likely whoever is debugging is interested in one voxel emitter sound at a time. Instead of connecting the in-game voxel debug to the global in-game audio debug or a single toggle, it is recommended to create a separate toggle per voxel emitter instance.

The `AttenuatedPosition` of the voxel emitter is a single emitter position to be passed into the audio engine. The corresponding sound event should work with existing debugging both in-game and in the sound debug window (or list). The sound debug window, which typically includes the sound event name, distance to sound, and maybe virtual/active state, can be customized for the voxel emitter sound. The spread and number of voxels processed, `voxels_processed`, are useful for debugging.[12]

Seeing the numeric value of spread may not be meaningful enough on its own. It can be difficult to distinguish from headphone listening how "spread" the sound is and if the spread value is changing rapidly. If your debug UI supports plots, capturing the history of spread can help catch hard-to-identify value changes or verify if spread is increasing as expected near voxel boundaries.

Lastly the debug images rendered for this book chapter, such as Figure 13.4b or Figure 13.6, provide detailed offline debugging. Given a position in the world, in a brute force fashion, x and y coordinates are iterated

---

[11] I found that drawing the voxels in-game using other options such as drawing lines or projecting a transparent overlay became too visually noisy.

[12] Using a UI toolkit like Dear ImGui, the sound debug window can be modified to hide the extra metrics of the voxel emitter in a collapsed dropdown. This is also where I added buttons to toggle on/off the in-game voxel debug.

(a)   (b)

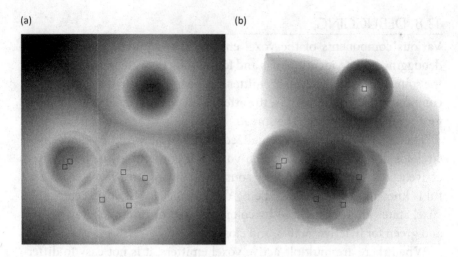

FIGURE 13.6 Sparse voxel emitter using a "distant only" weight function. (a) Estimated loudness at each point where white regions are louder. (b) Spread at each point where dark regions are higher spread.

over computing the attenuated position result and writing the spread or estimated loudness to a png file. Estimated loudness can be computed by

```
Max(0.f, (attenuation_range - closest_distance) / attenuation_range).
```

Rendering an image is helpful as anyone can file a bug with the world position and you can visually inspect the situation first without having to guess or try and listen for a possibly difficult-to-reproduce scenario.

13.9 WEIGHT FUNCTIONS

The attenuated position algorithm was developed for distance or large ambient bed-type sounds. The weight function defined in Equation 13.2 which is linear seemed like a natural fit.[13]

The attenuated position algorithm can also be used with smaller voxelized close-ranged emitting sources like energy beams, fire effects, or DoTs that create several emitting positions. Because the number of emitters is small or rapidly changing, the direction using a linear weight function might be too influenced by voxels farther away as in Figure 13.7a.

---

[13] Actually, the voxel emitter was the discretized version of an earlier algorithm to compute the attenuated position along a spline. Because the spline version was based on integrals, the choices in weight function were limited to analytical solutions. See Taylor [1] for more details.

(a)

(b)

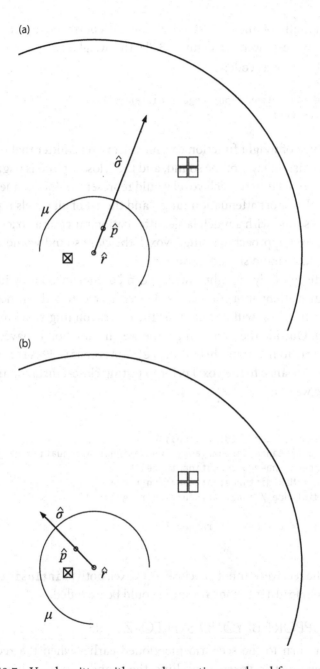

FIGURE 13.7 Voxel emitter with one close active voxel and four more distant voxels. (a) The direction of attenuated position is pointing away from the closest voxel using a linear weight. (b) The direction of attenuated position is pointing more in the direction of the closest voxel using a squared weight (and the spread has slightly increased).

The strength of the closest voxel can be controlled by raising the weight to some power. In Figure 13.7b, the weight is squared. That is $W'(\hat{v}) = W(\hat{v})^2$ or as code:

```
float weight = attenuation_range - distance;
weight *= weight;
```

Another type of weight function can model a voxel emitter that only represents the distant layer of the sound, and the "close" sound is triggered by a separate point emitter. Each voxel would represent an independent point emitter with a short attenuation range, and the set of all voxels represents the distant sound with a much larger attenuation range as a voxel emitter. As the receiver approaches a single voxel, the close sound would activate, but the distant sound should move away.

This "distant only" weight function can be implemented by introducing an inner attenuation range. As the receiver enters the inner range, the weight function will decrease for the corresponding voxel instead of increasing. Outside the inner range, the weight function behaves as normal. One way to integrate this into VoxelsToAttenuatedPosition() is to change the distance to the voxel prior to testing closest distance and computing the weight:

```
...
float distance = Length(direction);
// Assign a distance farther away inside inner_attenuation_range.
if (distance < inner_attenuation_range) {
  distance = Max(distance, attenuation_range *
    (1 - distance / inner_attenuation_range));
}
if (distance < attenuation_range) {
...
```

Because the receiver cannot get close to a voxel, both PointInsideVoxel() and GetNearFieldInterpolation() should be excluded.

13.10 SUPPORT BEYOND STEREO: Z AXIS

We now return to the scenario mentioned earlier when the receiver is between symmetric voxels cancelling the x and y axes to handle constraining the attenuated position along the z axis as in Figure 13.3. The result is most of the magnitude being applied in the z axis coordinate of $\hat{p}$ creating an unnatural-looking position if most of the voxels are in the same x–y plane.

If the z axis is unimportant for auralization, a simple change would be to track the closest voxel center as 3D for m but treat total weight and total direction as 2D. The z axis coordinate of the attenuated position would be assigned the same value as the receiver's z axis coordinate. However, if the z axis should be preserved to work with other auralization such as ambisonics or just to make the emitter behave more naturally for debugging, then one technique to try is projecting the vector $\hat{p}$ onto some plane perpendicular to the z axis. This will keep the z axis coordinate within a range that is closer to the voxels contributing to the attenuated position. When the voxels are above or below the receiver, the $\hat{p}$ should only change minimally. When the voxels have z axis coordinates similar to those of the receiver, then $\hat{p}$ may change significantly in direction.

To make sure the plane perpendicular to the z axis changes continuously as the receiver position changes, the new z axis coordinate can be set to the average weighted z coordinate observed from each active voxel. Equation 13.1 for total direction, $\hat{\sigma}$, already resembles the equation of a weighted average. The equation can be rewritten to apply to only the z coordinate $v_{i,z}$ where i is the ith voxel.

$$\sigma_z = \sum_{i \in V} v_{i,z} \frac{W(\hat{v}_i)}{\|\hat{v}_i\|} = v_{0,z} w_0 + v_{1,z} w_1 + \cdots + v_{N,z} w_N \qquad (13.8)$$

where w_i is the weight divided by magnitude of the voxel center $\hat{v}_i$. The weighted average z axis coordinate, σ_z, is then normalized so that the set of all weights Ω is equal to one:

$$\bar{\sigma}_z = \frac{\sigma_z}{\sum_{i \in \Omega} w_i} \qquad (13.9)$$

Thus, `VoxelsToAttenuatedPosition()` requires one additional tracking variable to accumulate Ω:

```
float total_weight_dir_ratio = 0.f;
Vector total_direction = { 0.f, 0.f, 0.f };
...
const float weight_dir_ratio = weight / distance;
// Accumulate the weight to distance factors.
total_weight_dir_ratio += weight_dir_ratio;
total_direction += weight_dir_ratio * direction;
...
```

The next step is to project the attenuated position $\hat{p}$ onto the plane at $\bar{\sigma}_z$. Let $\hat{z} = \{0,0,\sigma_z\}$ be a vector from the receiver and $\hat{p}'$ be the new projected position. That is $\hat{p}' = \{p'_x, p'_y, \overline{\sigma_z}\}$ for some new p'_x and p'_y.

The magnitude of $\hat{p}'$ is the same as the magnitude of $\hat{p}$ which is m. Let $\hat{p}''$ be the 2D vector going in the x, y direction of $\hat{p}$. This is will be in the same x, y direction as $\hat{p}'$. As shown in Figure 13.8, $\hat{p}''$ can be used to connect a right triangle. Then we can find projected position $\hat{p}'$ by normalizing $\hat{p}''$ and adding $\hat{z}$:

$$\hat{p}' = \frac{\hat{p}''\left(\sqrt{m^2 - \bar{\sigma}_z{}^2}\right)}{\|\hat{p}''\|} + \hat{z} \tag{13.10}$$

Because the projected vector has the same magnitude as the original vector, spread will be the same as if the attenuated position were unaltered. The difference is that the original vector's position would update smoothly, but $\hat{p}'$ has the potential to make large discontinuous jumps. We can use a method from earlier where we add one more level of spread. Let this fourth spread interpolation be μ_z. The interpolation can be the ratio of the original z component p_z to the new z magnitude $\bar{\sigma}_z$. Therefore, when there is minimal projection or $p_z \approx \bar{\sigma}_z$, the interpolation will be close to zero. The spread projected is

$$\mu_z = \left|\frac{p_z - \bar{\sigma}_z}{p_z}\right| \tag{13.11}$$

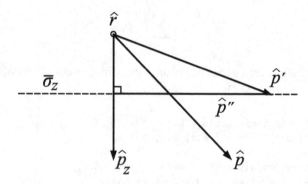

FIGURE 13.8 Side view of the projection of the attenuated position $\hat{p}$ to the plane of the average z coordinate $\bar{\sigma}_z$ to form $\hat{p}'$. The magnitude of $\hat{p}$ is equal to $\hat{p}'$.

13.11 SUPPORT BEYOND STEREO: 5.1 AND MORE

The average attenuated position outputs a single emitter for the audio engine, and because the audio engine handles the speaker configurations, the voxel emitter is already compatible for speaker configurations beyond just stereo. However, I was asked to explore how an approach that could work for 5.1 when sound might map to opposite speakers such as in Figure 13.9.

In this configuration, using the attenuated position with a single emitter, the voxels in the rear left increase the spread but not by enough to have much sound output from the rear-left speaker (or left surround speaker) in a 5.1 arrangement.[14]

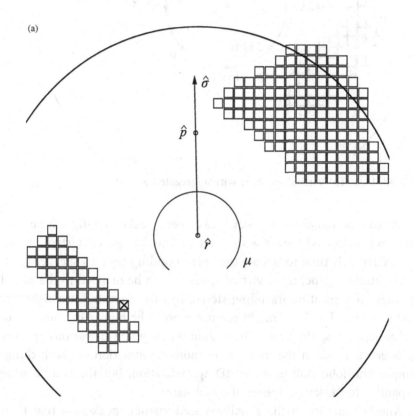

(a)

FIGURE 13.9 Voxel emitter in which voxels are on either side of the receiver. (a) Using the attenuated position algorithm with a single emitter.

---

[14] It is my opinion that the example in Figure 13-9 is somewhat contrived, and for a listener to notice a difference between the single emitter solution and the more complex algorithm below may be unlikely. However, there could be cases that I did not think of and the solution does have some interesting properties.

(b)

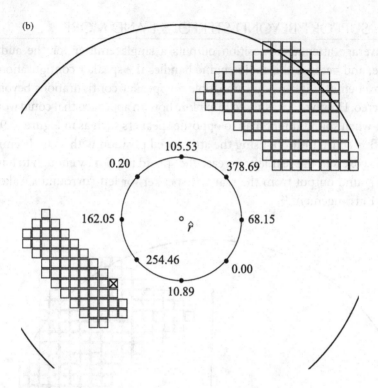

FIGURE 13.9 (b) Virtual speakers with aggregated weights.

Instead of handling a special case per speaker configuration, the approach below will start with a set of equally spaced virtual speakers. When it is time to update the corresponding sound's speaker gains in the audio engine, these virtual speakers can be mapped to the actual speaker configuration including stereo. In this example I use eight virtual speakers. For 7.1 it might require more. The higher the number of virtual speakers, the better the resolution mapping to various speaker arrangements but at the trade-off of more computation. To keep things simple, the following assumes 2D spatialization, but the code can be expanded to work with spherical coordinates.

Another quality of the equally spaced virtual speakers is that their angles relative to the receiver's forward direction stay constant. If the receiver rotates, changing the "center" direction of the speaker arrangement, the virtual speakers' positions remain constant, whereas the angles for the speaker arrangement (stereo, 5.1, etc.) have to be translated. Each virtual speaker is represented with a SpeakerData as an angle in the x, y plane and the total weight aggregated in the direction of the speaker.

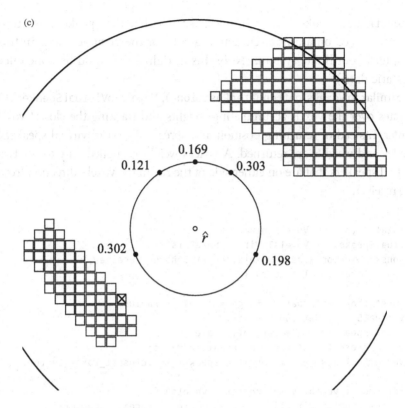

FIGURE 13.9   (c) Typical 5.1 arrangement mapped from virtual speakers.

```cpp
constexpr int kNumVirtualSpeakers = 8;

struct VirtualSpeakerSet {
  struct SpeakerData {
    float angle = 0;
    float total_weight;
  };
  std::array<SpeakerData, kNumVirtualSpeakers> speakers;
  Vector closest_voxel_center = { 0.f, 0.f, 0.f };

  VirtualSpeakerSet() {
    const float angle_dist = 2 * (float)M_PI / kNumVirtualSpeakers;
    int speaker_id = 0;
    // Initialize speaker angles evenly around a circle.
    for (auto& speaker : speakers) {
      speaker.angle = angle_dist * speaker_id++;
      speaker.total_weight = 0.f;
    }
  }
};
```

The `VirtualSpeakerSet` is initialized such that the speakers are uniformly spaced on a unit circle starting at $0°$ or the positive x-axis in this chapter's coordinate system. (Note this initialization could be done once in static data.)

Similar to `VoxelsToAttenuatedPosition()`, `VoxelsToVirtualSpeakers()` iterates over the voxels accumulating weights and tracking the closest voxel center. Instead of returning position and spread, the set of virtual speakers' angles and weights are returned. A voxel's weight is applied only to the two virtual speakers that are on either side of the ray in the voxel's direction from the receiver.

```
template<typename VoxelContainer>
VirtualSpeakerSet VoxelsToVirtualSpeakers(
  const VoxelContainer& voxels, const Sphere& receiver,
  const float voxel_extent) {

  const float attenuation_range = receiver.radius;
  VirtualSpeakerSet speaker_set;
  auto& speakers = speaker_set.speakers;
  float closest_distance = attenuation_range;
  Vector& closest_voxel_center = speaker_set.closest_voxel_center;

  for (const Vector voxel_center : voxels) {
    const Vector direction = voxel_center - receiver.center;
    if (PointInsideVoxel(direction, voxel_extent)) {
      closest_distance = 0.f;
      closest_voxel_center = voxel_center;
      // Evenly distribute the weight across all speakers for
      // full spread.
      for (auto& speaker : speakers) {
        speaker.total_weight = 1.f / kNumVirtualSpeakers;
      }
      break;
    }
    const float distance = Length(direction);
    if (distance >= attenuation_range) {
      continue;
    }
    if (distance < closest_distance) {
      closest_distance = distance;
      closest_voxel_center = voxel_center;
    }
    const float weight = attenuation_range - distance;
    float angle = atan2f(direction.y, direction.x);
```

```
  // Correct angle such that it is rotated positively.
  if (angle < 0.f) {
    angle += 2.f * (float)M_PI;
  }
  auto it_rhs = upper_bound(speakers.begin(), speakers.end(),
    angle,
    [](const float _angle, const SpeakerData& lhs) {
      return _angle < lhs.angle;
  });
  auto it_lhs = it_rhs - 1;
  // Handle wrapping around the circle.
  if (it_rhs == speakers.end()) {
    it_rhs = speakers.begin();
  }
  float rhs_angle = it_rhs->angle;
  if (rhs_angle < it_lhs->angle) {
    rhs_angle += 2.f * (float)M_PI;
  }
  const float angle_lerp = (angle - it_lhs->angle) /
    (rhs_angle - it_lhs->angle);
  // Apply weight to speakers left and right of the ray
  // to the voxel linearly interpolated by angle.
  it_lhs->total_weight += weight * (1.f - angle_lerp);
  it_rhs->total_weight += weight * angle_lerp;
  }
  return speaker_set;
}
```

On either the game engine side or the audio engine mixer, the virtual speakers need to be mapped to the current speaker configuration of the game. VirtualSpeakerSetToSpeakerArrangement() is similar to VoxelsToAttenuatedPosition() with a couple of changes. First the speaker arrangement is unlikely to have a speaker directly at 0°, and so a bit of extra care is required to wrap around the circle. The speaker angles are assumed to have already been translated to match the receiver's forward direction. Secondly after the weights are accumulated, they must be normalized to the desired gain values.

Wwise implementation: To trigger playback and get information about the authored sound's gain, the closest voxel center can be used as the emitter's position sent to the audio engine. Registering the callback AK_SpeakerVolumeMatrix can be used to alter the per-speaker gain values.

```cpp
template<int N>
std::array<float, N> VirtualSpeakerSetToSpeakerArrangement(
  const VirtualSpeakerSet& speaker_set,
  const std::array<float, N>& speaker_angles,
  const float gain_rms) {

  std::array<float, N> speaker_gains{};
  float total_weight = 0.f;
  for (const auto& virtual_speaker : speaker_set.speakers) {
    const float weight = virtual_speaker.total_weight;
    if (weight <= FLT_EPSILON) {
      continue;
    }
    float virtual_angle = virtual_speaker.angle;
    // Handle wrapping around 0 degrees.
    auto it_rhs = upper_bound(speaker_angles.begin(),
      speaker_angles.end(), virtual_angle);
    auto it_lhs = (it_rhs != speaker_angles.begin() ?
      it_rhs : speaker_angles.end()) - 1;
    if (it_rhs == speaker_angles.end()) {
      it_rhs = speaker_angles.begin();
    }
    float rhs_angle = *it_rhs;
    if (rhs_angle < *it_lhs) {
      rhs_angle += 2.f * (float)M_PI;
      if (virtual_angle < *it_lhs) {
        virtual_angle += 2.f * (float)M_PI;
      }
    }
    const float angle_lerp = (virtual_angle - *it_lhs)
      / (rhs_angle - *it_lhs);
    // Apply weight to speakers left and right of the ray
    // to the virtual speaker linearly interpolated
    // by angle.
    speaker_gains[it_lhs - speaker_angles.begin()] +=
      weight * (1.f - angle_lerp);
    speaker_gains[it_rhs - speaker_angles.begin()] +=
      weight * angle_lerp;
    total_weight += weight;
  }
  // Normalize speaker_gains.
  if (total_weight > FLT_EPSILON) {
    for (float& gain : speaker_gains) {
      gain = gain_rms * sqrtf(gain / total_weight);
    }
  }
  return speaker_gains;
}
```

To normalize the speaker set, VirtualSpeakerSetToSpeakerArrangement() is given the target gain value: gain_rms. Regardless of the receiver's forward direction, the gain for the voxels across the speakers should remain constant. Therefore, the output is normalized such that the RMS (or root mean square) of the speakers is equal to the target gain. Here I have used the following definition for RMS for multiple channels with each speaker weighted equally:

$$RMS = \sqrt{\frac{c_1^2 + c_2^2 + \cdots + c_n^2}{n}} \tag{13.12}$$

where c_n are the gain values per channel and n is the number of channels. In this case for 5.1, $n = 5$.

The speaker angles in the example were based on the ITU-R BS.775-3 reference loudspeaker arrangement as shown in Table 13.1. This representation may differ depending on the sound engine. Figure 13.10 shows the per-speaker gain from the example used in Figure 13.9. For simplicity, near field has been left out as well as the sound's authored spread which would also need to be applied to the normalized weights. This combination of managing the attenuation and the speaker arrangements may heavily overlap with the audio engine's functionality. Some care should be taken to not end up rewriting entire systems from the audio engine.

One improvement over the single emitter approach used in VoxelsToAttenuatedPosition() is that each virtual speaker could have its own occlusion value (or entirely separate DSP/signal processing chain for that matter). This extra control could model a setup like a river bend that goes behind a wall but only on the right-hand side relative to the receiver.

TABLE 13.1 Speaker Angles for a 5.1 Setup Based on the ITU-R BS.775-3 Reference Loudspeaker Arrangement

Channel	Degrees from Center	Coordinate
Left	30	$\pi/3$
Center	0	$\pi/2$
Right	30	$2\pi/3$
Right Surround	120	$7\pi/6$
Left Surround	120	$11\pi/6$

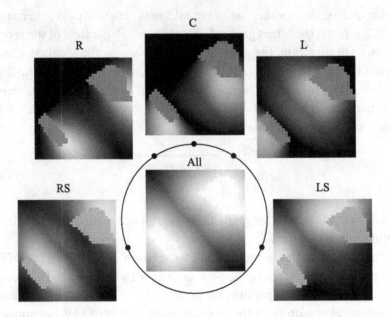

FIGURE 13.10 Gain plots of the five 5.1 speakers. The brighter areas are louder. (Notice there is no near field applied.)

Wwise implementation: In addition to SetPosition(), the Wwise API also includes SetMultiplePositions() and SetMultipleObstructionAndOcclusion() which take an array of positions and obstruction/occlusion pairs. The mode MultiPositionType_MultiDirections will treat the set of positions as a single sound. Like using a single position voxel emitter approach, using SetMultiplePositions() would depend on the audio engine to handle the details of specific speaker configurations. Before committing to the complexity of an algorithm like VirtualSpeakerSetToSpeakerArrangement(), it would be worth exploring if SetMultiplePositions() can be leveraged [2].

13.12 FINAL NOTES

This chapter extended the idea of using a grid or set of voxels to approximate the position of a sound that represents an area or volume of space. Integration of these approaches can involve a large commitment on development time as well as CPU and memory resources. As the feature's complexity grows, it may start to overlap functionality handled by the audio engine.

Yet in my mind, this chapter has hardly touched on the many number of ways to optimize with alternate algorithms or how to integrate with or modify the existing audio engine to avoid reverse engineering or duplicating code. Areas like spatial partitioning algorithms or approximation algorithms and even predictive models are spaces for inspiration to build on a functioning voxel emitter prototype.

REFERENCES

1. Taylor, Nic. "Approximate Position of Ambient Sounds of Multiple Sources." *Game Audio Programming Principles and Practices Volume 2*, edited by Guy Somberg. CRC Press, 2019, pp. 197–226.
2. Audiokinetic, "Integration Details - 3D Positions." *Wwise Documentation*, https://www.audiokinetic.com/library/edge/?source=SDK&id=soundengine _3dpositions.html.

CHAPTER 14

Improvisational Music

Charlie Huguenard

derelict.computer

CONTENTS

14.1 ALL THAT JAZZ

We tend to think of music in terms of composers. Composers are everywhere—in pop music, classical music, game music, electronic dance music, and more. Composers create a piece of music for a set of musicians (or machines) and then usually record a performance. When we hear a piece of music, it's usually the same every time, unless someone else is performing it, remixing it, or rearranging it. This works fine with the way we typically consume music, which is in a *linear* manner—listening to a record, dancing in a club, or attending a performance.

Video games and other interactive experiences are *non-linear*. Although many interactive experiences utilize cutscenes and "baked" animation to great effect, the player certainly notices when the game is not responding to them. Providing nothing but pre-composed music in an experience is akin to providing nothing but cutscenes. We probably need to look elsewhere for inspiration for our interactive music systems.

Thankfully we have many forms of non-linear music in our music history corpus. Baroque keyboardists such as Bach were well known for their ability to improvise and embellish while performing, and even written counterpoint is thought to be heavily influenced by on-the-spot music generation [1]. Hip hop artists—MCs, DJs, and dancers alike—have used improvisation to great effect throughout the music's history [2]. Perhaps the most well-known modern example of a music which emphasizes improvisation is jazz music, which itself is influenced by West African improvisation techniques [3]. Jazz composers typically write a static piece of music—a "head"—and then expect the musicians performing to *improvise* the rest.

Music improvisation is the embellishment of musical ideas. Those ideas can come from a composer, other musicians, or several musical "games" used to generate the basis for the improvisation. You can hear many examples of this embellishment by searching for a famous jazz piece and listening to each musician's version. Try "Autumn Leaves" by Joseph Kosma for total overload.

14.2 MUSIC SYSTEM FOUNDATIONS, LIGHTNING ROUND

Music improvisation is not possible without some foundational systems. Creating all these supporting systems could be its own chapter [4]. We will briefly cover some of them in this section. Each example is provided as pseudocode in hopes of easing the process of applying it to a given environment. An implementation using Unity3d is provided in the supplemental materials at https://www.routledge.com/9780367348045.

14.2.1 Sound Generator

In order to make music, you'll have to make some sound. We use all kinds of sound generators—horns, bells, drums, synthesizers, and a huge variety of software instruments.

There are many kinds of samplers with myriad settings. To demonstrate this system, all you need is what I like to call the "one-shot" sampler.

A one-shot sampler takes a single audio file and plays the file at different speeds based on incoming musical notes.

Let's assume we always create tonal audio files at middle C (261.626 Hz, MIDI note 60). If we wanted our sampler to play the file one octave above middle C (523.251 Hz, MIDI note 72), we would tell it to play the file two times as fast. Similarly, if we wanted to play one octave below middle C (130.813 Hz, MIDI note 48), we would tell the sampler to play the file half as fast. The formula for determining the playback speed based on a MIDI note is

$$speed = 2^{(midiNote-60)/12}$$

Every interactive audio engine you'll encounter provides a way to play a sound file at some pitch. In fact, most interactive audio engines are essentially very complex samplers. To make a sampler instrument, you need only to set up the existing audio file playback to respond to notes and scale the speed like this:

```
Sampler:
  SoundFile file
  FilePlayer player

  function Play(int noteNumber, float scheduledTime):
    player.pitch = pow(2, (noteNumber - 60) / 12)
    player.play(file, scheduledTime)
```

14.2.2 Clock

Most interactive music systems require something to tell time or to send a signal when a musical interval is encountered. We generally call this a clock or metronome (timer tends to imply something that's not precise enough for audio or musical timing). These musical clocks can be either discrete or continuous—a decision which affects the design of the music system.

For example, a traditional DAW timeline is typically continuous. This requires plugins such as beat-synced effects to poll the timeline to determine when beats are going to happen. Effects are required to detect "edges" to demarcate musical events like a quarter note.

A pulse-based clock like one you might see in a modular synthesizer is an example of a discrete musical clock. It sends out a "pulse" periodically, and pieces of the system use that pulse to trigger or otherwise manipulate sound. Many times, using a discrete clock is a subtractive process. If the initial pulse is at 16th note intervals, a clock divider in the chain might take every fourth pulse, creating a quarter note pattern. An additional clock divider could take every other quarter note, playing just the first and third quarter notes in a measure or shifting to the second and fourth. By chaining clock dividers and other logical modules, you can create all kinds of musical patterns. Even with a discrete clock, though, you are by no means limited to dividing the initial pulse (look up "clock multipliers" for examples of this).

For this example, we'll use a continuous clock, which looks something like this:

```
Clock:
  float tempo // in quarter notes per minute
  float startTime // in seconds using the audio engine clock
  bool playing

  function Play():
    startTime = currentEngineTime
    playing = true

  function Stop():
    playing = false

  // get the current time of the clock in bars (fractional)
  function GetTimeBars():
    if (!playing):
      return 0

    float now = currentEngineTime - startTime_
    float timeQuarters = (tempo / 60) * timeSeconds
    // stick to 4/4 time for this example
    return timeQuarters / 4

  // we'll need this later for scheduling sampler plays
  function BarsToEngineTime(float timeBars):
    float quarters = bars * 4
    float seconds = quarters / (tempo / 60)
    return startTime_ + seconds
```

14.2.3 Sequencers

"Sequencer" is an overloaded term, even when you narrow it down to musical uses. We could be talking about a MIDI sequencer tool like those found in a DAW or a groove box step sequencer. And there are several smaller kinds of sequencers that transform pitches, select pulses, and resequence breakbeat samples. The general definition I like to use is that a sequencer is something that processes *control* signals in a musical system, much like how an effect processes an audio signal. A control signal could be a pulse, a MIDI note, a knob, a chord, a sensor, or anything else that could eventually manipulate a sound.

14.3 MUSICIAN RECIPES

Now that we have a concept of the underlying systems that enable real-time composition, let's think about how to build the whole thing. I like to think of real-time music systems in terms of three layers:

- **The Conductor** determines the overall shape of the music and generates control signals.

- **The Musicians** process the control signals from the conductor.

- **The Instruments** turn the control signals from the musicians into sound.

Matching these layers up to the previous definitions, the Conductor would be a clock and some logic for controlling the overall composition, the Musicians would be sequencers, and an Instrument would be a sampler.

14.3.1 Designing the Conductor

We've taken care of the sampler instrument, and we'll get to the musicians shortly. Let's briefly look at what our conductor will do. We know that we'll need timing info from the clock. We'll also want to know what notes to play for any tonal instruments, for which we can provide some information about the key or chord changes in the music. Two pieces of information we can use are the note number (or pitch) itself, as well as how likely it should be to play. We could go with a direct probability value for notes, but we'll get a little more context if we introduce a concept of "strength." In music, there are notes in a chord or scale that can be played very often. Those are typically the root note and some of the other chord tones (such as the fifth). And then there are notes that belong in the scale but will sound dissonant if played often or on strong beats such as the downbeat of a measure. We can assign a strength value to notes and then use that in our musician logic for selecting notes to play. If we describe a note like so:

```
Note:
    int noteNumber // MIDI note number
    float strength // 0-1, how "comfortable" or "strong" is this note?
```

And then describe a chord as a collection of notes with a position in bars:

```
Chord:
    float posBars
    Note[] chordNotes
    Note[] scaleNotes
```

Using this information, we can have the conductor cycle through chord changes and notify the musicians:

```
Conductor:
    Clock clock
    Chord[] chords // chords, sorted by position
    float chordLengthBars // at what point do we loop?
    Musician[] musicians // we'll get to this in a minute

    function Update():
        if (!clock.playing):
            return

        float timeBars = clock.GetTimeBars()

        // get the current chord
        float chordTimeBars = mod(timeBars, chordLengthBars)
        Chord currentChord
        for each chord in chords:
            if (chord.posBars > chordTimeBars):
                break
            currentChord = chord

        // update the musicians
        for each musician in musicians:
            musician.SetChord(currentChord)
            musician.UpdateNotes(timeBars)
```

14.3.2 Musician Design Considerations

So, what do these musicians do? What kind of logic do they contain? Remember that a sequencer can be any kind of control processor. Following that logic, we can combine any number of existing musical techniques to create a complete, "intelligent" sequencer for each type of musician we would like to emulate. How you put those together depends on your project's requirements. If you're making a one-off music system for a game, it might be more efficient to hand-code each musician. If you're making a tool for sound creatives, you could create a system of sequencer modules and let your users patch them together to design musicians. In this section, we will talk about the former: programming bespoke musician logic. After learning how to assemble musical logic in this way, it should be straightforward to port these techniques to a modular system, but that will be left as an exercise for the reader.

Our musician interface, as referenced by the conductor above, looks like this:

```
Musician:
  Clock clock // hang on to a reference so we can do conversions
  Chord currentChord
  float lastTimeBars
  float intensity // 0.0-1.0, the amount of musical movement

  function UpdateNotes(float posBars):
    // to be implemented in each musician to follow

  function SetChord(Chord chord):
    currentChord = chord
```

We'll build on this for each of the individual musicians, and some additional "homework" for extending each musician will be found at the end of each section.

14.3.3 Funky Drummer

Many interactive compositions call for a rhythm section, so let's make a drumbeat generator. This "drummer" will output a beat based on a couple of inputs—tempo and intensity. For the purposes of this example, we will assume 4/4 timing.

A drumbeat can be conceptually broken down into the following:

- The drums in a drum kit and their roles in constructing a beat.

- Strong and weak beats and their effect on the "feel" when hit (or not hit).

- Embellishment, such as fills or shifted hits.

FIGURE 14.1   A regular-time drum beat in 4/4.

FIGURE 14.2   A drum beat in 4/4 with notes added.

A very simple drum kit might include a kick drum, snare drum, and hi-hat. The kick anchors the beat, so its most prominent hits usually end up on strong beats, such as the downbeat of every measure. The snare compliments the kick by providing a "back beat," typically landing on the weak beats of the measure (beats 2 and 4 in 4/4 time). The hi-hat fills in space and, depending on the feel, can land pretty much anywhere in the measure. Figure 14.1 shows one example of a regular-time drum beat in 4/4.

We could just play this beat back over and over, but that wouldn't be very interesting. One way to vary a beat is to add and remove notes to make it feel more or less "intense" or "busy," as shown in Figure 14.2.

As the intensity input changes, we add or remove these embellishments. Building on the musician interface above, a drummer that plays an embellished beat could look like this:

```
Drummer:
  Sampler kick, snare, hat
  Note[] kickNotes, snareNotes, hatNotes

  function UpdateNotes(float posBars):
    // find out the positions in 16th notes
    int last16th = floor(lastTimeBars * 16) % 16
    int this16th = floor(timeBars * 16) % 16
```

```
// update the position
lastTimeBars = timeBars
// skip if we haven't advanced
if (last16th == this16th):
  return

// find the hit time (in audio engine time)
int wholeBar = floor(timeBars)
float barFraction = this16th / 16
float hitTime = clock.BarsToEngineTime(wholeBar + barFraction)

// find the notes that are in this index
// and play them if they're at the right level
float minStrength = 1.0f - intensity
Note tmpNote = kickNotes[this16th]
if (tmpNote.strength >= minStrength):
  kick.Play(tmpNote.noteNumber, hitTime)
tmpNote = snareNotes[this16th]
if (tmpNote.strength >= minStrength):
  snare.Play(tmpNote.noteNumber, hitTime)
tmpNote = hatNotes[this16th]
if (tmpNote.strength >= minStrength):
  hat.Play(tmpNote.noteNumber, hitTime)
```

Homework

- Add more instruments.

- Add fills that could play every few bars.

- Omit or add embellishments using randomness to add variation.

- Switch between half, normal, and double time feels based on intensity.

14.3.4 All About That Bass

It's helpful to have a musician to anchor the key of the music and to provide a basis for the listener to recognize the improvisation of the other tonal instruments. In modern Western music, a bass line typically serves that purpose.

For each of the tonal instruments, let's add some helpers in a subclass of the existing musician:

```
TonalMusician:
  Sampler sampler // we just need one for these

  function GetNote(Note[] notes, float minStrength):
    Note[] tmpNotes
```

```
      for each note in notes:
        if (note.strength >= minStrength):
          add note to tmpNotes

      int idx = randomInt(0, tmpNotes.size)
      return tmpNotes[i]

  function GetChordNote(float minStrength):
    return GetNote(currentChord.chordNotes, minStrength)

  function GetScaleNote(float minStrength):
    return GetNote(currentChord.scaleNotes, minStrength)

  function PlayNote(int noteNumber, float timeBars):
    float engineTime = clock.BarsToEngineTime(timeBars)
    sampler.Play(noteNumber, engineTime)
```

Real bassists play around in the key quite a bit. But for the purpose of this example, let's assume the bass line should stick within the chord tones and primarily the root note of the chord. The bass musician might look like this:

```
Bass:
  function UpdateNotes(float timeBars):
    // find out the positions in 16th notes
    int last16th = floor(lastTimeBars * 16) % 16
    int this16th = floor(timeBars * 16) % 16
    lastTimeBars = timeBars

    // skip if we haven't advanced
    if (last16th == this16th):
      return

    // find the note time (in bars)
    int wholeBar = floor(timeBars)
    float barFraction = this16th / 16.0f
    float noteTime = wholeBar + barFraction

    // play roots on the downbeat
    if (this16th == 0):
      PlayNote(GetChordNote(1.0f), noteTime)
      return

    // usually play strong tones on the other quarters
    if (this16th % 4 == 0):
      if (random0to1() < intensity):
        PlayNote(GetChordNote(0.5f), noteTime)
      return
```

```
// sometimes play on the 8ths
if (this16th % 2 == 0):
  if (random0to1() < intensity - 0.25f):
    PlayNote(GetChordNote(0.25f), noteTime)
  return

// sometimes play on the 16ths
if (random0to1() < intensity - 0.5f):
  PlayNote(GetChordNote(0), noteTime)
```

Homework

- Use scale tones for embellishments, instead of just chord tones.

- Add "memory" to provide a sense of repetition.

14.3.5 Spacey Chimes

Texture provides harmonic context and movement. While many times you'll hear a guitar or piano play full chords, another approach to add texture is to *arpeggiate* the chords. Simply put, an arpeggio is a sequence of notes that move around in a chord. If you spent any time in music lessons, you probably practiced running scales and arpeggios. If not, the typical arpeggio goes up, then down a scale, skipping every other note, as shown in the figure below.

So, let's look at how to make an arpeggiator. Much of the logic from the bass generator can be reused to create a chord arpeggiator like so:

```
Chimes:
  Mode mode // Up, Down, Random
  int sequenceIdx = 0

  function UpdateNotes(float timeBars):
    // set the step size based on intensity
    int stepSize
    if (intensity < 0.4f):
      stepSize = 4
    else if (intensity < 0.7f):
```

```
    stepSize = 8
  else:
    stepSize = 16

  // find out the positions based on the step size
  int lastStep = floor(lastTimeBars * stepSize) % stepSize
  int thisStep = floor(timeBars * stepSize) % stepSize
  lastTimeBars = timeBars

  // skip if we haven't advanced
  if (lastStep == thisStep):
    return

  // find the note time (in bars)
  int wholeBar = floor(timeBars)
  float barFraction = thisStep / stepSize
  float noteTime = wholeBar + barFraction

  // get the index within the sequence
  int numChordNotes = currentChord.chordNotes.length
  int chordNoteIdx
  switch (mode):
    case Mode.Up:
      sequenceIdx = (sequenceIdx + 1) % numChordNotes
      chordNoteIdx = sequenceIdx
      break
    case Mode.Down:
      sequenceIdx = (sequenceIdx + 1) % numChordNotes
      chordNoteIdx = numChordNotes - (sequenceIdx + 1)
      break
    case Mode.Random:
      chordNoteIdx = randomInt(0, numChordNotes)
      break

  int note = currentChord.chordNotes[chordNoteIdx].noteNumber
  PlayNote(note, noteTime);
```

Homework

- Add more arpeggio modes, such as an up/down mode.

- Add optional scale runs in addition to chord arpeggios.

- Tie the mode to the intensity.

14.3.6 The Soloist

Now that we have a rhythmic and harmonic base, a melody will complete our "band." In jazz music, there are often pre-composed melodies in the *head* provided to the musician. As the performance progresses, solo musicians take turns reinterpreting these melodies or creating their own completely. The same strong and weak concepts regarding tones and rhythmic intervals apply here. Playing a weak tone on a strong beat can create tension, whereas sticking to strong tones can ground the melody. Too much tension, and the music can become challenging to listen to. Conversely, too little tension can make the music feel bland and uninteresting.

Another consideration is repetition. You may have noticed that the bass and chime instruments can meander and sometimes sound a bit too random. This is often acceptable for those types of instruments, but with a melody, too much wandering can leave the piece feeling without basis. One way to solve this is by introducing some "memory" to the musician logic. For example, in the first four bars, we could use similar stochastic methods as the bass musician to generate a melody. After that melody has been generated, we could store it and reuse it for another four bars to create a repeating eight-bar phrase.

The solo instrument might then look like this:

```
Solo:
    int recordBars = 4 // the length of the recording
    int repeats = 1 // how many times we want to repeat the recording
    int[] recordedMelody
    float repeatStartBar

    function UpdateNotes(float timeBars):
        // find out the positions in 16th notes
        int last16th = floor(lastTimeBars * 16) % 16
        int this16th = floor(timeBars * 16) % 16
        lastTimeBars = timeBars;

        // skip if we haven't advanced
        if (last16th == this16th):
            return

        // find the note time (in bars)
        int wholeBar = floor(timeBars)
        float barFraction = this16th / 16
        float noteTime = wholeBar + barFraction

        // get the index within the recording
        int recordingIdx = this16th + (wholeBar % recordBars) * 16

        // repeat the recording until the next time
        // we should generate a melody
```

```
  float repeatEndBars = repeatStartBar_ + repeats * recordBars
  if (timeBars < repeatEndBars):
    int note = recordedMelody_[recordingIdx];
    if (note != InvalidNoteNumber):
      PlayNote(note, noteTime)

// if we're recording, generate the melody
else:
  if (recordingIdx == 0):
    init recordedMelody with 16 * recordBars notes

  int note = InvalidNoteNumber

  // always play a strong note on the downbeat
  if (this16th == 0):
    note = GetScaleNote(1.0f)
  // usually play a note on the quarters
  else if (this16th % 4 == 0):
    if (random0to1() < intensity):
      note = GetScaleNote(0.5f)
  // sometimes play a note on the eighths
  else if (this16th % 2 == 0):
    if (random0to1() < intensity - 0.25f):
      note = GetScaleNote(0.25f)
  // sometimes play a note on the 16ths
  else if (random0to1() < intensity - 0.5f):
    note = GetScaleNote(0.0f)

  // record and play the note
  recordedMelody_[recordingIdx] = note
  if (note != InvalidNoteNumber):
    PlayNote(note, noteTime)

  // if we're done recording, start repeating
  int lastRecordingIdx = recordBars * 16 - 1
  if (recordingIdx >= lastRecordingIdx):
    repeatStartBar_ = Mathf.Ceil(timeBars)
```

Homework

- Modify the sampler and the solo musician to play sustained notes.

- Keep track of two recorded melodies to play an AABA sequence.

14.4 WRAPPING UP

There are so many ways to design interactive music that it can become overwhelming, but the process becomes a little simpler by looking at how humans make music on the spot. Jazz music provides a useful framework for autonomous music, thanks to its focus on improvisation and well-defined theory. Leaning on the composer, musician, instrument metaphor further grounds the concept such that we can visualize how the code components come together. Hopefully, these concepts and examples help you decide how to make your own improvised music systems.

REFERENCES

1. Massimiliano Guido. *Studies in Historical Improvisation: From Cantare Super Librum to Partimenti*. Routledge, Abington, New York, 2017.
2. David Nicholls. *The Cambridge History of American Music*. Cambridge University Press, New York, Cambridge, 1998. https://catalog.loc.gov/vwebv/search?searchCode=LCCN&searchArg=98003814&searchType=1&permalink=y
3. Don Michael Randel. *The Harvard Dictionary of Music*. Harvard University Press, Cambridge, MA, 2003. https://catalog.loc.gov/vwebv/holdingsInfo?searchId=28796&recCount=25&recPointer=0&bibId=13266550
4. Huguenard, Charlie. "Note-Based Music Systems." *Game Audio Programming Principles and Practices Volume 2*, edited by Guy Somberg. CRC Press, 2019, pp. 321–344

Index

Printed in the United States
by Baker & Taylor Publisher Services